Human Rights, Suffering, and Aesthetics in Political Prison Literature

Human Rights, Suffering, and Aesthetics in Political Prison Literature

Edited by
Yenna Wu and Simona Livescu

LEXINGTON BOOKS
Lanham • Boulder • New York • Toronto • Plymouth, UK

Copyright © 2011 by Lexington Books
First paperback edition 2013

British Library Cataloguing in Publication Information Available

Library of Congress Cataloging-in-Publication Data
The hardback edition was previously cataloged by the Library of Congress as follows:
Human rights, suffering, and aesthetics in political prison literature / edited by
Yenna Wu and Simona Livescu.
    p. cm.
 Includes bibliographic references and index.
 1. Political prisoners—Civil rights. 2. Prisoners' writings—History and criticism.
I. Wu, Yenna. II. Livescu, Simona.
  HV6254.H86 2011
  365-.45—DC22   2011012282

ISBN 978-0-7391-6741-0 (cloth : alk. paper)
ISBN 978-0-7391-8616-9 (pbk. : alk. paper)
ISBN 978-0-7391-6742-7 (electronic)

Contents

Preface   vii
   Yenna Wu

1   Introduction   1
      Yenna Wu

2   Reviving Muted Voices: Rhizomatous Forces in Political Prison
      Literature   17
      Yenna Wu

3   Surviving Traumatic Captivity, Arriving at Wisdom: An
      Aesthetics of Resistance in Chinese Prison Camp Memoir   47
      Yenna Wu

4   The Argument from Silence: Morocco's Truth Commission and
      Women Political Prisoners   87
      Susan Slyomovics

5   The Persistence of Spectacle in PRC Modes of Punishing
      Criminality and Deviance   107
      Philip F. Williams

6   The Cocoons of Language: Torture, Voice, Event   117
      R. Shareah Taleghani

7   A Primer for the Politics and Literature of Resistance:
      Apparitional Subjectivity in *The Collective Autobiography of
      the New York 21*   139
      Ramsey Scott

8   Remembering Pain in Uruguay: What Memories Mean in Carlos
      Liscano's *Truck of Fools*   163
      Eugenio Di Stefano

9   Deviating from the Norm?: Two Easts Testify to a Prison
       Aesthetics of Happiness   185
       Simona Livescu

Appendix: Cup Poems   207

Index   209

About the Contributors   215

Preface

Yenna Wu

This interdisciplinary volume of essays studies human rights in political prison literature, while probing the intersections of suffering, politics, and aesthetics in an interliterary and intercultural context. As the first book to explore the concept of global aesthetics in political prison narratives, it demonstrates how literary insight enhances the study of human rights. Covering varied geographical and geopolitical regions, this collection encourages comparative analyses and cross-cultural understanding. Seeking to interrogate linguistic, structural, and cultural constructions of the political prison experience, it highlights the literary aspects without losing sight of the political and the theoretical.

The contributors cross various disciplinary boundaries and adopt different interpretive perspectives in analyzing prison narratives, especially memoirs, from such diverse countries as China, Egypt, Morocco, Syria, Romania, Russia, Uruguay, and the United States. The volume emphasizes the literary works produced since the second half of the twentieth century, particularly since the political seismic shift in 1989. The authors treated range from the canonical to the less well known: Nawal El Saadawi, Varlam Shalamov, Zhang Xianliang, Cong Weixi, Wumingshi, Carlos Liscano, Fatna El Bouih, Nabil Sulayman, Faraj Bayraqdar, Hasiba 'Abdalrahman, Tahar Ben Jelloun, Nicolae Steinhardt, Irina Ratushinskaya, etc.

Critical issues investigated include how the writers represent their sufferings, experiences, and emotions during incarceration; their strategies of survival; and how political prison literature can reveal hidden violations of human rights, while resisting official discourse and serving other functions in society. Examining the commonalities and differences in global experiences of imprisonment, the eight chapters engage with the aesthetics of self-making and resistance, individual and collective memory, denial and conversion, catharsis and redemption, and the experiencing and witnessing of trauma.

Topics also include the politics of remembering and the politics of representation, such as the problematic relationship between narrative, language, and representations of torture. Similarly under discussion are prison aesthetics of happiness, the role of spectacle in the criminal justice system, and the intersection of prison, gender, and silences.

At a juncture when more and more people all over the world actively defy repressive regimes and demand political reform, this book makes a timely contribution to the advocacy and discourse of universal human rights.

ACKNOWLEDGMENTS

Enormous thanks are due to all the contributors for their wonderful chapters and conscientious cooperation. I am particularly grateful to Simona Livescu for her enthusiastic participation and various help throughout the process. We owe special thanks to Simone Weil Davis, who expertly did the initial editing of chapters 3, 7, and 9 in 2008. We are also appreciative of Alexander Elinson's participation and cooperation during the editing process, even though we regret not being able to include his chapter in the end due to copyright issues. I am extremely grateful for financial assistance from the Academic Senate of the University of California, Riverside.

We are indebted to Flagg Miller and Holly Carver for granting us permission to reprint two poems from Marc Falkoff, ed., *Poems from Guantánamo: The Detainees Speak* (Iowa City: University of Iowa Press, 2007), p. 35. Susan Slyomovics' chapter originally appeared in *Journal of Middle East Women's Studies* 1:3 (Fall 2005): 73–95. We thank Prof. Slyomovics and Kathryn Caras (Indiana University Press) for granting the permission to include this article in this volume.

I am grateful to Simona for typing out Slyomovics' chapter based on the article, and for her great help on the index. I also thank some colleagues and an outside reader for their advice on the manuscript. Each contributor is responsible for the content of his or her chapter. Being in charge of most of the editing, I am responsible for any errors that remain.

Finally, Simona and I would like to express our gratitude to our families and friends for their support. We dedicate this volume to those upright and innocent individuals who have suffered in, or are still incarcerated in, political prisons worldwide.

Chapter One

Introduction

Yenna Wu

This volume examines political prison narratives, a distinct literary genre which has gradually emerged in recent decades. What engages our attention are the works produced since the second half of the twentieth century, especially since the political seismic shift in 1989. Twenty years after the fall of the Berlin Wall, we are on the cusp of a new era in the study of prison literature. New public spaces and discourses are opened through the hard-won freedom resulting from the end of tyranny in a number of countries (such as the collapse of the former Communist governments of Eastern Europe or the end of apartheid in South Africa in 1994), and in some cases also due to recent access to the files and archives previously kept by secret police as well as the establishment of truth and reconciliation commissions. A great deal of political prison literature has been published, particularly in Eastern Europe and the Middle East.

The literary works under study were written about and mostly by political prisoners, a category which in its broadest definition would include not only those incarcerated due to their active or passive involvement in political activities but also prisoners of conscience associated with non-political activities such as religious practices. Many of those who advocate human rights and challenge their governments to institute political reforms or democracy are non-violent. Yet they are detained merely because of being suspected as anti-regime or harmful to the state. Indeed, under a dictatorship, political dissidents can be easily "disappeared," framed, detained, tortured, assassinated, or executed without any trial. Examples of extreme human rights abuse do not occur only in largely lawless countries or regions. In some countries, even if constitutions and laws theoretically exist, they are frequently by-passed and flaunted in reality and practice. Furthermore, an authoritarian regime that is also manipulative and hypocritical would justify its brutality by utilizing such pretexts as maintaining national stability, keeping law and order, or protecting ordinary citizens. For years some regimes have repeatedly adopted similar justifications so as to falsely accuse innocent individuals of subversion, arrest them, and incarcerate them for an inordinately long period. Regrettably, such a phenomenon could occasionally or temporarily occur even in countries claiming to be governed by a Western democracy that includes a system of checks and balances and rule of law.

While a number of individuals publishing political prison literature were already journalists, writers, or dissident authors before their arrest and incarceration, the others are what I would call "cell-made" writers—they did not take to creative or political writing until after experiencing imprisonment. The main reason for repressive regimes to round up dissidents and imprison them is to silence, subdue, and even brainwash them (as in Mao-era Chinese prisons, for example), and to keep them from ever engaging in any potentially "subversive" activities (such as organizing any oppositional groups or rallying other dissidents) or writing anything that can incite others to "sedition." Ironically for the regimes, however, the dehumanizing prison experiences not infrequently result in either transforming existing writers into more mature and effective ones or else turning some of the inmates into authors, motivating them to resort to writing. [1] They write either during their incarceration secretly or after their release for the purpose of bearing witness to the experiences or reaffirming their identity, conviction, and humanity. Some, like Uruguay's Carlos Liscano, are "fashioned" into writers through their imprisonment, and later change their former vocations to that of writing. There are also those who only compose literature temporarily within the duration of their incarceration. Some of the Guantánamo detainees, for example, become "amateur poets" while in prison, turning to "writing poetry as a way to maintain their sanity, to memorialize their suffering, and to preserve their humanity through their acts of creation" (Falkoff 3). In addition, some professional writers—who may or may not have been incarcerated—could be so inspired or moved by the testimonies of the ex-inmates they interview that they write about these experiences.

The group of works studied in this collection consists primarily of nonfictional memoirs and some fictionalized memoirs or novels. Selected by the contributors for analysis due to both their human rights and artistic values, these works were mostly composed after the authors' release, though some were based largely on the notes clandestinely kept by the authors while imprisoned. The narratives frequently document the various aspects of life—ranging from trauma, attempt at survival, denial, conversion, to resistance—which the authors and their cellmates might have experienced or witnessed while doing time. Also often described are the inmates' relationships with one another and with prison personnel. Occasionally the authors may reveal some of their personal histories, including their associations with their families, friends, and communities during the periods before and after prison. Thus from the narratives the reader sometimes obtains glimpses into how numerous people living under an authoritarian regime would become intimidated and "tamed," censor their own and others' thoughts, speeches, and behaviors, or even collaborate with the secret police and inform against other people for the sake of self-protection or benefit. Furthermore, from time to time we find the writers' various emotional reactions, meditations on suffering, political ideas, and philosophical reflections on life, society, and history. These works form a treasure trove containing a wealth of information on prison culture, economics, and politics, as well as previously hidden or suppressed individual and collective memory.

A good number of materials examined in this volume have been hitherto little known or inadequately studied, and many of them were originally written in languages other than English. Produced in such geographically diverse areas as East Asia, the Middle East, Eastern Europe, Latin America, and the United States, these narratives understandably vary from one another due to their cultural, linguistic, political, religious, and historical differences. Taken together, however, they surprisingly reflect universal suffering and global traumas induced by immense political repression and incarceration.

The contributors in this volume bring in interesting and innovative modes of analysis, having come from diverse backgrounds and disciplines—Anthropology, Middle Eastern and Islamic Studies, Asian Studies, Hispanic Studies, English, Gender Studies, and Comparative Literature. Most of the texts examined herein—including those written in foreign languages such as Arabic, Chinese, Spanish, Romanian, and others—are analyzed in depth in their original languages by scholars equipped with the linguistic expertise and capable of translating the cited passages by themselves. Taking different disciplinary angles, the contributors examine not only the writers' sufferings, reflections, and emotions during incarceration but also how they represent these experiences and, to some extent, what political implications the works might entail or how they function in society. Some of the chapters study the authors' experiences in a broad spatial and temporal perspective, including their carceral as well as pre- and post-carceral experiences in both individual and collective contexts. Rather than emphasizing merely suffering and human rights abuses, a few contributors investigate the writers' strategies of survival, aesthetics of self-making and resistance, and artistic features and merits.

I begin in chapter 2, "Reviving Muted Voices: Rhizomatous Forces in Political Prison Literature," by considering the controversy surrounding remembrances of atrocity. While aware of the pros and cons, I nevertheless argue that in the case of political prisoners, remembering is a much-needed "ethical act," and the healing process cannot begin if the truth of unjust suffering is forgotten even before it is uncovered, discussed, understood, and properly dealt with. I use "rhizome" (a rootlike stem) as a metaphor for political prison literature and discourse to underscore its powerful, protean, and creative potential. Containing rich resources and ethical value, political prison narratives offer crucial contributions to the process of remembering, understanding, and healing.

I call attention to the complex politics involved in the representation of suffering and in the writing, reading, publishing, as well as potential commodifying and politicizing, of political prison literature. Although narratives from various areas reveal numerous commonalities in global carceral experience, I caution against erasing differences. Instead, I advocate the need to emphasize the specificities and their particular circumstances, contextualize them, and engage deeply with the authors' subjectivities and interiorities. I also propose that cross-cultural, cross-literary, comparative, and interdisciplinary studies of this literature can fruitfully uncover the literature's multiplicities, resources, transformations, and connectedness. In particular, I highlight the importance of aesthetics and promote the investigation into the intersection of aesthetics and political prison literature from diverse perspectives, while recommending that we be conscious of the complexities and ambivalences embedded in this topic.

In chapter 3, "Surviving Traumatic Captivity, Arriving at Wisdom: An Aesthetics of Resistance in Chinese Prison Camp Memoir," I suggest that studying Mao-era Chinese political prisoners' experiences is relevant and timely because it reveals a continuing CCP (Chinese Communist Party) pattern of repression, denial, and deception. I explore how the Maoist regime adopted semi-starvation as a tactic to punish, control, and break prisoners in laogai ("remolding through [forced hard] labor") camps, thereby inflicting a sort of "prolonged, repeated trauma" (to borrow Judith Herman's term) upon them. Examples of inmates' responses to severe hunger are drawn from three representative memoirs: Wumingshi's (pseudonym of Bu Naifu, alias Bu Ning, a.k.a. Pu Ning, 1917–2002) interview-based, secondhand memoir, *Red Sharks* (*Hongsha* [1989] 1994, published in Taiwan), Cong Weixi's (b. 1933) laogai memoir, *The Heading into Chaos Trilogy* (*Zou xiang hundun sanbuqu*, 1998, including Part One, *Heading into Chaos* or *Zou xiang hundun*, 1989), and Zhang Xianliang's (b. 1936) memoir *My Bodhi Tree* (*Wode putishu*, 1994). Falsely labeled "rightists" in 1957, Cong Weixi and Zhang Xianliang both spent over two decades in labor camps. Wumingshi personally endured unjust incarceration and hard labor at least in 1958 and 1968–69 (Wu 128–30), though his *Red Sharks* memorializes the long-term laogai tribulations of a former Nationalist officer. These memoirs reveal multifaceted and sometimes even ambivalent aspects of carceral existence ranging from inmates' experiencing and witnessing trauma to their submission, collaboration, and resistance. However, I argue that by daring to divulge the hideous truth through their representations of prisoners' extreme deprivation and attempts at survival, the authors help expose the regime's deception and hypocrisy, thereby contributing—whether intentionally or not—to a collective discourse of resistance.

As a form of knowledge production, prison memoir writing can constitute an act of political protest and extend human rights discourse. The three laogai memoirs, for example, go beyond being expository and self-expressive. While pointing out the different political contexts underlying the composition of these memoirs, I also highlight some aspects of the three authors' artistic treatment of their materials, such as Wumingshi's use of metaphors, paradoxes, and visceral surrealism; Cong Weixi's art of restraint and encoded challenge; and Zhang Xianliang's skill in irony and generating multivalence. These aesthetic elements help enhance the memoirs' affective power, moving the reader to empathy while augmenting the reader's consciousness and understanding of the various dimensions of suffering. I propose that the memoirs can even be cathartic, recuperative, or cognitively and affectively instructive for both the authors and their readership.

Unlike China, a number of countries have since the 1990s undergone either regime change or serious political reform and have significantly improved their human rights conditions, opened up public spaces for free discussion, or even established truth commissions. Morocco is one such example. During King Hassan II's regime (1961–99), the so-called Lead Years or Years of Lead, many political dissidents disappeared, being illegally detained, tortured, and even killed by state police. Yet since the death of King Hassan II in July 1999, the government has committed itself to defend human rights.

In chapter 4, "The Argument From Silence: Morocco's Truth Commission and Women Political Prisoners," anthropologist Susan Slyomovics focuses on Moroccan women political prisoners' experiences of disappearance and rape. This chapter results from Slyomovics' long-term study of human rights issues in Morocco, drawing upon such resources as her firsthand fieldwork and interviews as well as dissidents' testimonies and prison memoirs. Comparing and contrasting South Africa's Truth and Reconciliation Commission with Moroccan Justice and Reconciliation Commission (since 1999), she points out the Moroccan commission's special emphasis on "identifying, verifying, and reporting the process of uncovering the truth about arbitrary detention and secret torture sites." Slyomovics deftly contends that the victims' screams are "silent about facts but not emotions" and that "silence is informative."

A representative figure examined in this chapter is the Moroccan activist Fatna El Bouih, who was incarcerated in 1977–82. Fatna El Bouih's *Hadith al-'atama* (*Talk of Darkness*, published in Arabic in 2001) includes not only her personal account but also two other women prisoners' oral histories. Slyomovics insightfully notes the author's strategies to overcome shame in

relating the repression and torture specific to female prisoners and their bodies. While disclosing how the police would use gender-based intimidation
and violence to silence women, El Bouih's prison memoirs also reveal wom-
en's individual or collective response and resistance to sexual harassment
and rape. Through her careful engagement with testimonies and memoirs,
Slyomovics effectively explores political women prisoners' particular experience of disappearance and rape as well as its "articulation (or lack of
expression) in language."[2]

If Slyomovics' chapter investigates the complex intersection of punishment, gender, and silences, Philip F. Williams's chapter, "The Persistence of
Spectacle in PRC Modes of Punishing Criminality and Deviance," draws our
attention to the equally complex intersection of prison and spectacle. Ap-
proaching prison literature from a primarily social sciences perspective,
Williams analyzes the continuing role of spectacle in China's criminal justice
system, as evidenced by mass sentencing rallies held in stadiums and other
public gathering places and a recurring series of well-publicized Party-led
campaigns to "deal severe blows" to criminal offenders and suspects. The
chapter advances the theoretical debate on the historical development of
punishing crime and deviance by demonstrating that making a public spectacle out of punishing convicts in a "medieval" or premodern fashion can
actually co-exist with a system that usually punishes inmates through "modern"-style incarceration in prisons and labor camps. Williams correctly
points out how an aesthetics of spectacle is used to support the Party-state's
manipulation of public feelings against prisoners, and how, depending upon
the different phases of the internment process as well as other factors, the
state may utilize or eschew public spectacle with the aim of achieving calculated result.

The authoritarian regime can choose to make their torture of political
prisoners a spectacle, public knowledge, or secret. While generally denying
the use of torture, the regime might wish to intimidate would-be dissidents
(and its populace) with the knowledge of the state's brutality. Whether to
narrate one's experiences of torture or not can thus present a quandary.
Narrating torture and making it widely known is imperative from a human
rights perspective. However, this may inadvertently and paradoxically benefit the regime, strengthening its power to terrorize. "How" to narrate and
represent one's experiences of torture becomes a tricky question.

In chapter 6, "The Cocoons of Language: Torture, Voice, Event," R.
Shareah Taleghani rightly calls attention to this dilemma. She further investigates the problematic representation of torture as an embodied and inscribed
event in vastly different works of contemporary Syrian prison literature,
ranging from Maher Arar's story to fascinating narratives by Nabil Sulayman, Faraj Bayraqdar, and Hasiba 'Abdalrahman. Torture, especially in the
well-disseminated analysis of Elaine Scarry, is often understood as destruc-

tive of language or the tortured subject's ability to speak. By comparison, Taleghani examines how particular authors provide works that actually function to efface or disrupt this language-destroying capacity of torture.

Taleghani's chapter offers a careful comparison of the representations of torture in writer and critic Nabil Sulayman's novel, *al-Sijn* (*The Prison*, 1972); Faraj Bayraqdar's poetic prison memoir, *Khiyanat al-Lugha wa al-Samt* (*The Betrayals of Language and Silence*); and Hasiba 'Abdalrahman's *al-Sharnaqa* (*The Cocoon*, 1999). According to Taleghani's analysis, Sulayman's novel is a social realist text that depicts "the endurance and resistance of both the individual, 'committed' political prisoner and a group of political detainees." By comparison, Bayraqdar's memoir "works self-reflexively to interrogate the idea that torture can ever be accurately represented." Bayraqdar's memoir comprises of "a series of fragments" he wrote while incarcerated. After his release from prison in 2000–2001, he "compiled them into a memoir," which was left unedited and exists in the form of an unpublished manuscript. It is an intriguingly "hybrid" narrative that focuses less on the author's own suffering than on "the physical and psychological agony experienced by his fellow prisoners." An example of the self-questioning found in Bayraqdar's text is: "Can you be faithful to your duty of the necessity of exposing the entirety of the experience, from the first rattle to the last hell?" Pointing out the dilemma confronted by Bayraqdar in his reflections, Taleghani contends that he "evokes his sense of betrayal—not just his betrayal at the hands of agents of the Syrian state, but the betrayals of the language at his disposal and the betrayals of a subjugating but at times unavoidable silence."

Taleghani focuses her study upon *al-Sharnaqa* (*The Cocoon*), a "novel" written by human rights activist Hasiba 'Abdalrahman eight years after her release and based on her prison diaries and writings. This work is unique because it is the first novel about Syrian prison by a former female political prisoner and also because its narrative is "non-linear" and "polyphonic." Taleghani's reading of this unusual work is both sensitive and perceptive. Using the cocoon as a metaphor, Taleghani suggests that 'Abdalrahman offers "the uneven fabrication of a cocoon of language, of speech and voice against the silencing produced by torture and other events."

While Taleghani scrutinizes the relationship between narrative, language, and representations of torture in selective works of contemporary Syrian prison literature, in chapter 7, "A Primer for the Politics and Literature of Resistance: Apparitional Subjectivity in *The Collective Autobiography of the New York 21*," Ramsey Scott inspects the problematic subjectivity behind the production of a collective "autobiography" published in the United States in 1971. The text examined in Scott's brilliant chapter—*Look For Me in the Whirlwind: The Collective Autobiography of the New York 21*—is a crucial, almost forgotten document from the Black Liberation Movement. *Whirlwind* has not attracted significant critical attention since the negative reception it was given upon publication by the *New York Times*. And yet, its provocative structure challenges fundamental principles of autobiography and life-writing, suggesting that this collaborative work deserves consideration as a model of innovative writing rooted in (and serving as historical witness to) an influential dissident movement. Scott suggests that *Whirlwind* succeeds as a work of what some might call "experimental" literature because its structural idiosyncrasies embody the political beliefs and philosophies espoused by its contributors. In *Whirlwind*, sixteen of twenty-one Black Panthers arrested as part of a thorough-going NYPD infiltration of the Panthers' New York offices combine narrative fragments and anecdotes as they await trial, recording their own stories and inscribing an image of unity ultimately destroyed by the government's undercover agents. In coining the term "apparitional subjectivity" to describe the products of their labor, Scott subtly argues that *Whirlwind*'s composite textual body, comprised of the various linguistic prostheses its individual contributors donate, constitutes an original and potentially adaptable paradigm through which resistance movements might organize and represent themselves amid state repression.

Ramsey Scott's insightful analysis of the politics of representation in a collective "autobiography" can be productively juxtaposed with Eugenio Di Stefano's interesting discussion of the politics of remembering in a Latin American prison memoir. The conclusions reached by Scott and Di Stefano may vary, yet they complement each other and prove to be thought-provoking. Di Stefano's chapter, "Remembering Pain in Uruguay: What Memories Mean in Carlos Liscano's *Truck of Fools*," takes a special perspective on the recent past in Uruguay. A political dissident, Carlos Liscano (1949–) was incarcerated and tortured by the military regime at the age of twenty-three. Released after thirteen years of imprisonment, Liscano gradually developed into one of Latin America's renowned creative writers. Liscano's *Truck of Fools* (2001) is not only a testimonio of his incarceration and torture but also a memoir containing his remembrances of childhood as well as his reflections on humanity and language. Di Stefano offers an original reading of Liscano's *Truck of Fools*, questioning the political meaning of the left's commitment to representations of torture and incarceration and its relationship to neoliberalism in Uruguay. Like Taleghani's chapter, this chapter also analyzes representations of torture, though from different perspectives such as the politics and discourse of remembering. This chapter centers on culture and politics in Uruguay's postdictatorship. Yet Di Stefano's conclusions might be potentially applicable to the rest of Latin America and even the United States, as he addresses the question of political torture, confinement, and violence on the one hand, and the depoliticization of politics under neoliberal regimes on the other.

Whereas Di Stefano interrogates the meaning of memory and the impact of an important memoir from the perspective of history and politics, Simona

Livescu combines literary and philosophical perspectives in examining four prison memoirs from the Middle East and Eastern Europe in the last chapter, "Deviating from the Norm? Two Easts Testify to a Prison Aesthetics of Happiness." Livescu indicates that a number of memoirs, including these four, attest to a unique feature: while narrating their harrowing prison experiences, quite a few authors in fact tried to write about "a *modus felicitatis*—a state of happiness or bliss," which, as they argued, took them "out of psychological traumatic zones." Already long in existence in a number of prison narratives, this motif has so far been rarely noticed—let alone studied—by critics, partly due to their predominant attention to the traumatic aspects in incarceration. Livescu cites illuminating examples of "epiphanic experience" from four remarkable works exhibiting very different religious and ideological outlooks: Nawal Saadawi's *Memoirs from Women's Prison* (Egypt, 1986), Tahar Ben Jelloun's *This Blinding Absence of Light* (France-Morocco, 2002), Nicolae Steinhardt's *Jurnalul Fericirii* (The Diary of Happiness; Romania, 2003), and Irina Ratushinskaya's *Grey Is the Color of Hope* (Russia, 1989). In this seminal study, the "paradoxical prison aesthetics of happiness" identified by Livescu is not simply defined "as a trope, but also as a social attitude relevant to community life and political interaction on a larger scale." Aside from considering this "epiphanic experience" as a "phenomenological state," a resistant strategy, and a form of "aporetic survival" during the dissidents' incarceration, Livescu examines its post-prison political implications.

The appendix features two brief poems composed by Shaikh Abdurraheem Muslim Dost, a Pakistani writer who was incarcerated for about three years in Guantánamo Bay. They were entitled "Cup Poem 1" and "Cup Poem 2" because some of the detainees used small stones or spoons to etch their poems into foam cups (Falkoff, ed., 35). These poems are a chilling reminder of the controversial human rights abuses unfortunately accompanying the post-9/11, ongoing (global) War on Terrorism.

Indeed, while exulting in the end of the Cold War, apartheid, and some other dictatorships, we cannot help but notice how various wars are still going on, a number of repressive regimes continue to operate with little change, egregious violations of human rights are still rampant, and world peace is still elusive. More and more people aspire to freedom and genuine democracy, yet quite a few authoritarian governments still hold fast to their tight domination, refusing to give up their monopoly of power. Admittedly these regimes are repressive at different levels. For example, crimes against humanity continue to be committed in the Democratic Republic of the Congo due to a long period of violent armed conflict. By comparison, Zimbabwe ostensibly has an emerging opposition party and a system for direct election of its president. In reality, however, there is a great deal of government corruption, intimidation, and brutality toward dissidents, especially as exposed by the alleged fraud in the election and the prolonged post-election unrest in 2008.

As in the case of Zimbabwe, vote rigging in the Iranian presidential election was similarly suspected in 2009, leading to a series of massive post-election protests. A repressive theocracy that boasts also of its 1979 Constitution, Iran witnesses how its current government has been cracking down on demonstrations and illegally assaulting, arresting, detaining, torturing, and killing the dissenters. Religions, including Islam, usually encourage peace, yet a state-controlled religion can harldy counter political repression. Similarly, while Buddhism ought to be conducive to peace, it failed in Myanmar (formerly Burma), a primarily Buddhist state, to relieve people of an abusive regime. The military junta in Myanmar has held strict control over its people since 1962, intimidating its citizenry into submission and robbing them of many rights. Aung San Suu Kyi (Nobel Peace Prize laureate in 1991), the non-violent leader of the opposition party since 1989, has been repeatedly placed under house arrest, while her co-workers or followers have been jailed or persecuted. Clearly the religions in these two countries have been abused, exploited, or co-opted by the regimes.

Some Western academics designated China and Vietnam "post-socialist" primarily because of the economic and political reforms these two countries claimed to have implemented (since 1978 in China and 1986 in Vietnam). Such a designation may be somewhat acceptable for describing the economic reality, but it is inaccurate, or at best premature, for describing the current political reality. Though at different stages of economic development, China and Vietnam have indeed partially incorporated market economy and capitalism into their system and allowed their people far more economic freedom than before. Politically, however, these two countries remain authoritarian one-party socialist states in which the Communist Party reigns supreme, controls all government organs and armies, and brooks no political dissent. The CCP (Chinese Communist Party) brutally crushed the Tiananmen Square protests of 1989 and has censored all mention of this bloody event even now.

Since 1989, Chinese people have obtained far more economic and social rights than before, but their political rights continue to suffer. Despite being non-violent, countless pro-democracy activists have been jailed, "exiled," harassed, or persecuted to various degrees. The famous environmental and AIDS activist Hu Jia was sentenced to jail in April 2008 on charges of "inciting subversion of state power"; despite his imprisonment, Hu won the European Parliament's prestigious Sakharov Prize for Freedom of Thought in 2008—much to the fury of the PRC government.[3] In 2008, prominent human rights activist Liu Xiaobo supported the drafting of—and later signed—the online petition "Charter 08" ("Lingba xianzhang," in imitation of "Charter 77" from Czechoslovakia in January 1977), which called for political reform, rule of law, and such basic civil rights as freedom of expression and peaceful assembly in China. Even a harmless, peaceful petition of this sort led to the government's persecution of Liu and many other signatories. Taken from his home in December 2008, Liu Xiaobo was detained until June 23, 2009, when he was "formally arrested" on the charge of inciting "subversion of the state."[4] To intimidate its citizens at large, the regime routinely punishes not only political dissidents but also those involved in non-political activities such as non-violent Falungong practitioners and ordinary petitioners, including even their sympathizers, supporters, and rights-defenders.

Human rights violations in the above-mentioned countries might vary in their extent and intensity, yet as far as secrecy is concerned, perhaps none of them could compare with North Korea, the iron-curtained socialist state that has been dominated and terrorized by a totalitarian, hereditary dictatorship for several decades. While we might at least hear—if only intermittently—fragmentary reports of human rights abuse as well as voices of protest from the above-mentioned countries, we have hardly heard any protesting voices from North Korea. In the age of computer technology, some of the authoritarian governments have enhanced their control through more complicated surveillance and internet censorship. For example, China has developed advanced technology in surveillance and censorship, replacing its former "iron curtain" with far more sophisticated "firewalls." I cite these repressive examples not only to curb some of our premature complacency about global democratic development, but also to stress the importance of the emerging creative works on political prisons. In revealing the various aspects of carceral suffering and bringing us close to that previously buried reality, these works also enable us to imagine the undisclosed realms of torment still in existence.

As more and more political prison narratives are being written in different languages and published by individuals of diverse nationalities and ethnicities in various parts of the globe, the topic of human rights issues in literature is also receiving growing international attention. The carceral aspect, however, is but one piece—albeit an extremely crucial piece—of the vast fabric of pain manufactured by the gigantic repressive machinery. Viewed from a panoramic perspective, political prison literature is interwoven with other contemporary publications about the various aspects of life under dictatorships, and plays a major role in the larger context of human rights discourse.

It is enormously heartening for those of us who care about human rights in literature to find the 2009 Nobel Prize for Literature awarded to none other than Romanian-German writer Herta Müller. After living in Romania under the dictatorship and suffering in the hands of the secret police for years, Müller was finally allowed to emigrate to West Germany in 1987. Her mother, in addition, had endured life in a Soviet Union labor camp for a few years after World War II. Intellectuals like Müller who have experienced political repression are less likely to take freedom for granted. In Müller's own words, "I felt [in 1987] that I could breathe, and it was only when the dictatorship fell in 1989 and I felt I wouldn't be threatened any more."[5] In Germany, Müller not only depicts extensively in her fiction "the brutality suffered by modest people living under totalitarianism" but also courageously speaks out "against oppression and collaboration."[6]

A number of the authors studied in this collection had lived through repressions similar to Müller's, and experienced similar or longer and worse types of incarceration than Müller's mother. They would certainly resonate with Müller's musing on what her works attempt to represent, question, and investigate: "My writing always had to do with the question—how could a handful of powerful people seize a country. What gave them that right? . . . You can also count the Nazi regime, the concentration camps, military dictatorships and the religious dictatorships in some Islamic countries. So many people are crushed by them, so many lives ruined."[7] Just as writers of conscience like Müller have started to re-create what it was like living under dictatorships during the Cold War, so the authors in this volume have been recapturing for us the well-hidden secrets of outrageous human rights abuses under authoritarian regimes—the political prison experiences.

Through the conferral of the crowning literary honor upon Herta Müller, the international community's attention would be riveted upon human rights in literature even more than before. In addition, her works reconfirm this volume's conviction that human rights and aesthetics can coexist and flourish through their symbiotic relationship, and that literature that reveals the human truth of life under oppression can powerfully resist the deceptive discourse of a repressive regime.

To some extent, political prison narratives constitute part of the global protest literature or "resistance literature." The term, "resistance literature," was first used in 1966 by the Palestinian writer Ghassan Kanafani in his study of literature in occupied Palestine (Harlow 2). In her impressive book, *Resistance Literature* (1987), Barbara Harlow examines a number of "Third World" texts (from the Middle East, Africa, and Latin America, exclusively), including resistance poetry or narratives, and prison memoirs. These "Third World" works are called "resistance literature" particularly in the sense that they are revolutionary and activist. Harlow focuses on this literature's connection with resistance movements and the historical and cultural struggle against colonialism and imperialism.

This current volume, however, differs from Harlow's study in several aspects. While by no means claiming to be global or comprehensive, this volume goes beyond Harlow's coverage of the "Third World" texts to include Eastern Europe, China, and the United States, for example. The texts selected for analysis herein are rarely of the "revolutionary" type concerned with fighting for liberation from Western "imperialist" colonialism. When incorporating sociopolitical and historical contexts into their studies, most contributors of this volume are not talking so much about foreign oppression and postcolonialism as about state or government oppression, or what can be called a type of internal hegemony and domestic "colonialism." I use the word "colonialism" here because of a somewhat similar paradigm, and because the oppression suffered by dissidents is in some sense akin to that suffered by the "colonized." The oppression experienced by political dissidents during Morocco's "Lead Years," for example, came from within the country, not from foreign influences. The massive imprisonment and repression during the Mao era in China did not result from foreign oppression, but were self-inflicted. Moreover, in terms of approaches to studying political literature, significant emphases and discussions on selected works' aesthetic aspects also set the current volume apart from Harlow's.

Political prison narratives may overlap somewhat with *testimonio* (which is part of the resistance literature), yet remain distinct. According to John Beverley, "*testimonio* coalesces as a new narrative genre in the 1960s and further develops in close relation to the movements for national liberation and the generalized cultural radicalism of that decade"; as such, it is considered a "component" of the "resistance literature" (13). Beverley defines *testimonio* as "a novel or novella-length narrative in book or pamphlet . . . form, told in the first-person by a narrator who is also the real protagonist or witness of the events he or she recounts, and whose unit of narration is usually a 'life' or a significant life experience" (12–13).[8] By comparison, though the narratives examined in the present collection reflect struggles for civil rights, most of them have less connection to "the movements for national liberation."[9] The "significant life experience" presented in these narratives seldom covers as many aspects of "repression, poverty, subalternity" as the "life" in *testimonio* does; rather, it centers on the political repression related to and surrounding incarceration. If in *testimonio* the "protagonists" or "witnesses" of the events, along with the victims they represent, tend to come from the poor, peasants, and working classes, a good number of political prison narratives in fact feature "bourgeois" intellectuals.

Furthermore, while *testimonio* is a "protean" form that includes many "textual categories," whether literary or not (Beverley 13), most of the texts in this collection are selected not for being mere testimonies or testimonial documents but rather for their literary and artistic values. Unlike *testimonio*, which is "told in the first-person" by a narrator "who is either functionally illiterate or, if literate, not a professional writer" (Beverley 15), the texts under study were largely written by literate or well-educated people, including professional writers, who occasionally adopted novel narrative strategies.

The study of the multicultural political prison narratives from interdisciplinary perspectives is an emerging, rather than waning, field. We notice that the numerous discussions of the Latin American *testimonio* in the 1980s and 1990s have made some critics wonder if the once marginal, subaltern litera-ture has become "institutionalized" (through "canonization").[10] For example, Georg Gugelberger asks, "what is left of that which the academic Left had considered for so long as exemplary of a 'poetics of solidarity,' a possible center of 'resistance literature'?" (1). Gugelberger's concern is certainly le-gitimate, and his warning should be heeded. However, I would suggest that academic study of global political prison literature is still at a relatively early stage, and what is needed the most at present is to discover more works and explore innovative ways to study them.

While focusing on narratives, this collection would hopefully encourage studies on other genres, voices, media (especially films), and art forms sur-rounding the subject of political prison. It also hopes to offer a more catholic spectrum of perspectives that go beyond class-centered Marxist ideology and the "academic Left's" viewpoint and approach. I believe that persistent intel-lectual diversity in methodology would keep the study of the genre vibrant even after it has become "institutionalized."

This volume presents careful studies of political prison narratives that cross geographical and geopolitical boundaries. The contributors engage with the varied texts, pointing out new aspects in them for exploration, while adopting interesting approaches to examine them. The nine chapters fruitful-ly interrogate linguistic, structural, and cultural constructions of the political prison experience.

So far, studies on political prison narratives have tended to emphasize their human rights and sociopolitical aspects, while overlooking—sometimes even dismissing—their literary and aesthetic dimensions. Yet the volume crosses various disciplinary boundaries, studying the texts not only from historical, sociopolitical, and anthropological, but also from philosophical, psychological, and literary perspectives. Analyzing the literary aspects with-out losing sight of the political and the theoretical, the volume breaks new ground in examining a global aesthetics in political prison narratives and in fusing the study of human rights and suffering with that of the aesthetics.

Finally, in drawing attention to the heterogeneous, complex nature of the political prison narratives and experiences, the volume aims to open up con-structive discussions on them. The contributors may not all agree with one another's political outlook or theoretical approaches. Nevertheless, by allow-ing diverse—even conflicting or opposing—views to be aired in the same public discursive space provided herein, this volume embodies a democratic platform for a free yet civil exchange of ideas for the contributors; and by enabling the readers to engage with various perspectives, it aspires to con-struct a bridge to potentially healthy, fruitful, and mutually respectful debates in the future. In this regard, the volume also hopes to serve as a versatile educational tool that encourages further intercultural, interliterary, and inter-disciplinary research into political prison literature.

NOTES

1. In the case of Chinese authors, for example, Wumingshi shifted from writing about love and philosophical quest to writing about the Chinese Communist Party's political repression only after he had been imprisoned; the journalist and budding writer Cong Weixi developed into a mature author because, he declared, his many years in labor camp provided inspiration for him; and Zhang Xianliang became a full-blown writer only after his long jail experience. See also my discussion below and in chapter 3.

2. In conjunction with Slyomovics' excellent chapter, I would like to mention Alexander Elinson's interesting article, "Opening the Circle: Storyteller and Audience in Moroccan Prison Literature" published in *Middle Eastern Literatures* 12.3: 289–303 (2009). Elinson observes that some of the prison narratives tell stories "by creating a strong link between the speaker and the audience to the point where often, the boundary between the two is obscured," and the stories themselves are "circular and interactive, unbroken chains of telling/listening/re-telling" (290). Elinson examines two fascinating novels that adopt such narrative strategies: Abdellatif Laâbi's (1942–) *Le chemin des ordalies: roman (Path of Ordeals: A Novel)*, published in 1982, after Laâbi's release from prison, and Khadija Marouazi's (1961–) *Sirat al-Ramad: Riwaya (Biography of Ashes: A Novel)*, published in 2000 when human rights reforms had been launched. Significantly, as Elinson indicates, these two works attempt to go beyond a state-imposed "monolingual (literary Arabic) and officially circumscribed national identity, and a monovocal rendering of post-independence Moroccan history" (301). Elinson's paper was originally submitted to and accepted by the editors of this volume in 2008. I deeply regret that I am unable to include Elinson's article in this volume due to difficulty in obtaining the permission to reprint for free or at a low cost. I would still like to thank Elinson for his cooperation during the editing process.

3. See the report, "Hu Jia Wins European Rights Prize," October 23, 2008, http://news.bbc.co.uk/2/hi/asia-pacific/7686026.stm (accessed October 25, 2008).

4. Michael Bristow, "China Activist Formally Arrested," June 24, 2009, http://news.bbc.co.uk/2/hi/asia-pacific/8116044.stm (accessed June 25, 2009). Postscript: One year after I wrote this introduction, the jailed Liu Xiaobo was awarded the Nobel Peace Prize (on October 8, 2010), to the immense delight of all the supporters of China's human rights. The PRC government (which had previously warned the Nobel Peace Prize committee against awarding the prize to Liu) immediately "condemned the award, saying it could damage China-Norway relations." See "Nobel Peace Prize awarded to China dissident Liu Xiaobo," October 8, 2010, http://www.bbc.co.uk/news/world-europe-11499098 (accessed October 9, 2010). While the PRC regime is unlikely to release Liu, and would lead ordinary Chinese people to see the award as the West's "attack" on their nation's image, the award to Liu is extremely timely and significant in that it greatly boosts the morale of all China's rights defenders (especially those signing "Charter 08") and draws international attention and support to them.

5. Cited in "Germany hails literature Nobel honor for Herta Mueller," October 8, 2009, http://www.dw-world.de/dw/article/0,,4775947,00.html (accessed October 10, 2009).

6. Ibid.

7. Ibid.

8. Also quoted in Georg M. Gugelberger, "Introduction," 9.

9. However, see Eugenio Di Stefano's intriguing chapter in this volume on Carlos Lisca-no's "testimonio," *Truck of Fools* (2001), and Di Stefano's discussion of the MLN-Tupamaros (*Movimiento de Liberación Nacional*, National Liberation Movement) in Uruguay, an organ-ization of Marxist urban guerrilla fighters.

10. See the insightful argument in Georg M. Gugelberger, "Introduction."

Chapter 1

REFERENCES

Beverley, John. 1989. "The Margin at the Center." *Modern Fiction Studies* 35.1 (Spring): 11–28.

Bristow, Michael. 2009. "China Activist Formally Arrested." June 24, http://news.bbc.co.uk/2/hi/asia-pacific/8116044.stm (accessed June 25, 2009).

Elinson, Alexander. 2009. "Opening the Circle: Storyteller and Audience in Moroccan Prison Literature." *Middle Eastern Literatures* 12.3: 289–303.

Falkoff, Marc. 2007. "Notes on Guantánamo." In *Poems from Guantánamo: The Detainees Speak*, ed. Marc Falkoff, 1–5. Iowa City: Univ. of Iowa Press.

_____, ed. 2007. *Poems from Guantánamo: The Detainees Speak.* Iowa City: Univ. of Iowa Press.

"Germany Hails Literature Nobel Honor for Herta Mueller." October 8, 2009, http://www.dw-world.de/dw/article/0,,4775947,00.html (accessed October 10, 2009).

Gugelberger, Georg M. 1996. "Introduction: Institutionalization of Transgression: Testimonial Discourse and Beyond." In *The Real Thing: Testimonial Discourse and Latin America*, ed. Georg Gugelberger. Durham: Duke Univ. Press.

Harlow, Barbara. 1987. *Resistance Literature.* New York: Methuen.

"Hu Jia Wins European Rights Prize." October 23, 2008, http://news.bbc.co.uk/2/hi/asia-pacific/7686026.stm (accessed October 25, 2008).

"Nobel Peace Prize Awarded to China Dissident Liu Xiaobo." October 8, 2010, http://www.bbc.co.uk/news/world-europe-11499098 (accessed October 9, 2010).

Wu Yanna (Yenna Wu). 2004. "Chuangshang de shengyin: Pingxi Wumingshi de 'Daqiang wenxue' zhuzuo" (The Voice of the Wound: A Critique and Analysis of Wumingshi's "Prison Literature"). In *Wumingshi de wenxue zuopin tansuo yu jihuai* (Exploring and Remembering Wumingshi's Literary Works), ed. Wang Zhilian, et al., 123–161. Taipei: Wenshizhe chubanshe.

Chapter Two

Reviving Muted Voices

Rhizomatous Forces in Political Prison Literature

Yenna Wu

THE MISSING CRY

W. H. Auden (1907–73) began in his famous poem "Musée des Beaux Arts" (1940) with a reflection on suffering.[1] The poem was inspired by Auden's contemplation of Pieter Brueghel's (c. 1525–69) painting *Landscape with the Fall of Icarus* (c. 1558) and some other paintings in the Museum of Fine Arts in Brussels in 1938. In Greek mythology Icarus fell into the sea while escaping with his father from the exile and imprisonment ordered by King Minos. If not alerted by its title, any first-time viewer of this landscape painting might have easily missed the tragic fall depicted therein. Occupying but a small area in one corner of a rather crowded canvas, Icarus' failed flight appears trivial and inconsequential. Nor does it seem to ruffle the peaceful atmosphere pervading the rest of the landscape. The title is what prompts us to search for the fall and to espy the two tiny white legs sinking into the water. It is up to the viewer to imagine the missing cry from the falling boy in the picture.

What Auden notes in the artist's representation is not only the individual suffering but also other people's (and creatures') apathy to the calamity. He imagines that the plowman probably heard Icarus' cry, but paid no attention (198). Brueghel could have "represented" the cry or the splash by depicting someone in the picture cocking his or her ear in an attempt to listen, or else looking in the direction of Icarus' plunge. Yet, as depicted by the painter, none of the characters in the canvas gazes at the sinking legs or looks even slightly concerned. Whether they have noticed or heard Icarus' cry or not,

17

these people simply continue with their business, seemingly too preoccupied with their own living to mind others' pain. Mundane life goes on as usual, undisturbed by a fleeting event.

Absent Brueghel's own explanation, however, it is difficult to judge how he expects his viewer to interpret his representation of humanity. Did he intend to suggest that some people may have heard a cry, yet did not pay attention to it, or that Icarus' cry was hardly audible to bystanders, or else that Icarus did not utter any cry at all? Even if we assume the first case, we also do not know for sure if the painter's view of human reaction (or in this case, lack of response) to others' suffering is positive, negative, neutral, or mixed. For example, should the people in the painting be criticized for paying no heed to the tragedy or be commended for not being distracted and for ignoring the individual tragedy and moving on, focusing on their everyday life, routine, and goal? There are a number of ways to look at and interpret the painting. Viewers' responses to this artistic representation can thus vary considerably.

Through his poem Auden performs the role of an imaginary, perceptive and empathetic viewer. He chooses an ethical reading. Deducing a somewhat cynical message from the painting, he ponders upon human ignorance of and indifference to other people's sufferings. His musings, however, go beyond what is depicted in this painting. Auden turns his attention to one of the archetypal patterns of man-made suffering that involves perpetrators and their henchmen, victims, and possibly also other spectators. Written during the late 1930s, the poem might reflect some of the poet's impressions of the contemporary political unrest, persecutions, and wars. Employing images that make sense literally yet also have figural significance, Auden tells about how martyrdom takes place in some messy place in which the "dogs" continue leading their own life, and the horse that carries the torturer stands idly, rubbing its bottom on a tree.[2] Auden's elliptical, satirical, and somewhat humorous lines prompt us into further reflections of human position and responsibility regarding man-made disasters: Acts of atrocity committed in places dominated by repressive, corrupt regimes or groups often occur in an inconspicuous corner. While major perpetrators are surely guilty, the responsibility of their accomplices—either willing or coerced—is less easy to measure. And would those who accompany the torturer to the scene but do not perpetrate the crime (such as the role metaphorically indicated by the horse) be deemed "innocent"? What about the spectators—other than the victims, the torturers, and their company who also witness the scene—who either knowingly attend the scene or happen to pass by and inadvertently come upon the scene? Should they be held somewhat accountable? And should those who live near the scene of atrocity, who may have heard about the acts, and who continue to lead their own lives instead of trying to report the atrocity to the outside world, be completely exempt from blame? Just as the painting(s) inspired Auden to contemplate on issues beyond what has been represented within the frame of the painting(s), so Auden's poem encourages ethical interpretations and philosophical reflections beyond what the poem denotes or connotes. Without being explicitly didactic or exhortative, the poem performs a moral act.

TO REMEMBER OR NOT TO REMEMBER

Perpetrators of atrocious acts would often hide their acts from public view, though depending upon circumstances, they might create a spectacle in order to intimidate the public. By comparison, those in the midst of persecution would yearn desperately for the truth to be out, for the spectators to be sympathetic, and for the outside forces to come to their rescue and stop their suffering speedily. After the event, the perpetrators as well as their accomplices and supporters may then attempt to erase the bloody traces from public memory, or else justify their acts by distorting the truth and putting the blame on the victims instead. As we know, it is part of our human nature to evade painful memories. Naturally, most spectators and even some individual survivors of atrocity would wish to forget about it and go back to their normal life as soon as possible. Nevertheless, a majority of the surviving victims, especially those of collective suffering, would hope (even if they might not dare voice it) that the truth of their ordeal be known to the outside world and be remembered, and that justice be done and redress made.

Writing in less than a decade after Auden's poem, a young Polish writer named Tadeusz Borowski (1922–51) would similarly perform an ethical act by revealing, in unsentimental terms, atrocities of an unimaginable magnitude. A survivor of Nazi concentration camps, Borowski obviously felt compelled to reveal Nazi crimes against humanity which he had witnessed. For these prisoners, the most imminent of their hopes was of course for some strong forces from outside to stop the massacre immediately. Failing that, they would still hope for the hideous reality to be known to the outside world one way or another.

In "A Visit" (1948), one of the prose narratives Borowski wrote soon after the liberation in 1945, the narrator recalls how those emaciated, sickly Jews, on their way to the gas chamber, "begged the orderlies loading them into the crematorium trucks to remember what they saw. And to tell the truth about mankind to those who do not know it" (155). In utter desperation and unable to find anyone they can trust for help, victims have no choice but to appeal to the humanity of the perpetrators' "accomplices" (whether forced, reluctant, or willing) and implore them to serve as witnesses to their suffering and to report the truth to the outside world.

For those who are unjustly detained, incarcerated, tortured, or soon to be put to death, and who might have no recourse to justice in their lifetime, the only vindication they can hope for is that the truth of their suffering will eventually be known to other people, be recorded in history, and not be forgotten. Numerous political prisoners tried their best to survive in order to bear witness. As Terrence Des Pres demonstrates, the desire to "survive as a witness" is essential to the Holocaust survivors' survival and identity (31–35). The inmates might also establish some kind of network to ensure that at least someone would bear witness to their agony in the future. Furthermore, a number of them would like to see their misery represented. As Susan Sontag observes when discussing the long siege of Sarajevo, "the Sarajevans did want their plight to be recorded in photographs: victims are interested in the representation of their own sufferings" (112).

The desire to "survive as a witness" is similarly strong among many Chinese political prisoners. Traditionally, the Chinese regard the purpose of history as teaching later generations not to repeat previous mistakes. Therefore, these prisoners particularly wish to have their pain recorded in writing, known to posterity, and thus serve as a lesson in history. The Chinese writer Cong Weixi (b. 1933) was falsely labeled a "rightist" in 1957 and spent over two decades in Mao's laogai (forced hard labor) camps. In the 1960s, a senior fellow "rightist" inmate urged Cong Weixi to record their sufferings: "You used to be a journalist and writer. Do commit this span of history to memory as best as you can. If someday you are able to write again, you must write all this down without mixing in any falsehood—doing this is not for the sake of exposing shortcomings, but rather for China's future" (Cong 293). A few other fellow inmates made similar requests. Though their motivations might vary somewhat, Cong's fellow inmates must have wished for the catastrophic event to be truthfully documented and remembered so that it would not happen again. Cong Weixi did compose his laogai memoirs (published in 1989 and 1998), and despite being cautious about not offending the authorities, he insisted on the authenticity of his records while expressing the hope for future generations to learn lessons from this part of history.

Besides writing, various other mediums have been adopted to bear testimony or represent suffering. In her book, *Regarding the Pain of Others* (2003), Sontag examines the medium of photography as offering one of the many opportunities in modern life for regarding others' suffering from a distance (13). Indeed, images of cruelty can compellingly allow us to regard others' pain from not only a spatial distance but also a temporal or cultural distance. Yet the images perceived by a viewer positioned at a distance might risk the danger of seeming blurred or unreal. Furthermore, photographs without captions or any accompanying explanations can be confusing or misleading; and photographs can be fabricated, manipulated, and even deceptive.

Depending upon their positioning, viewers can possibly have rather diverse responses. While some viewers would be prompted to sympathize with the victims or take concrete actions to help, others might feel skeptical, cynical, or indifferent. Distanced observation could easily make some feel complacent, lacking in sympathetic engagement and a sense of crisis. Aware that photographs of atrocity may "give rise to opposing responses" (13), Sontag nevertheless contends that these images could tell us, "This is what human beings are capable of doing—may volunteer to do, enthusiastically, self-righteously. Don't forget" (115). Controversial as they might be in their uses, photographs still constitute one of the most direct means to record and show, and to shock us into recognizing, the human capacity for cruelty.

I would suggest that political prison narratives are among the most useful resources for us to discover, reflect upon, and remember the acts of atrocity as well as the victims' misery. Similar to photographs of atrocity, these narratives of suffering also force us to recognize brutality and injustice which some regimes still try to hide. The works convey the same message: "Don't forget" and "Never again!" As the saying goes, "A picture is worth a thousand words." Photographs can create an instantaneous impact. Though not as speedily sensational as photographs, these narratives not only can accomplish similarly positive achievements but often affect us in a far more complex and nuanced manner. Rather than offering merely visual fragments of an event, a narrative may present sequences of events in the form that gives the impression of a series of connected "snapshots," and would often explain what comes before and after the events. Accounts of suffering typically cover more dimensions spatially and temporally than photos, and can potentially be more powerful and enduring in their impact. Survivors' memoirs can particularly lend insight into inmates' identity and survival. In general, narratives are far more capable than photos in manifesting the meandering complexity of the human mind. Considering their strengths and weaknesses, I find these narratives to be superior to photos as a medium of representation.

If "to photograph is to frame, and to frame is to exclude" (Sontag 46), the narratives can result from an even more complex process of the writers' framing, selection, and exclusion of materials than photos. This issue would be further complicated in the cases of multiple authors, heavy-handed editors, interview-based works, or second-hand memoirs. Translation poses another layer of complication, especially in the cases when translators abridge the original, select only certain parts for translation, change the order of the chapters, mistranslate certain words or sentences, or fail to capture the authors' meanings, voices, tones, and nuances.[3] Furthermore, issues of authenticity in an account would often be contested. It would be debatable, for example, whether a work can be deemed authentic if its narration of the experience is not completely truthful to the objective reality yet the overall affect it evokes is truthful to the experience. While the writers' motivations might be under scrutiny, the readers' responses could vary or even clash with one another, depending upon their perspectives.

Generally speaking, we find diverse reactions to an atrocious act from different parties and positioning—such as to stop it immediately, uncover and condemn it, refuse to know the truth, neglect or condone the act, or hide the truth and lie about it. We also confront differences of opinion as to whether the event should be remembered afterward, why it needs remembering, what is to be remembered, how to remember it, and how much and for how long it should be remembered. Sontag points out a paradoxical situation: "Remembering *is* an ethical act, has ethical value in and of itself. . . . And too much remembering (of ancient grievances: Serbs, Irish) embitters. To make peace is to forget" (115). Indeed, remembrances can play controversial roles in certain contexts. Many, no doubt, would like to see the opposing parties in a feud or war bury their hatchets, reconcile with one another, and forget about past rancor and bloodshed. Spectators of atrocity often wish to forget and move on, rather than bearing witness in investigations.

For certain ex-inmates, freedom from incarceration means not only being physically released but also being mentally released and free from past rancor and resentment. Nelson Mandela, laureate of the 1993 Nobel Peace Prize, exemplifies the spirit of forgiveness. In *Living History*, Hillary Rodham Clinton relates how, when in jail, Mandela "learned to control his emotions in order to survive"; Mandela also reminded Clinton that "gratitude and forgiveness, which often result from pain and suffering, require tremendous discipline" (235–36). When Mandela was released from prison (February 11, 1990), he remarked inspiringly, "As I walked out the door toward the gate that would lead to my freedom, I knew if I didn't leave my bitterness and hatred behind, I'd still be in prison" (Clinton 236). Mandela's resolve to leave his "bitterness and hatred behind" is surely not just a strategy for a more comfortable personal survival; it also marks a superior type of individual who, tempered by his suffering, has grown to be truly generous and compassionate at heart, and developed the capability to embrace all humanity, including former enemies. However, while "to err is human, to forgive divine," as Alexander Pope famously stated, not every ex-inmate or victim's surviving family member can forgive easily. And while forgiving usually entails some forgetting, it is not the same as forgetting.

I would suggest that in the case of political prisoners, remembering—especially bearing witness—is a much-needed "ethical act," and forgetting too soon will not bring genuine peace. To speak metaphorically, if such a "wound" is left unattended, it would fester, worsen, and even spread to other parts of the body, however imperceptible it may be; and an untreated disease of this type would not go away by itself, but is likely to deteriorate or recur. A first step toward preventing a catastrophic event from recurring might be to conduct an objective investigation into exactly what had happened, and why and how it had happened. I believe that the healing process cannot begin if the truth of unjust suffering is forgotten even before it is uncovered, discussed, understood, and properly dealt with. Before true forgiveness and peace can set in, there ought to be a process of healing which involves independent investigation and truth finding, open discussions, negotiations, public apology, legal actions to ensure justice, or even reparation from the perpetrators or their representatives, and finally, reconciliation. "Embittering" as remembering may be, it serves a crucial function in eventually healing the wound and restoring lasting peace. In this respect, political prison narratives play a crucial role in truth finding, witnessing, and testifying, whether specific individuals prefer to remember the event or not. Consequently, we find much "ethical value" in the narratives of pain that enhance public consciousness and remembrance of, as well as discourse on, unjust suffering.

At the same time, however, we cannot afford to be unaware of the daunting complexity in the discourse of remembering and representation. We would need to discern the increasingly complex politics in the remembrances and representation of suffering, and in the writing, reading, publishing, as well as potential commodifying and politicizing, of political prison literature. This is a field of study that both requires and can particularly benefit from intellectual diversity.

READING SPECIFICITIES IN POLITICAL PRISON NARRATIVES: COMMONALITIES AND DIFFERENCES

Given the rich historical significance and ethical value inherent in creative works about the political prison experience, how can we best tap into those resources? I would suggest that a fruitful way to accomplish this goal is to read broadly, gain breadth of exposure, and study the texts comparatively—for example, cross-culturally, cross-literarily, and cross-disciplinarily—and at the same time, read the materials deeply, examining the specificities and engaging with the authors' and narrators' subjectivities and interiorities.

Reading prison narratives from diverse areas, we observe how frequently the human rights abuse and psychological trauma suffered by political prisoners transcend national borders as well as historical specificities. We cannot help but notice some of the remarkable commonalities. The patterns of repression can be similar, whether the authoritarian regimes genuinely, or for mere convenience, espouse such ideologies as fascism, communism, socialism, nationalism, militarism, or others. Time and again, we also witness how some heroes of liberation movement can be corrupted by their acquired power and turn into military dictators themselves, who blatantly contradict their original idealistic slogans for freedom and social equality and desire only to cling to their power for as long as possible. Political repression worsens when the regime has complete internal hegemony armed with a monopoly of executive, legislative, judicial, and military powers, while unrestrained by the rule of law or checks and balances. Prompted by the "paranoia" about any opposition to their dictatorship, the leaders of autocratic regimes engage in similar oppression and secretive surveillance. Various regimes share comparable features in their deceptive tactics, illegal arrest, detention, and torture of real and imagined dissidents, as well as carceral practices and prison regimens. For example, the former Soviet Union's repressive and carceral practices exerted much influence on the PRC and the formerly Communist European states during the Cold War.

We realize that in different regions, the prison culture, the suffering caused by massive imprisonment and repression, and prisoners' responses and reactions to oppression also have much in common. For example, state censorship on reading and writing can go to such an extreme in political prisons that pen and paper are prohibited. When incarcerated in 1968–69 during the Mao era, Wumingshi (pseudonym of Bu Naifu, alias Bu Ning, a.k.a. Pu Ning, 1917–2002) composed a number of poems. Lacking writing instruments to write them down and dreading additional punishment if the poems were discovered, he decided to memorize the poems instead. Retrieved or reconstructed from his memory later, twenty-two of these poems were published in Taiwan in a collection of his poetry, *Yuzhong shichao* (Poems Composed in Prison) (1984).

Nawal El Saadawi's experience of censorship resembles yet also differs from Wumingshi's. In her memoir ([1986] 1994) about the women's prison in Cairo in 1981, Saadawi reported that the prison head rejected the political women prisoners' request for pen and paper, saying, "Easier to give you a pistol than pen and paper" (49). This line struck her like "a line from a farce," and she reflected: "I had not imagined that pen and paper could be more dangerous than pistols in the world of reality and fact" (49). Saadawi nevertheless defied the rule and managed to keep a diary, writing secretly after midnight, sitting "on top of the overturned bottom of the jerry can" in the lavatory, while using "toilet rolls and cigarette papers" for writing (81–82). By hiding the diary entries she had written inside her hair rollers (189–90), she eventually packed them in her suitcase and took them out safely upon her release. Saadawi was resourceful enough to exploit some advantages exclusive to female prisoners as well as her prison's relatively lax surveillance so as to write and "smuggle" out her writings.

We find an interesting parallel to Saadawi's experience in the case of the Syrian writer Faraj Bayraqdar. He also wrote down his thoughts on cigarette paper. Though without recourse to any gender-specific advantages, he later managed to have the series of fragments smuggled out of prison, and compiled them after his release (in 2000–2001) into a memoir, *Khiyanat al-Lugha wa al-Samt* (The Betrayals of Language and Silence).[4]

Even in the 21st century, writing materials were denied to most of the Guantánamo detainees during the first year of their detention. According to Marc Falkoff, the detainees managed to "inscribe their words" on Styrofoam cups with pebbles or "trace out letters with small dabs of toothpaste," then "pass the 'cup poems' from cell to cell." These cups would eventually be collected and dumped as trash, yet some of them were later "reconstructed from memory" (Falkoff 3).

While we cannot ignore the commonalities, we also have to be cautious so as not to conflate one narrative with another or flatten out their differences. A closer look at political prison literature would reveal its distinct multiplicities and a wide array of specificities. Tied to specific political situations and locations, prisoners' experiences could be very different. Even in such common human rights abuses as depriving prisoners of the freedom to write, significant variations exist synchronically and diachronically.

In Mao-era China, for example, Zhang Xianliang (1936–) went through different types of jails and labor camps from 1957 to 1978. He once claimed that during the twenty-two years he was forbidden to keep a diary: "If I tried to write a diary, someone would inform on me the following day"; nor did he have the habit of keeping a diary (Zhang 1987, 91). Yet later he discovered a small booklet of a "diary" dated from 1960, and based on its meager record, he wrote his memoir *My Bodhi Tree* (*Wode putishu*, 1994).[5] Apparently in 1960 Zhang was in a less stringently guarded camp in a rural area in Ningxia, China's remote Northwestern region. Serving as the scribe of his group, Zhang could keep his pen and some paper; he also managed to keep a tiny diary secretly. Because of his special position and circumstances, he enjoyed a little more freedom to write relative to his contemporary fellow inmates. Of course, he still needed to constantly exercise self-censorship and be cautious about what he wrote.

By comparison, the writer Wumingshi was strictly guarded in a prison in the city of Hangzhou after his arrest in 1968—during the early period of the Cultural Revolution (1966–76) when CCP-coordinated surveillance, censorship, mutual denunciation, and struggle sessions were rampant. As mentioned above, unable to write down the poems he composed in prison, he could only commit them to memory. Yet even after his release in 1969, he was still too intimidated to write down those poems. Whether inside or outside the prison, he felt and dreaded the Orwellian surveillance and paranoia of censorship pervading China—an enormous jail—at that time. Only after Mao's death in 1976 did he dare write these poems down from memory. And only after he had left China in 1982 did he publish these poems (1984).

Somewhat similar to prisoners of Mao such as Wumingshi, prisoners of Stalin such as Varlam Shalamov (1907–82) also found the overwhelming paranoiac censorship intimidating even outside the prison. Shalamov did not start writing his tales about the Soviet forced-labor camps in desolate Kolyma until after Stalin's death. The manuscripts of Shalamov's masterpiece, possibly written during the mid- to late-1950s, were later smuggled abroad for publication.[6]

Specific issues such as denying inmates the access to pen and paper can vary through time and circumstances even for the same prisoner or group of prisoners in the same location. As reported by Saadawi, the official, despite his initial refusal, finally granted the request of Saadawi and her cellmates for pen and paper so they could write and ask their family to bring them clothes (Saadawi 51, 56). In this case, writing to one's family to request clothing is deemed innocuous enough to win inmates at least one-time access to writing materials. However, creative writing or writing down one's thought and feelings is held suspect in this and many other cases. In Marc Falkoff's account, the Guantánamo detainees were given access to writing instruments after the first year in which such access was denied (3). Some sent their poems out to the volunteer lawyers. Yet many of the poems were "destroyed or confiscated" or forbidden to be made public because the Pentagon argued that poetry "presents a special risk" to national security due to its "content and format" (4). The above-mentioned examples exhibit both commonalities and differences. When we pay attention to the specificities and compare variations on common themes in diverse texts, we are able to better understand the specific circumstances surrounding the political incarceration, and better appreciate the creative work.

UNDERSTANDING CONTEXTUALLY AND COMPARATIVELY: CROSS-CULTURAL AND CROSS-LITERARY ENCOUNTERS

Reading cross-culturally and cross-literarily, we are struck by an amazing range of diversity and complexity in the different contexts of these narratives as well as in their content, form, technique, and style. This prompts us to not only examine the specificities but study them contextually. Even looking merely at the content level and the rudimentary aspects of prison regimens, we would already confront a wide spectrum of diversity resulting from different governments, political cultures, historical times, geographical areas, ethnicities, religions, and socioeconomic conditions. Furthermore, when encountering varied literary expressions of the political prison experiences, and when reading works originally written in a language different from our own, we would benefit from some understanding of their literary tradition, conventions, or even theories. Indeed, adopting a comparative approach to studying these different aspects would be both imperative and highly illuminating.

While we often encounter descriptions of hunger, deprivations, and hard labor in these narratives, the intensity as well as the representations can vary substantially. The labor camp in China's northwestern province Ningxia in 1960, as described in Zhang Xianliang's *My Bodhi Tree* (*Wode putishu*, 1994), shares quite a few similarities with the Soviet gulag described by Varlam Shalamov and Solzhenitsyn,[7] but still differs considerably from the Soviet camp. Differences exist also within the Soviet gulag or the Chinese laogai respectively, as, for example, Solzhenitsyn admits that Shalamov's experience in the freezing Kolyma camps (in northeastern Siberia) was "longer and more bitter" than his own (Glad 8). The labor camp conditions depicted in Zhang's memoir resonate with—yet also depart from—the conditions of the 1950s' Qinghai camps, as documented by Wumingshi in his interview-based account, *Red Sharks* (*Hongsha*, [1989] 1994a, published in Taiwan); unlike in Zhang's memoir, the inmates in Wumingshi's account about Qinghai did not have a preexisting "camp" to settle in and must initially serve as "frontiersmen" to build their own. Taken together, the carceral experiences depicted by these four authors far "surpass" the experiences of the Egyptian woman writer Nawal El Saadawi in terms of the intensity in hardships and miseries. Yet even the relatively less harrowing conditions experienced by Saadawi in a Cairo prison in 1981 can still make some other prisons (in contemporary U.S., for example) seem rather comfortable by comparison.[8]

From these works we also discover how prisoners of one country sometimes try to imagine, form ideas, or harbor illusions about the living conditions of the inmates in another country, particularly when they feel desperate or hopeless about their own conditions. For example, in his *Gulag Archipelago*, Solzhenitsyn observed how some Russian inmates imagined that life in China was much better. He related the prisoners' thoughts during a transport in which they had no knowledge of their destination: "We even supposed that it might be somewhere quite close to the Chinese border (and this made some of us happy, since they had yet to learn that China was even worse than our own country)" (1976, 54). It was years later when those prisoners discovered that the conditions in China at that time were much worse.

Zhang Xianliang seems to largely agree with the assessment made by Solzhenitsyn here about the Russian gulag conditions being still better than those of Chinese laogai. Claiming that he has read a number of works about the former Soviet and East European gulag, he ventures to compare the living conditions of the Chinese prisoners with those of the former Soviet and East European inmates in the 1950s and 1960s. He finds the latter far superior to the Chinese case due to their much better-constructed prison compounds, better-equipped facilities and services, much more abundant material resources, higher standards of hygiene, and so forth (1994, 265–277).

Deeming the Soviet prisoners far more fortunate than their Chinese counterparts for being able to enjoy "wonderful facilities" and services, Zhang Xianliang asserts—without irony—that what he envies the most about the Soviet prisoners is their having "laundry rooms," "bathhouses," regular haircuts and changing of underclothes, and well-equipped hospitals. He complains that when he was twice incarcerated in formal laogai camps, for a total of about seven years, he never had the opportunity to enjoy taking a bath or change his underclothes. As a result, his underclothes were constantly full of lice (268). Of course, we would assume that writing after their release from prison camps, both Solzhenitsyn and Zhang must have been equipped with more knowledge and broader perspectives and could better judge and analyze their former prison conditions than when they were confined.

Reading Zhang Xianliang's comparison of the Soviet and Chinese labor camps by itself, a reader would tend to trust Zhang's judgment and therefore take his evaluative statements for granted. However, it is necessary to keep in mind that the location of the Chinese camps used by Zhang for comparison was confined to the Ningxia region, and was not necessarily typical of all the Chinese camps. Zhang's understanding of the Soviet gulag might have also been somewhat limited, since his conception seems to be based on his reading of only some selectively translated materials. [9]

Yet, only when we read more broadly the diverse narratives from both the Soviet and Chinese ex-inmates, and read them comparatively and contextually, can we obtain more complex perspectives from both sides and form a more truthful and comprehensive picture. For example, those who have also read Shalamov's *Kolyma Tales* and known about the horror of Kolyma (where, according to a historian's estimate, three million people died; Glad 7) would find it difficult to agree with Zhang's sanguine assessment readily. Shalamov spent close to seventeen years in Kolyma from roughly 1937 to 1954 (Glad 12). The camps in Kolyma, as described by Shalamov, were in quite a few aspects no better than Zhang's, and were in some ways (such as the unbearable cold and the criminal convicts' bullying of political prisoners) much worse. Had Zhang read Shalamov's "In the Bathhouse," for example, he would have realized that in fact many Soviet prisoners often referred to the bathhouse sessions as "tyranny" (Shalamov 39), and regarded the bathhouse as "a negative event, a burden in the convict's life" (40). Required even in severe weather conditions, the bathhouse sessions were devised to be more like torture than comfort.

Considering the particular contexts of the two works, we would realize that both writers are actually "similar" in that what they complain about are extremes. Both are "accurate" in their negative portrayal of the conditions: Zhang grumbles about Chinese camps' lack of resources and facility for sanitation, thereby forcing prisoners to live in filth for years, while Shalamov grouses about the Soviet camps' unreasonably rigid rule and impractical practice surrounding the bathhouse sessions. When reading Shalamov's and Zhang's narratives side by side, we could provide an imaginary space for the two authors to cross linguistic barriers and "converse" with each other across space and time. Had such a meeting of the minds been possible, Shalamov's detailed explanations of why the bathhouse sessions became a torture would have disabused Zhang to some extent of his misconception in this regard. Conversely, had Shalamov had an opportunity to converse with Zhang, he might have written about the bathhouse sessions and other experiences some-what differently. It is through our cross-cultural and cross-literary interpre-tive lens that different authors can imaginably "engage" with one another, so to speak, and some of the unexpected, problematic, and complex aspects of the works would surface. The knowledge thus produced would be able to dispel illusions and false conceptions about the reality of varied prison expe-riences.

Political prison narratives encourage a broad range of comparative, inter-literary reading. It would be fruitful to examine possible intertextual links and how the works of such earlier masters as Shalamov and Solzhenitsyn have influenced later writers, and to investigate how later works react to or even reverse earlier models in order to creatively craft their own individual styles. It would be interesting to compare, for example, Solzhenitsyn's *Gulag Archipelago* with the memoirs that have been partially inspired by it such as Wumingshi's *Red Sharks* and Zhang Xianliang's *My Bodhi Tree*. In addition, to what extent are the works of Wumingshi, Zhang Xianliang, and Cong Weixi informed by—and to what extent do they respond or react to—their indigenous or Western literary traditions in general, and by the works about the former Soviet and even East European gulag in particular? Furthermore, it would be productive to look into how different artistic expressions may influence one another. Scholars have noted, for example, how a type of Moroccan performance space, the *halqa* (chain link; ring; circle), which joins "the performer and the audience, the insider and the outsider" appears to inform "the performative act of telling and listening" in some remarkable Moroccan prison narratives (Elinson 2009, 290). Through examining Guantánamo detainees' verses in the context of Islamic poetic genres and traditions, Flagg Miller skillfully compares the imagery, language, and style of Guantánamo detainees' verses and those of the "self-proclaimed militant *jihadists*," and convincingly argues for their differences (11–12). Our cross-cultural encounters with political prison literature would thus enhance our cross-literary understanding and competency, encouraging us to further plumb the depth of different literary traditions and individual subjectivities.

ENGAGING SUBJECTIVITIES

Just as Auden's poem revives Icarus' cry, which is not represented in the painting and can only be imagined by the sympathetic viewer, so the prison literature analyzed in this volume revives some of the voices, sobs, and screams that have long been muted by repressive regimes and official discourse, or by the general public's neglect and amnesia. Moreover, this body of literature performs an ethical act in ways that are somewhat analogous to the photos of atrocity—yet due to its complexity it also goes beyond the latter in this function. It reveals the hidden reality of the political prison through various representations of a broad spectrum of experiences—including not only oppression, atrocity, submission, suffering, death, but also resilience, survival, agency, resistance, transformation of identity, and others—thereby inspiring the reader to recognize the reality and truth, correct the illusion previously manufactured by official discourse or propaganda, remember the victims' misery, and reflect upon human nature, history, and the future.

Human suffering has many faces, depending upon the specific time, place, people, and circumstances. What might seem similar to the outsiders can appear widely different from the insiders' perspective. For example, Sontag points out that the Sarajevans want their suffering "to be seen as unique" (112). Though Sontag detects "a racist tinge" in the Sarajevans' protest against a photographer's exhibiting photographs of their plight alongside those showing the sufferings in Somalia (113), it is understandable that due to identity, pride, self-esteem, and other reasons beyond simply racism or elitism, victims of different catastrophic events would view their own misery as special. Holocaust survivors would hardly regard their suffering as exactly the same as any other genocide. Indeed, prisoners of different regions, ethnicities, class, gender, cultures, political ideologies, religions, and even those imprisoned due to different reasons in the same jail might assert the uniqueness of their own suffering and identity. For example, political prisoners in the former Soviet gulag and Mao-era laogai camps frequently felt humiliated by or even resentful about being jailed with criminal offenders.[10] Whether agreeing or disagreeing with the authors, the reader might need to try to understand, respect, and accept the fact that a number of writers consciously distinguish political prisoners from other types of inmates.

Indeed, many political prisoners are concerned not only about "outsiders'" (lack of) recognition of the uniqueness of their situations but also about the very representation of that uniqueness. Depending upon their familial, educational, and other backgrounds, some writers could be crafting their individual or group's uniqueness or asserting their identity or agency more than the others. Furthermore, quite a few authors intentionally differentiate themselves from other prisoners or writers through their works. Some would pay more attention to realistic details or to affect, while others to individual psyche. Some of the authors are also highly self-reflective; they might calculate the effect of their writing, or they might wonder if language can sufficiently or accurately convey their experiences and feelings, if the meaning of their works would be distorted by the regime, if others can truly understand them, and so forth. Reading these narratives thus requires us to go beyond surface meanings and engage deeply with the authors' subjectivities.

Varlam Shalamov is one of the writers that consciously represents their prison experiences in unique ways. Of course one may argue that his experience itself is unique enough. Like some other writers, Shalamov records much suffering from the camps, including the extreme cold and hunger. Yet his keen observation and deep reflection enable him to select and depict some highly exceptional and even ironic episodes. For example, in "Lend-Lease," one of Shalamov's famous Kolyma tales, the narrator sees crowds of starving prisoners vying with one another to get a taste of the less-than-half-a-barrelful American machine grease (175). The struggle for getting a taste of the inedible machine grease underscores the extent of the prisoners' hunger, while we cannot help but be struck by the irony in the fact that what the inmates in a supposedly superior "socialist" state vie for is the machine grease produced in "capitalist" America.

Shalamov permits the reader some glimpses into his interiorities by creating an observant, curious, introspective, and reflective narrator (his persona). In the same story, the narrator witnesses a horrendous scene: "A grave, a mass prisoner grave, a stone pit stuffed full with undecaying corpses of 1938 was sliding down the side of the hill, revealing the secret of Kolyma" (178). The scene is focalized through the narrator, as he notes the gruesome remains that reveal the suffering these "skeleton-like corpses" must have endured: "the twisted fingers, the pus-filled toes which were reduced to mere stumps after frostbite, the dry skin scratched bloody and eyes burning with a hungry gleam" (179). Shalamov creates a distinctive persona through the narrator, who, though starving and fatigued like his cellmates, still preserves the capability of observation, imagination, and reflection. Noticing the injuries sustained by the corpses, the narrator imagines the hardships those inmates must have endured while alive, and asks sharp questions:

> With my exhausted, tormented mind I tried to understand: How did there come to be such an enormous grave in this area? I am an old resident of Kolyma, and there hadn't been any gold mine here as far as I knew. But then I realized that I knew only a fragment of that world surrounded by a barbed-wire zone and guard towers that reminded one of the pages of tent-like Moscow architecture. Moscow's taller buildings are guard towers keeping watch over the city's prisoners. That's what those buildings look like. And what served as models for Moscow architecture—the watchful towers of the Moscow Kremlin or the

guard towers of the camps? The guard towers of the camp "zone" represent the
main concept advanced by their time and brilliantly expressed in the symbolism of architecture. (179–180)

Stumbling upon the macabre secret generates an epiphanic experience for the
narrator. The sight of the enormous grave filled with frozen corpses shocks
him into the realization of the incredible scope of the despotic Soviet regime's victimization. A sudden recognition of the connection between politics and punishment triggers his notice of the architectural similarity between
the guard towers in both Kremlin and prison camps, and his reflections on the
permeating repressive surveillance represented through their architectural
symbolism. All these ignite in him the vision of a massive political persecution network that stretches from Moscow to Kolyma. The whole nation
seems like a gigantic prison to the narrator at that moment of insight.

When engaging with the authors' subjectivities, the reader would notice
that despite often containing narrations of physical and mental torture and
suffering, these works by no means limit themselves to describing pain
alone. In fact, to the extent that they also express and convey individual
subjectivities, these narratives not uncommonly depict moments of calm,
peace of mind, triumph, and even happiness for either an individual or a
group of prisoners.[11] Such depictions are of course separate from the type of
hypocritical "happy prison" narratives written primarily for the purpose of
the regime's propaganda and for some other ulterior motives.

Unique subjectivities often surface in narratives relating how political
prisoners strategize for survival and preserving identities. Prisoners' strategies to find calm and support vary according to such factors as their personalities, upbringing, or family and educational backgrounds. Some prisoners
find inspiration and spiritual support from religion, philosophy, literature, or
other sources. Aung San Suu Kyi, whom the Myanmar regime has repeatedly
placed under house arrest since 1989, is an exemplary of a successful survivor. Through her education and disciplined way of life, belief in Buddhist
philosophy, and Buddhist practices such as daily meditation, she has maintained tranquility, resilience, and a sense of humor, though facing enormous
pressure.[12] Neither fearing nor hating her captors, she has persisted in her
non-violent struggle for democracy.

Literature, spiritual tradition, or aesthetic education can provide succor to
those facing extreme conditions. Ariel Dorfman relates how a Chilean woman prisoner tortured by Pinochet's secret police in a cellar in Santiago "repeated to herself those verses sent from some dead poet . . . as a way of
differentiating herself from the men who were treating her body like an
object, like a piece of meat." The woman's repeating of the verses "protected
her besieged identity" from the jailers and helped her endure the "pain and
humiliation" (Dorfman 69). Creative writings carried out in prison—often

clandestinely—can also provide similar protection for the inmate's identity and dignity, while offering spiritual support. The attempt to express oneself through creative writing in prison could be ambivalent for sure. For example, Flagg Miller indicates that poetry itself can be "constraining" for the Guantánamo detainees not only due to its structural limits but also due to the authorities' censorship and the detainees' "self-monitoring" (Miller 14). Nevertheless, in the end, poetry still can "provide a welcome salve even when its formal devices prove insufficient to express the reality of a tragic situation" (Miller 14–15).

Some of the authors consciously reflect on human capabilities in adapting and finding strategies to survive when faced with extremities. While remembering and repeating some of the previously acquired literature or knowledge could serve as a strategy for survival, some authors discover that selective memory or partial "self-brainwashing" by filtering out the negative appears to work sometimes to the inmates' benefit. The narrator in Shalamov's work, "Dry Rations," remarks, "A human being survives by his ability to forget. Memory is always ready to blot out the bad and retain only the good" (66). Forgetting the painful while remembering and hoping for the good can also serve as a survival strategy for the incarcerated.

Even when writing about prisoners' seemingly endless sufferings from extreme cold, hunger, exhaustion, beatings, and other miseries in Kolyma, Shalamov inserts sporadic brighter scenes into the generally bleak panorama. In "A Child's Drawings" (135–38), while foraging at a heap of garbage, the narrator suddenly comes upon a child's drawing book and recalls some of the happier, but irretrievable, moments during his childhood; he enjoys a brief respite in reminiscing, though his fond memories are mixed with a little sorrow and a sense of irony.

Shalamov also depicts experiences that resemble self-healing, such as an individual's joyous reawakening from depression as well as a group's temporary mood shift from despair to ecstasy. The narrator in "Sententious" (70–76) describes a period of time when he gradually "wakes up" from severe impoverishment of language and emotions: complete indifference disappears, while pity for the animals returns. One day the word "sententious" suddenly returns to his tongue, much to his joy, though his mind does not comprehend the word's meaning until much later. The story ends with an ecstatic scene in which the inmates are running excitedly to the village where a newly arrived record player "was playing symphonic music" (76). Shalamov thus beautifully captures the evanescent moment of joy either in an individual's sudden discovery of the return of some cognitive intellect and emotion or else in a group's unexpected brief encounter and engagement with classical music.

Somewhat resembling Shalamov, Nawal El Saadawi emerges as a strong personality in her prison memoirs. Similar to Shalamov, she records moments of aesthetic pleasure or reflection, and sometimes writes poetically about her emotional responses to such moments and her captivity: for example, her heart "beat forcefully" on hearing the sweet voice of the curlew (which she could not see); she jammed her head "between two steel bars" trying to see the bird; and she describes the curlew as singing "like a mother's voice . . . like a child's abrupt, long laugh, or like a single scream in the night" (83). These impressionistic metaphors lyrically reflect her sadness, anguish, yearning for freedom, but also a tinge of joy of living.

Like Aung San Suu Kyi, Saadawi persevered in preserving her identity, integrity, and dignity during imprisonment. Ever courageous and resourceful, Saadawi not only writes about her suffering but also dwells on the occasions of contentment. For example, she describes the satisfaction derived from establishing harmonious relationships and female solidarity with the other inmates—despite occasional disputes—and succeeding in jointly pressing the prison administration to meet some of their demands ([1986] 1994, 40, 44–45). She relates how she kept her body and mind sound by continuing to do physical exercises daily. She writes about being so happy as to sing a song when she could take a shower for the first time since being detained (64), and how her back pains disappeared due to her delight in making friends with a young girl (82–83).

Saadawi certainly counts among the more resourceful, adaptable, and successful survivors. By initiating a request, Saadawi obtained the opportunity to plant vegetables, and enjoyed the digging and gardening (84, 98). This type of activity seems therapeutic for her because, instead of continuing to be plagued by uncertainty and waiting, she started to reminisce about her childhood and forgot about time. She admits at one point, "I forgot that I was in prison" (85).

Saadawi's experiences in a Sadat-era women's prison offer illuminating contrasts and comparisons with those of many other political prisons. For example, Saadawi's mood was lifted by doing the manual "labor" she requested, yet in the Soviet gulag or the Mao-era laogai camps, labor means something very different to the inmates who were routinely forced to do hard work for long periods of time even when half-starved. Furthermore, in contrast to many inmates who were strictly forbidden to write, Saadawi's engagement in secret writing while incarcerated, which became a sort of nocturnal ritual for a while, allows her to differentiate herself from her captors and even cellmates, and helps preserve her dignity and identity as a free-thinking writer. Similar to our encounter with Shalamov's work, reading Saadawi's memoirs carefully would enable us to appreciate the uniqueness of her prison experience, engage with her exceptional personality and interiority, and respect her subjectivity and agency.

THE NECESSITY OF INTERDISCIPLINARY STUDIES: WHEN AESTHETICS AND POLITICAL PRISON INTERSECT

Political prison narratives tend to be construed as truth-telling testimonials that have uses for such studies as human rights, law, politics, and history. However, this group of literature can be complex enough as to warrant a wide range of interdisciplinary and cross-cultural studies. For example, when examining women political prisoners' life in postwar Greece, Janet Hart suggests that we pay attention to "prisons as places of residence, marked by quotidian practices, rituals of communication and survival, negotiations of power and desire" (491). Indeed, when examining prison culture and litera-ture, we find that anthropological and sociological approaches can intersect fruitfully with political science and history. Saadawi's memoir, for example, not only contributes to studies of human rights and history, but also lends itself very well to analyses adopting literary, psychological, or women's studies approaches.

While suggesting the potential and necessity of cross-disciplinary re-search, I would like to focus my discussion on a seemingly incompatible "intersectioning" for the time being: can politics or ethics intersect with aesthetics in the study of political prison literature? A thorny question in reading political prison literature is whether we should or could contemplate it aesthetically. When "regarding the pain of others," is it appropriate for us to look for the "aesthetic" in the victims' suffering? Is it ethical for us bystanders to "appreciate" or "savor" the spectacle of a sufferer's pain? Barbara Harlow contends that prison literature should not be read for aesthet-ic enjoyment as other types of literature: "Reading prison writing must in turn demand a correspondingly activist counterapproach to that of passiv-ity, aesthetic gratification, and the pleasures of consumption that are tradi-tionally sanctioned by the academic disciplining of literature" (4). In the context that political prison literature generally performs an ethical act, Har-low's argument for readers' political "activist" approach is understandable. Many scholars, including the contributors to this volume, intend to encourage understanding of, and empathy for, political prisoners' pain, and would hard-ly take the approach of "aesthetic gratification," advocate taking the prison-ers' pain as "material" for distanced observations, or encourage the reader to unsympathetically appreciate the spectacle of victims' suffering.

Nevertheless, prison literature merits more approaches and angles of anal-ysis than merely the political, "activist" approach. I believe that we should embrace more diverse interpretive strategies in our academic study of this topic. Our study of the aesthetic of prison literature is justified for a number of reasons. For example, it can be argued that whether the authors compose their works in jail or after their release, they must have obtained some degree of aesthetic pleasure from the process of creative writing. The joy, as Shala-mov describes, in the prisoner's finding the difficult word "sententious" sud-denly returning to his tongue, has to do with the pleasure of intellectual re-engagement. We can also ascertain that Saadawi, hiding in a corner writing her secret memoir while everybody else was asleep, was happy during those moments. Despite the fear of censorship and other restraints, the emotion involved in writing—a sort of intellectual exercise—would include some degree of happiness derived from a temporary sense that your mind is free even if your body is not. There may also be some satisfaction derived from a sense of achievement for having overcome obstacles and accomplished something meaningful. This joy of freedom and creation is a kind of aesthetic pleasure similar to what one feels when engaging in musical or artistic activ-ities. In a sense, some narratives therefore occasionally embody the aesthetic joy of creative writing, however fleeting or elusive it may be.

Furthermore, many factors contribute to why the narratives and the nar-rated prison experiences would be aestheticized to some degree. For exam-ple, the writers who composed their narratives of suffering aesthetically might have done so for one or more of the following reasons: they chose to abide by their artistic standards and styles, they desired to enhance the texts' affective power and attract more readership, they might attempt to avoid censorship or wish to subvert official discourse, and so forth. Aware of the difficulty in representing the pain, some may adopt aesthetic interventions or experiment with aesthetic strategies in order to better convey the experiences and emotions. Writers sometimes aestheticize their prison experiences, and even write about their aesthetic experience of pain. Comparing different prisons and prison cultures, we also find a few of them more amenable to some degree of aestheticizing than others. Even when confined under abject and degrading circumstances, some prisoners' inclination and yearning for the beautiful and good still shine through. In addition, as suggested by Janet Hart (1999), aestheticizing the experiences in prisons can be for some a tactic for transforming their attitude and life, survival, and resistance.

While refraining from "consuming" the suffering depicted in any given prison narrative with "aesthetic gratification," we may not want to overlook the aesthetics in the narratives' form, style, and content, either. Nor should we ignore the fact that some authors do write about their occasional "aesthet-ic" experiences during incarceration or even in the midst of pain. Just as we should not disregard the parts of the narrative which delineate non-painful or even pleasant experiences, so we cannot discount the aesthetic strategies adopted by authors for self-expression or for their identities and subjectiv-ities. Failure to take these materials and factors into account could be "uneth-ical" of the reader in the sense that he or she is not doing complete justice to the authors and the texts.

Immanuel Kant's (1724–1804) theory of aesthetics as explicated in his monumental *Critique of the Power of Judgment* (a.k.a. *Critique of Judgment*, 1790) (2000, 55–230) is well-known to literary critics: he proposes that judgments of taste (beauty) are based on subjective feelings of pleasure that are entirely disinterested, and that they are distinctive, objective, and universal.[13] Building upon Kant's ideas of beauty and the sublime, Friedrich von Schiller (1759–1805) developed his aesthetic concept of the "pathetic" that is "sublime"—the effect generated through the human's confronting and triumphing over suffering. In his famous essay, "On the Pathetic" (1793), Schiller explains the effect: "The moral independence of the human reveals itself all the more gloriously, the portrayal becomes all the more pathetic, and the *pathos* all the more sublime" (1993, 53). While all these concepts are useful for application in studying political prison literature, Schiller's aesthetic principle of sublime pathos is particularly germane to our study of suffering.

Of course, the aesthetics relevant to this body of literature should not be limited to the Kantian or Schillerian aesthetic. It would be very worthwhile, for example, to explore the aesthetic concepts in the different cultural and literary traditions of the various works discussed in this volume. For now, however, I would only single out Pierre Bourdieu's idea for discussion. In his book analyzing class tastes and lifestyles, Bourdieu identifies the "popular aesthetic" while also arguing for the importance of the socio-economic contexts in the judgment of taste. He observes that "there is no area of practice in which the aim of purifying, refining, and sublimating primary needs and impulses cannot assert itself, no area in which the stylization of life . . . does not produce the same effects." And he proposes that "nothing is more distinctive . . . than the capacity to confer aesthetic status on objects that are banal or even 'common' . . . or the ability to apply the principles of a 'pure' aesthetic to the most everyday choices of everyday life" (5).[14] Such a broadly defined, context-specific concept of the aesthetic departs from Kant's pure judgment of taste or notion of beauty as disinterested pleasure.

Inspired by Bourdieu's sociological analysis of the aesthetic, Janet Hart suggests a "political prison aesthetic"—a "stylized response to oppression" (often mingling with "routine practices, with recurring dreams, nightmares and coping mechanisms") that "helpfully transforms the most dire circumstances into a fabrication which is a source of pride, can be appreciated as a compelling act of creation, engages the senses, and has a lasting value for those who are able or care to remember" (487–88). It is from such an anthropological perspective that Hart discovers what is unique about this special prison culture. For example, she finds that the Greek prisoners "reinterpret the fate of death by execution and the death-row category as the macabre elements of political theater, involving song, dance, and satire, thereby forcing a kind of ritual 'enjoyment'" (488). This type of "aesthetic" group ritual demonstrates some agency, bonding, and resistance, while serving as a "coping mechanism" for survival.

Hart's research and insight encourage scholars to be sensitive to aesthetics in political prison and its literature, and to examine the various representations and uses of such aesthetics. Hart argues that aesthetics "provide a means of gaining control and of mobilizing interest and commitment" and are "profoundly tied to memory as a way of altering and of coming to terms with events over which we have not enjoyed full control" (504). She notices that the texts emphasize "humor, dignity, and force of will," though they also narrate "the painful dilemmas and injustices political prisoners faced" and convey "the sheer monotony of daily life" (503). Through her interviews, she discovers that some prisoners were reluctant to reveal in detail the many conflicts among themselves—so as not to "endanger the aesthetic profile" (503). Clearly, these prisoners consciously craft their "aesthetic profile," and the aesthetics they produce in their daily life is crucial to their survival. The authors of the prison narratives also attempt to represent their experiences with aesthetics in mind. The emphasis on "dignity" and "force of will" seems an attempt to create the aesthetic effect of the "sublime pathos." We recall similar emphases in a number of prison memoirs. Saadawi's memoir, for example, highlights her struggle, friendship, small triumphs and happiness, and strategies for survival.

Let us digress at this point by considering two extremely brief poems: (A) "What kind of spring is this,/ Where there are no flowers and/ The air is filled with a miserable smell?"; and (B) "Handcuffs befit brave young men,/ Bangles are for spinsters or pretty young ladies." Just as we might not have noticed Icarus' fall in Brueghel's peaceful landscape had we not been alerted by its title, so we might not have known that the poems were composed by a Guantánamo detainee had we not been informed of the context of the titles, "Cup Poem 1" and "Cup Poem 2."[15] Of course a competent reader who discerns the ironic gap resulting from the juxtaposition of "spring" with "no flowers" and "miserable smell," and the juxtaposition of the telling word "handcuffs" with its contrast "bangles," would suspect these poems might have something to do with incarceration, just as a careful viewer who pays attention to minute details in Brueghel's painting would note the two puny sinking legs as well as the unequal juxtaposition and uneasy relationship between this incongruous tiny figure and the rest of the landscape. The process of gradually exercising the imagination to figure out the clues and understand the context of the poems brings aesthetic pleasure to the reader. Before affecting us readers, the aesthetics of these poems might have served as part of a "coping mechanism" for the survival of the writer and his cellmates, since the aesthetics might help "provide a means of gaining control and of mobilizing interest and commitment," as Hart suggested.

In connection with our discussion of the intersection of political prison literature and aesthetics, we could also consider an oft-cited remark of Theodor W. Adorno, "to write poetry after Auschwitz is barbaric" (1967, 34). This famous yet controversial statement is often taken out of the original context. On the surface, the remark seems to suggest that poetry-writing should be suspended or stopped altogether after the Holocaust. Yet one can easily retort, "What is the rationale for that? Why should poetry-writing be singled out as barbaric?" Of course, the extreme, massive brutality and horror of the Holocaust might have shocked a number of philosophers into rethinking about humanity, culture, and the arts. Nevertheless, does the Holocaust necessarily render poem-writing "barbaric"? Does it also reduce other artistic creations to meaningless, frivolous activities?

Made in Adorno's hallmark spirit of "negative dialectics," this statement originally appears at the end of his essay "Cultural Criticism and Society" (published in 1949). In this famous essay, Adorno boldly proclaimed, "Neutralized and ready-made, traditional culture has become worthless today":

> Cultural criticism finds itself faced with the final stage of the dialectic of culture and barbarism. To write poetry after Auschwitz is barbaric. And this corrodes even the knowledge of why it has become impossible to write poetry today. Absolute reification . . . is now preparing to absorb the mind entirely."
> (1967, 34)

In this context, Adorno's remark about writing poetry after Auschwitz forms a part of his overall disappointment with and severe critique of "culture" and "absolute reification," which he fears would "absorb the mind entirely." Poetry-writing could be a "semblance of freedom." Yet in Adorno's thinking, "the semblance of freedom makes reflection upon one's own unfreedom incomparably more difficult than formerly when such reflection stood in contradiction to manifest unfreedom, thus strengthening dependence. . . . Such moments . . . result in the regression of spirit and intellect. . . . In accordance with the predominant social tendency, the integrity of the mind becomes a fiction" (1967, 21). In his argument, poetry-writing is barbaric because it can lead to the "regression of spirit and intellect" and deprive the mind of freedom and integrity.

Adorno would "obsessively" repeat this idea a few times in his publications. At one point, he seems to relent somewhat when he admits the remark may have been wrong (c. 1966): "Perennial suffering has as much right to expression as a tortured man has to scream; hence it may have been wrong to say that after Auschwitz you could no longer write poems" (1973, 362).[16] In a similar vein, he observes in another essay, "To say something out loud is to put some distance between oneself and the immediacy of suffering, just as screaming helps mitigate great pain" (1984, 171). In other words, he recognizes the emotional need (and the right) for expressing suffering through poetry. We would think that if writing poetry is to express one's suffering, like screaming, then it can help alleviate pain and should be justified. Nevertheless, Adorno belabors his original claim elsewhere (c. 1965), "I have no wish to soften the saying that to write lyric poetry after Auschwitz is barbaric; it expresses in negative form the impulse which inspires committed literature" (1979, 60). It is interesting to note that in this passage he refers to "lyric poetry," rather than such genres as narratives or other artistic forms. To lyricize a calamity wrought by utter evil could conceivably be deemed "barbaric," and such horror and pain as the Holocaust could simply be beyond expression. What concerns Adorno is that literature's existence after Auschwitz could be a "surrender to cynicism," and artistic representation of pain could be consumed by the public with enjoyment (1979, 61). The last point, as we mentioned previously, is a central concern of scholars such as Harlow.

This "aporia" or insoluble contradiction perceived by Adorno exists to some extent also in the creation of political prison literature. On the one hand, carceral suffering yearns for expression, and there are various needs for the pain to be expressed and documented. On the other hand, skeptics can find many reasons against the writing and publishing of such literature. For example, can one lyricize suffering? Can language adequately express the pain or would it distort the reality instead? How can authors represent political prison experiences in ways that evoke in the reader their intended responses (including aesthetic feelings) without being trivialized or misunderstood? And as critics like Adorno would worry, would this literature be fetishized and mass-consumerized? We can neither resolve the difficulty nor control the general public's ways of reception or consumption. Yet we can at least caution ourselves and others about cynicism, fetishization, and unethical consumption, and try to keep a balanced stance and exercise judicious judgment in our study, in the hope of influencing or educating the general public to understand this literature better and respond more sensitively.

The intersection of aesthetics and political prison is one of the controversial yet fruitful areas deserving cross-disciplinary research. Taking interdisciplinary perspectives enables the scholar to discover complex meanings and uses of various activities in prison culture. Furthermore, adopting diverse literary approaches allows the critic to drill into the often neglected parts of the texts and mine the hitherto untapped resources. We find that certain writers deliberately cultivate a "political prison aesthetic" both in their prison life and in their memoirs composed after their departure from incarceration. The special "aesthetic" regimen or ritual is one of the possible strategies that could help them gain some measure of "control," keep physically and mentally fit, be more resilient and better survivors, and form more solid camaraderie with others. Attempts at transforming themselves and forging a stronger identity could change their relationship with the prison environment for the better, and after their release, could continue to exert a positive impact on their life, enabling them to work for improving human rights.

RHIZOMATOUS FORCES

Political prison narratives can be likened to rhizomes. A rhizome is a horizontal plant stem such as ginger that continuously grows roots below and shoots above, and can be found either underground or aboveground. By the same token, these narratives, depending upon circumstances, can continuously grow roots below (in the sense of existing as fragments, manuscripts, or simply ideas in would-be authors' minds) and shoots above (in the sense of being published and coming to light, for example), and can be found either underground or aboveground (published and uncensored). Like the rhizome, a well-written narrative is organic, has a life of its own, and possesses internal forces that enable it to sprout and grow shoots in various directions, transform in shapes, and propagate in unpredictable ways. It is not mechanically cut to fit the ideological gears of a regime. Just as rhizomes send out shoots and roots from their nodes and can entangle one another, so these narratives can creep, spread, and reproduce, endowed with the potential to connect with one another, either above- or underground, and either through some sort of relatively visible network and contact or through invisible forces emanating from the works.

In employing "rhizome" as a metaphor for political prison literature (and discourse), I particularly wish to underscore the latter's powerful potential. It is creative, adaptive, resilient, persistent, and recurring. It can be camouflaged (such as appearing in a fictional, non-realistic form), can have offshoots in different forms and directions, and possesses strongly protean quality. This body of literature constitutes a major part of the underground discourse, continuously challenging, interrogating, and contesting official discourse. It can help mobilize grassroots movements or help nongovernmental forces resist the repression from an authoritarian regime.

Since these narratives often deal with the writers' life, memories, or interiorities, comparing them to the rhizome also accords somewhat with the way Carl G. Jung (1875–1961) employs this metaphor. For his autobiography Jung chooses to write about his encounters with the unconscious—which stays in his memory—instead of external events and people (3–5). He finds the unconscious to be like the rhizome:

Life has always seemed to me like a plant that lives on its rhizome. Its true life is invisible, hidden in the rhizome. The part that appears above ground lasts only a single summer. Then it withers away—an ephemeral apparition. When we think of the unending growth and decay of life and civilizations, we cannot

escape the impression of absolute nullity. Yet I have never lost a sense of
something that lives and endures underneath the eternal flux. What we see is
the blossom, which passes. The rhizome remains. (4)

Through his extended analogy, Jung rightly contrasts the ephemerality of the
visible, surface part of life (a point that seems to echo, to some extent, the
Buddhist conception about the impermanence of life and worldly phenomena) with the unconscious that "endures underneath the eternal flux" and
remains. The shoots and growth of the narratives may flourish, bloom, with-
er, or be stymied and even prematurely cut off, depending upon the change-
able political winds and other socioeconomic factors. Yet the buried memories and interiorities, along with their rhizomatous forces, will not disappear
completely, but will return to life, growth, and reproduction, given the right
circumstances.

Gilles Deleuze and Félix Guattari not only recognize that "the rhizome is
precisely this production of the unconscious" (18), following Jung, but exploit the potential of this metaphor to its fullest for describing a new type of
research, which they conceive as a departure from the so-called arborescent
schema:

> The rhizome is an antigenealogy . . . the rhizome pertains to a map that . . . has
> multiple entryways and exits and its own lines of flight. . . . In contrast to
> centered (even polycentric) systems with hierarchical modes of communica-
> tion and preestablished paths, the rhizome is an acentered, nonhierarchical,
> nonsignifying system without a General and without an organizing memory or
> central automaton. (21)

Using "rhizome" and "tree" as metaphors to describe theory, these two eru-
dite philosophers have attempted to contrast the "horizontal," decentralized
rhizome with what they perceive as the traditional Western, "hierarchical,"
tree. The attempt to free up theoretical and research methods in the West is
most welcome. The acknowledgment of the rhizome having "multiple entryways and exits" and being "acentered, nonhierarchical" is especially pertinent to our study of political prison narratives.

Four and a half centuries ago, Pieter Brueghel captured and embedded in
his painting the sense of suffering in the mythical story about the incarcerated Icarus' failed flight and escape. Seventy years ago, Auden detected in this
painting Icarus' cry before his death, while registering the bystanders' apathy
to another individual's suffering. The story of Icarus' fall has spawned myriad representations, which in turn give rise to multiple interpretations. Somewhat similarly, the story of the political prison has emerged in many narratives (and other art forms) that encourage various interpretations. While these
"rhizomes" possess great potential, it is partly up to us readers and critics to
help free, rather than stifle, the imprisoned cries, realities, memories, and

interiorities. Affirming the "ethical" act of remembering, we nevertheless recognize how people can remember sufferings differently. When reading narratives from diverse historical, cultural, sociopolitical, religious, literary, and linguistic backgrounds, we cannot help but be impressed by the overwhelming commonalities in political prison experience. However, we also advocate the need to avoid erasing differences, study the specificities and their particular circumstances, contextualize them, and engage deeply with the authors' subjectivities and interiorities. Furthermore, cross-cultural, cross-literary, comparative, and interdisciplinary studies of this literature can generate synergy by fruitfully uncovering the literature's multiplicities, resources, transformations, and connectedness. While promoting the investigation into the intersection of political prison literature and aesthetics from diverse disciplinary perspectives, we must be aware of the complexities and ambivalences involved in this topic. Complex politics in the discourse of remembering and representation, as well as in the writing, publishing, reading, and possible commodifying of this literature, also deserve our attention. Non-dogmatic approaches and theories are called for in order to do justice to this group of literature that has "multiple entryways and exits and its own lines of flight." In these ways, we would more likely be able to help adequately release the forces in these narrative "rhizomes," enabling them to take their own lines of flight.

NOTES

1. See W. H. Auden's poem, "Musée des Beaux Arts," in *Modern Poetry*, edited by Maynard Mack et al., p. 198. I cannot quote any line from this poem due to copyright limitations.

2. Some of the scenes described in Auden's poem are obviously not from Brueghel's *Icarus*, which is the only painting specifically mentioned in the poem. In this stanza Auden might be describing and alluding to scenes from a few other paintings.

3. For example, when Wumingshi's (pseud. of Bu Naifu, alias Bu Ning or Pu Ning) second-hand memoir *Hongsha* (*Red Sharks*, [1989] 1994a) was translated into English (*Red in Tooth and Claw: Twenty-six Years in Communist Chinese Prisons*, 1994b), the translator omitted many paragraphs and sentences, and the editor inverted the original sequence of the first two chapters.

4. See the chapter by R. Shareah Taleghani in this volume.

5. Note that the Chinese version of Zhang Xianliang's memoir, *Wode putishu*, has been translated into English by Martha Avery as two books: *Grass Soup* and *My Bodhi Tree*. See next chapter.

6. See Shalamov's *Kolyma Tales* (1980), for example.

7. See, for example, the descriptions in Shalamov's *Kolyma Tales* or Solzhenitsyn's *One Day in the Life of Ivan Denisovich*.

8. Both Saadawi and I attended a screening of Cheryl Dunye's film about prison life, *The Stranger Inside* (2001), on May 20, 2009. After watching this impressive film, however, we both came to the conclusion that the conditions of the modern U.S. women's correctional facilities represented in the film are far superior to either the Egyptian or Chinese prisons.

9. Zhang Xianliang mentioned, for example, that he had read Solzhenitsyn's *Gulag Archipelago*. While we can assume that Zhang most likely had read the work in Chinese translation, we do not know which version or PRC edition of the Chinese translation he had read and whether that edition was complete, abridged, or somewhat revised.

10. Descriptions of Russian criminals' harsh and cruel treatment of political prisoners can be seen in Varlam Shalamov's *Kolyma Tales*, 107–127, and Solzhenitsyn's *The Gulag Archipelago*, vol. 1, 500–502, for example. Although Chinese writers occasionally note the humiliation of having to be jailed with common criminals, they rarely depict the encounter between political prisoners and criminals to be as violent as that in the Russian case. See, for example, Cong Weixi, *Zou xiang hundun sanbuqu*, 301–307.

11. See Simona Livescu's chapter on prisoners' experience of a "state of happiness or bliss" in this volume.

12. See, for example, Aung San Suu Kyi's conversations with Alan Clements in *The Voice of Hope* (1997).

13. According to Kant's argument, for example, "Taste is the faculty for judging an object or a kind of representation through a satisfaction or dissatisfaction without any interest. The object of such a satisfaction is called beautiful. . . . The beautiful is that which, without concepts, is represented as the object of a *universal* satisfaction" (2000, 96).

14. Most of this quote is also cited in Hart 487.

15. These two poems were written by Shaikh Abdurraheem Muslim Dost. See Marc Falkoff, ed., *Poems from Guantánamo*, 35. They were called "cup poems" because, lacking writing instruments, some detainees used small stones or spoons to etch their poems into foam cups.

16. I thank my former colleague, Georg M. Gugelberger, an expert on Theodor W. Adorno, for his help in locating some of Adorno's quotes.

REFERENCES

Adorno, Theodor W. 1967. "Cultural Criticism and Society." In *Prisms*, trans. Samuel and Shierry Weber, 19–34. London: Neville Spearman.

——. 1973. *Negative Dialectics* (1966). Trans. E. B. Ashton. New York: Seabury Press.

——. 1979. "Re-View: On Commitment" (Continued). Trans. Francis McDonagh. *Performing Arts Journal* 3.3 (Winter): 58–67.

——. 1984. *Aesthetic Theory*. Trans. C. Lenhardt. Ed. Gretel Adorno and Rolf Tiedemann. London: Routledge & Kegan Paul.

Auden, W. H. 1963. "Musée des Beaux Arts." In *Modern Poetry*, ed. Maynard Mack et al., 198. Englewood Cliffs, NJ: Prentice-Hall.

Aung San Suu Kyi, with Alan Clements. 1997. *The Voice of Hope*. New York: Seven Stories Press.

Borowski, Tadeusz. 1967. *This Way for the Gas, Ladies and Gentlemen*. Trans. Barbara Vedder. New York: The Viking Press.

Bourdieu, Pierre. 1984. *Distinction: A Social Critique of the Judgment of Taste*. Trans. Richard Nice. Cambridge, Mass.: Harvard Univ. Press.

Clinton, Hillary Rodham. 2003. *Living History*. New York: Simon & Schuster.

Cong Weixi. 1998. *Zou xiang hundun sanbuqu* (The Heading into Chaos Trilogy). Beijing: Zhongguo shehui kexue chubanshe.

Deleuze, Gilles, and Félix Guattari. 1988. *A Thousand Plateaus: Capitalism and Schizophrenia*. Trans. Brian Massumi. London: Athlone Press.

Des Pres, Terrence. 1976. *The Survivor: An Anatomy of Life in the Death Camps*. New York: Oxford Univ. Press.

Dorfman, Ariel. 2007. "Where the Buried Flame Burns." In *Poems from Guantánamo: The Detainees Speak*, ed. Marc Falkoff, 69–72. Iowa City: Univ. of Iowa Press.

Elinson, Alexander. 2009. "Opening the Circle: Storyteller and Audience in Moroccan Prison Literature." *Middle Eastern Literatures* 12.3: 289–303.

Falkoff, Marc. 2007. "Notes on Guantánamo." In *Poems from Guantánamo: The Detainees Speak*, ed. Marc Falkoff, 1–5. Iowa City: Univ. of Iowa Press.

_____, ed. 2007. *Poems from Guantánamo: The Detainees Speak*. Iowa City: Univ. of Iowa Press.

Glad, John. 1980. "Foreword." In Varlam Shalamov, *Kolyma Tales*, 7–17. New York: W. W. Norton.

Harlow, Barbara. *Barred: Women, Writing, and Political Detention*. Middletown, CT: Wesleyan Univ. Press, 1992.

Hart, Janet. 1999. "Tales from the Walled City: Aesthetics of Political Prison Culture in Post-War Greece." *Comparative Studies in Society and History* 41: 482–509.

Jung, Carl G. 1963. *Memories, Dreams, Reflections*. Ed. Aniela Jaffé. Trans. Richard and Clara Winston. New York: Vintage Books.

Kant, Immanuel. 2000. *Critique of the Power of Judgment*. Ed. Paul Guyer. Trans. Paul Guyer and Eric Matthews. Cambridge: Cambridge Univ. Press.

Miller, Flagg. 2007. "Forms of Suffering in Muslim Prison Poetry." In Marc Falkoff, ed., *Poems from Guantánamo: The Detainees Speak*, 7–16. Iowa City: Univ. of Iowa Press.

Saadawi, Nawal El. (1986) 1994. *Memoirs from the Women's Prison*. Trans. Marilyn Booth. Berkeley: Univ. of California Press.

Schiller, Friedrich. 1993. "On the Pathetic." Trans. Daniel O. Dahlstrom. In Walter Hinderer and Daniel O. Dahlstrom, eds., Essays, 45–69. New York: Continuum.

Shalamov, Varlam. 1980. *Kolyma Tales*. Trans. John Glad. New York: W. W. Norton.

Solzhenitsyn, Aleksandr I. 1963. *One Day in the Life of Ivan Denisovich*. Trans. Ralph Parker. New York: E. P. Dutton.

Solzhenitsyn, Aleksandr I. 1974. *The Gulag Archipelago, 1918–1956: An Experiment in Literary Investigation*, vol. 1. Trans. Thomas P. Whitney. New York: Harper & Row.

_____. 1976. *The Gulag Archipelago, 1918–1956: An Experiment in Literary Investigation*, vol. 3. Trans. Harry Willetts. New York: Harper & Row.

Sontag, Susan. 2003. *Regarding the Pain of Others*. New York: Farrar, Straus and Giroux.

Wumingshi (pseud. of Bu Naifu, alias Bu Ning or Pu Ning). 1984. *Yuzhong shichao* (Poems Composed in Prison). Taipei: Liming wenhua shiye.

_____. (1989) 1994a. *Hongsha* (Red Sharks). Taipei: Liming wenhua shiye.

_____ (Pu Ning). 1994b. *Red in Tooth and Claw: Twenty-six Years in Communist Chinese Prisons*. Trans. Tung Chung-hsuan. New York: Grove Press.

Zhang Xianliang. 1987. *Xie xiaoshuo de bianzheng fa*. Shanghai: Shanghai wenyi chubanshe.

_____. 1994. *Wode putishu* (My Bodhi Tree). Beijing: Zuojia chubanshe.

Chapter Three

Surviving Traumatic Captivity, Arriving at Wisdom

An Aesthetics of Resistance in Chinese Prison Camp Memoir

Yenna Wu

Relatively little critical attention has been paid to the painful experiences in Mao-era Chinese prison camps (1949–76). Here I focus particularly on the experiences shared by the countless political prisoners—mostly intellectuals—who were sent to forced labor camps during the early 1950s or the "Anti-Rightist Campaign" of 1957–58, many of whom spent over two decades in prisons. To confront the traumatic memory of the Holocaust, scores of memorials and museums have been erected in commemoration, meetings have been held for communal remembrances and discussion, and numerous memoirs and studies have been published.[1] By contrast, the current PRC (People's Republic of China) government prohibits almost all public discussion of the "Anti-Rightist Campaign," while engineering public amnesia with a view to eventually erasing this large-scale persecution from collective memory.[2] Indeed, for fear of losing its authority and "legitimacy in ruling," the CCP (Chinese Communist Party) regime has so far been reluctant to admit its wrongdoings.[3] Surviving victims or victims' families and friends have been, for the most part, too intimidated to speak out, and the victims' painful experiences of incarceration have remained largely hidden from public discourse. Under such circumstances, to write and publish memoirs or truthful accounts about these traumatic memories can constitute a valuable resistance to the amnesia and falsified history constructed by the regime.

In this chapter, I suggest that selected prison camp memoir and fiction effectively reveal some of the suppressed traumatic memories, thereby enhancing public awareness of both the laogai ("remolding through labor"; forced-labor prison camp) system and, to some extent, the "Anti-Rightist Campaign."[4] Examining three memoirs while focusing on the role of severe hunger as a wielded weapon of torture and manipulation, I demonstrate that these authors help us broaden our understanding of strategies of state control. Depending upon the writer's position vis-à-vis the CCP and aesthetic preferences, I also explore varying tactics of authorial resistance, from overt condemnation and visceral surrealism to irony, multivalence, and encoded challenge.

A CCP PATTERN OF REPRESSION, DENIAL, AND DECEPTION

Studying Mao-era Chinese political prisoners' experiences is especially relevant now in light of China's recent (2008) crackdown on protesters in Tibet. Such study can reveal the hidden side of the CCP, alert us to its patterns of oppression, and prepare us for the tactics of denial and deception it has been adopting. In the case of the crackdown, the regime blocked foreign reporters' access to Tibet while dispatching armed troops there to put down the demonstrations with force. The BBC reported how China has been "aggressively censoring international media in an attempt to lock down information about the violent demonstrations in Tibet's capital, Lhasa" (Davis 2008). As a result, no foreign journalist could witness the violence and repression, or find out how many Tibetans were arrested, detained, or sent to prison—most likely without a proper public trial. According to the official version fabricated by the CCP, troops were sent there to control "rioters" and restore peace, and it was an internal matter of "law and order." The regime further alleged that the riot was a conspiracy (instigated by the Dalai Lama) to "sabotage" the Beijing Olympics.[5] In other words, the government represents itself as the potent defender of national security and stability—which many people believe to be essential to China's development—while at the same time inciting people's nationalist fervor and resentment against Tibetan protestors and Western media. Time and again through domestic and even foreign media, the authorities categorically insist on official versions that misrepresent the repression.

The CCP's manipulation of the media during and after its suppression of the Tibetan protests is reminiscent of its political censorship of the June 1989 Beijing Tiananmen Square Massacre. As pointed out by scholars, the CCP has insidiously adopted the "tactics of amnesia" for generations; and it employed the tactics first of "truth-inversion" and then of "diminution," in order to erase any memory of the June 4th Massacre.[6] The government has almost complete control over the domestic media and, consequently, enormous influence on its public. Its tactics have worked—to a large extent, if not completely successfully.

The "Anti-Rightist Campaign" of 1957–58 is another case in point. The regime committed atrocities with impunity, never admitting its crimes of persecution. Even after Mao's death, the government has insisted on the "correctness" of the CCP's actions in purging the so-called rightists.[7] In the late 1970s, Deng Xiaoping began to remove rightist labels from many intellectuals, whose help with China's modernization was urgently needed by the state, yet in a CCP "Resolution" adopted in 1981, the Party "still views the Anti-Rightist Movement as having been proper" (White 1987, 254, 266–67). The regime would acknowledge that at most only a total of 550,000 people were "labeled as rightists" in 1957–58. However, according to Ding Shu, an expert residing in the United States who has investigated and researched the "Anti-Rightist Campaign" for years, over 1.2 million people were persecuted as "rightists" at that time (Ji 2008).[8] Over the past three decades, no truth and reconciliation commission has been established, and there has been no investigation into this man-made catastrophe. The regime has neither apologized to the victims and their families, nor made any reparations.

Instead, through strict ideological control, the CCP has ensured that the "Anti-Rightist Campaign" would not be discussed, remembered, or commemorated in public. The regime appears to be employing stalling tactics in an attempt to "wait it out": when those who suffered during the "Anti-Rightist Campaign" or witnessed it have all eventually died, this part of history will die along with them. In addition to this delay tactic, the government has covered up historical truth and manipulated historical knowledge so that its version of the past monopolizes all public arenas and educational programs (which still include much ideological inculcation and thought remolding), as well as most cultural productions.

The regime's various tactics have been so successful that younger generations know nothing about the "Anti-Rightist Campaign"—indeed many who were born after the mid-1980s do not even know about the Tiananmen Square Massacre in June 1989. Conceivably, the recent crackdown in Tibet will be subjected to the same treatment: having first established its official (and largely deceptive) version of the event as *the* dominant narrative and insisting on it through continuous propaganda, the CCP would then gradually erase alternative versions of the incident from public memory, at most keeping only the official version in history.

Furthermore, many Chinese people's reaction to the crackdown serves as a sobering example illustrating how in recent years the "official and nonofficial perspectives within China have moved closer together" than in the 1980s.[9] Having no access to foreign reports on the unrest in Tibet, the Chinese must depend solely upon the official reports on state-controlled media. As a result, many of them actually trust the official narrative and side with the government. Believing that the Tibetans were committing violent crimes and it was legitimate of the government to send troops to Tibet to control "rioters," these people also condemn Western media for being biased against China.

Of course, nowadays neither the "nonofficial" nor even the "official" perspectives are monolithic (Murray 2005). Yet, for a number of reasons, voices of dissidence have become weaker and have found less resonance and sympathy among the people than during the 1980s. In general, numerous people are either uninformed about the regime's violations of human rights or unconcerned about political reform. Some are too intimidated to speak out against the regime, while others simply want to look after their own interests or are content enough with economic and social development as to refrain from taking issue with the government. Other reasons include technological advances in the CCP's surveillance and control as well as many people's ultranationalist fervor.

The last three decades have witnessed China's economic reform, rapid development, and military buildup. Admittedly, the Chinese government has adopted some fine policies, particularly those that have allowed a number of people more economic and social freedom. One of the common assumptions in the West is that economic development would necessarily lead to positive political reform and democracy.[10] However, despite its transformation into an economic superpower, politically the PRC remains a single-party Leninist regime in which the leaders hold exclusive military power and control all the executive, legislative, and judicial branches. The ever-dominant CCP has cleverly turned its people's attention from democratic reform to money-making. In a society that has grown to be "capitalistic" and consumerist to a great extent, many people are so busy pursuing profit, fame, and fun as to become apathetic to political reform. Economic development has enabled the regime to employ its carrot-and-stick tactic fairly successfully. It can maximize the police force in charge of the surveillance and detention of key dissidents, easily deprive dissidents of their livelihood and terrorize them, exile some vocal ones abroad, use economic incentives in exchange for some people's silence, and even recruit civilian help in policing.

We would in general assume that computer technology and the internet would permit Chinese people to learn more about democracies abroad, thereby helping China head toward democratization. According to a recent estimate, "China has the most online users in the world with more than 250 million."[11] Yet technological development actually works both ways. While potentially enabling more Chinese to aspire for democracy, it is also exploited by the regime to abuse human rights and obstruct any democracy movement. In fact, advanced technology not only helps enhance the CCP's arsenal, making China an even more formidable military threat to other countries and regions than before, but also helps the CCP immensely in its surveillance and control of the media and the people. Aided by advanced computer and communication technology, the CCP can control and censor media (including the internet), cover up or distort truth, inculcate political ideology, and manipulate people's perceptions and thought in an even more skillful and sophisticated way than was the case thirty years ago.

Moreover, as scholars have noted, "Since the 1990s, especially among the youth of the PRC, a renewed and invigorated nationalism has taken root."[12] The PRC regime has successfully instilled ultranationalist fervor and extreme patriotism in many people, particularly in the susceptible younger generations. As a result, instead of criticizing their own government for its political repression, many Chinese today become angry with foreign media's reports of China's human rights violations, regarding such reports not as criticism on the "regime" alone but as conspiratorial attacks on "China," "the Chinese people," their national pride, and themselves.

Curiously, a number of modern Chinese cultural studies scholars appear to take the side of the CCP official ultranationalist discourse to some extent. They view China as a victim of continuous aggression from a "hegemonic" West, thereby regarding Western broadcasting of news about China's human rights abuses as an attempt to "demonize China and thus affirm Western moral supremacy."[13] This view does not seem to take into account such facts as China's long history as a hegemonic empire vis-à-vis its neighboring countries and regions (including Tibet), a deep-seated Han chauvinism along with a sense of superiority over the non-Han ethnicities and foreigners, and the PRC regime's military threat and hegemonic aggression toward Taiwan and Tibet.[14] And in fact, China's violations of human rights have not been criticized only by people from the West. Critical voices have also been raised by people in non-Western parts of the world such as Asia and Africa, including, for example, the South African Archbishop and Nobel Peace Prize laureate Desmond Tutu. Furthermore, for various reasons, the so-called hegemonic West, particularly the United States, has over the last decade become too weak to assert "moral supremacy" over such a strong world power as the PRC.[15] The influence Western broadcasting of Chinese government's human rights abuses can possibly exert on the regime has also dwindled.

The CCP has not only suppressed dissidence at home but has also vociferously condemned foreign criticism of its human rights violations. The regime has attempted to silence censure abroad through wielding its formidable economic power and adopting a carrot-and-stick approach, while continuing to employ its tactics of denial and deception. Under current circumstances, I would suggest that selected Chinese prison camp memoirs and fictional works can actually supply some urgently needed dissident voices and thus function as an unofficial corrective to the CCP's distorting narrative.

PRISON CAMP MEMOIRS AND FICTION

Chinese prison camp memoirs and fiction constitute a rather diverse group. Ex-inmates' memoirs are perhaps the most authentic and authoritative in their first-hand description of prison camp experiences. A number of memoirs about Mao-era imprisonment were published abroad, ranging from earlier works by Lai Ying (1969) and Jean Pasqualini (Bao and Chelminski 1973) to later ones by Peng Yinhan (1984) and Harry Wu (1994), for example.[16] Since late 2001 the Laogai Research Foundation in Washington, D.C., founded by Harry Wu, has been publishing a number of prison camp memoirs in Chinese in a series called "Black Series: New Stories from the Laogai."[17] Notable memoirs published in China were from Cong Weixi (1989/1998) and Zhang Xianliang (1994), two ex-inmates who, after spending over twenty years in prison camps, became well-known writers since the 1980s. The tone of these two writers, who still reside in China and are currently CCP members, is understandably much less critical and strident than that found in memoirs such as Harry Wu's.

The writing of prison camp fiction started during the post-Mao cultural thaw of the late 1970s and early 1980s. Cong Weixi (b. 1933) and Zhang Xianliang (b. 1936) are two of the most famous in this subgenre, and their prison camp–related fictional works were mostly published in the 1980s. While using the labor camps as their settings and possibly incorporating some of the authors' laogai experiences, these works tend to dramatize unrealistically romantic, even heroic situations. These fictional works are often ambivalent "hybrids," in the sense that they contain both truthful and false information about prison experiences. The famous PRC writer Liu Binyan was angered by the "new false realism" in Cong Weixi's "happy prison fiction" (Kinkley 1991, 106). Huang Wenfan, a translator in Taiwan of Solzhenitsyn's *Gulag Archipelago*, criticizes some of Zhang Xianliang's descriptions of the labor camps in his fiction as inauthentic and contrary to the depictions in *Gulag Archipelago*, and wonders if these PRC novelists have to write about the prison camp falsely for fear of censorship (Huang 1990, 448). Indeed, at that time these novelists did have to avoid censorship, while also making their works entertaining enough for readers in order to ensure a successful reception. The sentimentalized and unrealistic accounts in these fictional works can repel more knowledgeable readers and mislead those readers unfamiliar with more typical conditions in Mao-era laogai prison camps. Yet as critics we do not need to impose the same burden of authenticity on "fiction" as on "nonfiction," though we should try to understand the author's intention, and should work to discern between accurate and falsified moments in the text.

Similar discernment should be exercised even in reading non-fictional prison writing like reportage, journalistic writings, and interviews. Some of the authors may have been motivated by a sense of moral duty and the desire to uncover hidden history. Wumingshi's (pseudonym of Bu Naifu, 1917–2002) interview-based account, *Red Sharks* (*Hongsha* [1989] 1994a, published in Taiwan), is an example.[18] While Wumingshi himself had been temporarily imprisoned, in *Red Sharks* he focuses exclusively on retelling the experience of an ex-inmate, Hong Xianheng (pseudonym, b. 1918), whom he interviewed a number of times over a long period. A former Nationalist Party (KMT, Kuomintang, a.k.a. Guomindang) military officer, Hong suffered in PRC prisons and laogai camps from 1951 to 1978. Wumingshi repeatedly affirms that the account is truthful, though he adds to it some "fictional style" (Wu 2006a). This partially fictionalized biography or memoir interspersed with reportage provides some detailed literary portrayal of the Mao-era laogai prison camps in Qinghai.

Such interview-based accounts are also written by authors who have never been incarcerated in the laogai, such as Yang Xianhui (1946–), a contemporary PRC writer. As a "sent-down youth" in Gansu province between 1965–81, Yang vaguely heard from some ex-inmate workers about the previous existence of a certain Jiabiangou Farm (a labor-remolding camp) in a barren region in Gansu as well as the tragic outcome of its numerous rightist inmates in 1959–60 (Yang Xianhui 2002b, 355).[19] He returned to Gansu in 1997 to conduct investigations and interviews and, though denied access to official archives, he wrote up the interview-based accounts, and published them in the guise of short stories in *Shanghai Literature* (*Shanghai wenxue*) in 2001. Framed within the interviews and in "fictional" guise, the embedded accounts are narrated by several different individual ex-inmates, and detail the painful experiences of many "rightists" in Jiabiangou labor camp.

Given that the PRC official history makes no mention of the rightists incarcerated in the Jiabiangou labor camp, and that whatever remnants of the camp site have mostly disappeared, Yang Xianhui's "stories" bring back to life the vanished geographical and historical vestiges. His disguised interviews give voice to the hitherto voiceless survivors, thereby indirectly defying the government's cover-up. Furthermore, they provide the readers with a good deal of unofficial narrative and perspective, and encode a challenge to them. Like Wumingshi, Yang Xianhui was prompted to write these accounts by a sense of justice and moral courage, as well as the hope that this part of history would be remembered. In the epilogue to a collection of his stories, Yang Xianhui explains that the long-forgotten "Jiabiangou incident" is the "history of suffering of over 2400 rightists," and that he tells the stories to reopen this page of history, "hoping that such a tragedy will not be repeated," and at the same time to "console" the souls of the dead, letting them know that "history will not forget Jiabiangou." Yang Xianhui concludes, "To pay close attention to the history of our forerunners is to pay close attention to ourselves" (2002b, 356). Through these explanations and justifications, Yang Xianhui assumes the responsibility of an unofficial historian and implicitly challenges his readers to apply the lessons of history to their present circumstances, and to guard against the regime's repetition of large-scale violation of human rights.

According to Jeffrey C. Kinkley, "Big Wall literature" (prison-camp literature) can be regarded as one subgenre of "legal system literature" (2000, 294). As Kinkley demonstrated in his book, the genre—"legal system literature" or crime fiction—underwent plenty of state intervention and was a product born of "a three-way compromise between official, liberal, and commercial interests" (2000, 296). We can see a spectrum of conflicting interests in the prison literature published in the PRC. Whether fictional or nonfictional, a great deal of it follows the official perspective to a certain extent and caters to commercial interests. In contrast to such serious and "authentic" works as those penned by Wumingshi and Yang Xianhui, some other journalistic writings and interviews of prison inmates seem to have been written to gratify general readers' curiosity about the topic and often follow the Party line in representing prison personnel as effectively remolding the incarcerated (Williams and Wu 2004, 158). Works written for public consumption and for profit often focus on criminal offenders (*xingshi fan*, or "ordinary criminals") instead of ideological offenders (*sixiang fan*, or *zhengzhi fan*, "political/ intellectual prisoners"); depicting prisons as helpful correctional facilities in which inmates repent and reform, these works might warn or educate readers to steer clear of crime, or reassure them of the state's capability to maintain security. Such narratives are less likely to dwell on inmates' pain or resistance, or take the perspective of political prisoners.

The prison literature that is the most extreme in championing the official discourse is the type promoted by prison authorities. These most propagandistic works (whose authors may also include current inmates) tend to fully affirm the Party-state's legal and moral supremacy, extol the regime's capability in matters of law and order as well as correction and discipline, praise the hard work of prison cadres in reforming prisoners, and so forth. I will bracket these off in the present discussion. This chapter will instead focus on three memoirs—Wumingshi's second-hand memoir *Red Sharks*, Cong Weixi's laogai memoir, *The Heading into Chaos Trilogy* (*Zou xiang hundun sanbuqu*, 1998, including Part One, *Heading into Chaos* or *Zou xiang hundun*, 1989), and Zhang Xianliang's memoir *My Bodhi Tree* (*Wode putishu*, 1994).[20] Highlighting these relatively more authentic voices and more trustworthy accounts of traumatic experiences of incarceration, I will explore the various aesthetic strategies of authorial resistance.

MAO-ERA PRISON CAMPS

A brief introduction of the Mao-era prison camps is in order.[21] The PRC's prison camp system had been officially referred to as "the laogai system" since May 1951. To explain the complicated system simply, there were three types of prison regimens: "laogai" (remolding through labor), "laojiao" (re-education through labor), and the "jiuye renyuan" (retained ex-inmate worker). There was some sort of court hearing or legal procedure (often formalities only) before a person was sentenced and sent to "laogai." By contrast, a "troublemaker" could be sent to a "laojiao" labor camp merely through an administrative order and without any sort of court hearing or legal procedure (Williams and Wu 2004, 2–3). The "jiuye renyuan" refers to a prisoner who had completed his term but was forced to accept "job placement in the vicinity of the camp" (*liuchang jiuye*) (Harry Wu 1992, 108, 124). During the Mao era, the state's proclaimed goal for laogai was "remolding" (*gaizao*)— to remold supposedly deviant prisoners into "socialist new men," or rather, obedient and useful subjects (Williams and Wu 2004, 19). Prisoners were supposed to "remold" themselves through hard labor and discipline. In actuality, the laogai system's unstated goals were punishment and production. As punishment, prisoners had to suffer extreme deprivation of basic human needs, forced hard labor, and constant physical and psychological abuse. To accomplish the goal of production, the system had to exploit prisoners' labor to the utmost. In December 1994, the PRC formally placed all of its carceral institutions under the term of "the prison system" (*jianyu zhidu*) (Yang and Zhang 1999, 3). Despite the shift in terminology, along with some improvement and other changes during the post-Mao era, China's prison system still retains quite a few characteristics from the Mao-era laogai. For example, the *ad hoc* system of "laojiao" administrative detention has not yet been discontinued. Such practices of illegal arrest and detention seriously infringe citizens' basic rights, and have been condemned both at home and abroad. In July 2008, over 15,000 Chinese scholars signed a petition to urge the government to abolish the laojiao system and protect human rights.[22] So far all such requests for reform have been to no avail.

SEVERE HUNGER AS "PROLONGED, REPEATED TRAUMA"

Depending upon specific historical period, region, and local laogai administration, prisoners' living and working conditions varied widely. Nevertheless, despite diverse depicted situations, the three prison camp memoirs by Wumingshi, Cong Weixi, and Zhang Xianliang exhibit some common themes such as deprivation, violence, suffering, trauma, and death. As far as the affective side of prison experiences is concerned, what a reader can most easily find in the texts are accounts of fear, anxiety, sorrow, and pain, though one would not categorically exclude some sporadic descriptions of rare moments of relaxation, relief, and even pleasure. Amid narratives of prisoners' acquiescence and submission, we occasionally find depictions of their passive and even active resistance. For example, in his *Red Sharks*, Wumingshi consciously provides narratives of resistance within the testimonials of pain. In chapter 2, "Tilanqiao Prison's Roaring Whirlwind" (*Tilan biaoxiao*), he describes how once in Shanghai's Tilanqiao Prison in the early 1950s many inmates organized a prison revolt under the leadership of a medical doctor, and how the revolt was quashed and the hero executed. Such large-scale active resistance, understandably, was exceptional. On the whole, we can interpret the three authors' act of writing laogai memoirs as a gesture of noncompliance in itself. To varying degrees, these works also exhibit an aesthetics of resistance through literary representations of the prisoners' traumatic experience.

Judith Herman's study of trauma (1992) can shed some light on our examination of the laogai experiences articulated in the memoirs. Herman indicates that the captor's coercive methods are "based upon the systematic, repetitive infliction of psychological trauma," which are the "organized techniques of disempowerment and disconnection," "designed to instill terror and helplessness and to destroy the victim's sense of self in relation to others" (77). The captor often punishes the victims by depriving them of human dignity and breaking them down. For prisoners, many factors can cause trauma: arrest, enforced separation from one's beloved, various kinds of torture, dehumanizing prison conditions, deprivation of food and sleep, forced hard labor, the captor's and warden's control and coercion, forced self-criticism, other prisoners' denunciation, and so forth. Some of these traumatic events clearly belong to the "prolonged, repeated" type which, as Herman explains, "occurs only in circumstances of captivity" and differs from the "single traumatic event" that "can occur almost anywhere" (74). These three memoirs all instantiate the "prolonged, repeated trauma" inflicted by the captor. The authors unfurl a panorama of long-term suffering as the narrators, presumably following the course of remembering, recapture the physical and emotional traces of some of the incarcerated in the Mao-era laogai camps.

In current studies of trauma, hunger rarely emerges as an important factor worthy of examination. Yet based on my reading of the Chinese prison camp memoirs and fiction, I would suggest that acute hunger stands out as perhaps the most unbearable of the various factors contributing to traumatic captivity, and the greatest of the various kinds of "prolonged, repeated trauma" experienced by laogai prisoners.[23] The PRC regime often subjected inmates to semi-starvation, adopting it as a "technique of disempowerment and disconnection" for a "systematic, repetitive infliction of psychological trauma." The regime's propaganda has always claimed that its correctional system follows the guiding principle of "socialist humanitarianism" (*shehuizhuyi rendaozhuyi*), yet some of the works here under discussion reveal how the laogai authorities often inhumanely used hunger as a tactic to control, punish, and even destroy prisoners. Through their representations of prisoners' extreme deprivation and attempts at survival, the writers directly or indirectly point out a significant form of inmate resistance—refusing to die. At the same time, by daring to divulge the hideous truth, the authors help to expose the regime's deception and hypocrisy, thereby contributing—whether intentionally or not—to a collective discourse of resistance.

The hunger experienced by many Mao-era prisoners resulted from a system of stringent rationing according to the inmate's rank and labor output. Depending upon camp hierarchy, higher-level cadres would receive better fare than lower-level guards, while among prisoners, the "trusties," cell bosses, some group chiefs, and privileged prisoners would have opportunities to obtain more food than their fellow inmates. Normally the degree to which a prisoner fulfilled or undershot the production quota could affect his food ration. At the same time, the authorities routinely withheld food from the incarcerated to punish them and force them to submit. Camp cadres typically limited food parcels from a prisoner's relatives or friends to one per month, and imposed stringent weight limitations on the food.[24] The camps' policies were designed to assert the party-state's supreme power and to remold inmates into obedient masses by controlling their stomachs.

Prisoners' experiences of prolonged hunger varied according to the operation of the local camp cadres, the camp's location, and the historical period. The variation in the intensity of prisoners' hunger depended upon whether the camp cadres' control and the rationing policies were lenient or strict, whether the camp's surrounding areas provided any possible food sources, whether the types of labor forced upon the prisoners were heavy or relatively light, and so forth. During normal times, a prisoner's daily fare would consist of two or three meager meals of rancid hardtack buns (*wotou*) and half-rotten vegetable soup.

Hunger was worst during the catastrophic famine from 1959 to 1961, when a total of around 30 million Chinese died of starvation. Already suffering from artificial stringent rationing of food, prisoners starved even more due to the pandemic famine which affected in particular rural areas, where laogai camps were mostly located. Mao's instruction to "substitute low ration [of grain] with gourds and vegetables" was in fact a euphemism meaning that prisoners had to eat mainly wild plants/greens (*yecai*), or rather, grass or weeds (Zhang 1994, 15–16). While numerous prisoners died from starvation, camp authorities did not dare to reveal the true reason of the mass deaths, nor did they dare to criticize Mao's food policy; instead, they attributed the cause of inmates' death to digestive problems (Zhang 1994, 278–79). As evidenced in laogai memoirs, from 1959 to 1960, each prisoner's monthly ration first dropped from 20 catties (about 22 pounds) of grain to 15 catties, and then to 9 catties, or even to 3 catties, in some cases (Zhang 1994, 129, 292).[25] Even when the ration was set at 9 catties, prisoners rarely had 9 catties of grain each because most of it had been "embezzled" by camp administrators and guards, pilfered by cooks, or even given to privileged prisoners (Zhang 1994, 104–105). Such a starvation diet naturally drove prisoners to be obsessed with nothing but food acquisition.

Laogai memoirs are teeming with descriptions of hunger and foraging. Famished prisoners would steal cucumbers, turnips, beets, or cabbage leaves from crop fields, and attempt to smuggle any edibles they thus obtained through the inspection line back into their cells.[26] In addition to foraging for wild plants, many prisoners also caught and devoured animals which they would not have normally considered edible, including field mice, crickets, locusts, toads, grapevine worms, grasshoppers, insect larvae and eggs, and poisonous snakes.[27] Camp authorities usually prohibited and punished this sort of foraging, and guards routinely searched prisoners' bodies and cells for any contraband.

For the regime to "instill terror and helplessness and to destroy the victim's sense of self in relation to others," deprivation of food has proved to be an easy and effective tactic. A prisoner could not help but be reduced to behaving like a desperate animal when his body suffered from constant gnawing hunger. Prolonged semi-starvation gradually destroyed his preexisting sense of identity and moral compass. To alleviate his hunger pangs he began to grovel, steal, cheat, or fight for food, relinquishing his self-respect. He might have become so intent on acquiring food that he lost any former affection for his family.

While this kind of dehumanization is sad and hard for any inmate, well-educated memoir writers occasionally betray a sense of elitism in distinguishing the responses from two groups of prisoners—criminal offenders and ideological offenders. The narratives sometimes depict how a criminal convict might steal from other prisoners, rob or commit further crimes for the sake of survival, but did not feel compunction or any loss of face. Considering themselves as part of an intellectual elite that were wrongly persecuted, some of the authors might delineate an educated-thought prisoner as having a stronger sense of ethics, morality, and shame—and therefore, ironically, suffering more from such remolding through "hunger"—than a criminal convict. Sometimes the authors seem to evince envy when relating how criminal convicts turned out to fare better at survival and group solidarity than intellectual political prisoners. Of course, in actuality, prisoners consisted of more than these two groups, and even within each of these two often overlapping groups, there were a variety of individual differences. There were those among the "ordinary criminals" who had a powerful moral compass, and those among the "intellectual prisoners" who lost moral compunction quickly.

While we avoid overgeneralizing two contrasting groups and replicating the elitism that may occasionally exist in some memoirs, we are nevertheless impressed by the authors' accounts of prolonged semi-starvation and how it devastated the inmates both physically and psychologically. Even though individual inmates' responses might differ, a number of prisoners were conscious of how they had devolved as a result of the dehumanizing effect of remolding-through-hunger, and became so ashamed as to be further traumatized by the sense of self-loathing and helplessness. Severe long-term hunger could break down the inmates' will to resist. Yet the memoirists' revelation of the inmates' pain and self-awareness paradoxically serves to resist the regime's manipulation of historical truth.

DOCILITY OR RESISTANCE?

While comparisons of Chinese and other concentration camp prisoners' behaviors would be valuable, we can only afford a brief aside here. Using Freudian psychoanalysis, Bruno Bettelheim claims that those confined in Nazi concentration camps regressed to being childlike, and that old prisoners especially identified with some of the camp authorities, accepting them as positive, "all-powerful father-images" (1979a, 79–81). Bettelheim praises individual prisoners' acts of defiance as autonomous and heroic, as triumphs for "human dignity and freedom" even when they meant death for the individual; and on the issue of surviving, he insists that true survivors would feel guilty for "having been so lucky as to survive the hell of the concentration camp," and this feeling of guilt is what makes us human (1979b, 302, 313–14).

Terrence Des Pres argues against Bettelheim's assertions about concentration camp inmates' behavior and survival. While Bettelheim declares that inmates tended to wet and soil themselves like infants, and were preoccupied with excretory functions, Des Pres correctly counters this argument by pointing out that these prisoners were "in extremity," in which the guards deliberately humiliated them, forcing them to worry about excretory functions. This differs from the situation in which someone in "civilized circumstances" is preoccupied with excretory functions—this latter case would indicate the person might be suffering from some kind of neurosis (56–57). Des Pres also contends that the "heroic" defiance Bettelheim celebrates is "still suicide" (161) whereas the apparently submissive "struggle for life" of the prisoners (whom Bettelheim deems "childlike") achieves survival, and that is what really counts. [28]

Unlike the Jews held in the concentration camps, who were imprisoned for a rather homogeneous reason, Chinese prisoners were incarcerated for a whole host of reasons, from speech and belief to theft and murder. Prisoners' responses to their detention could be very diverse, ranging from complete submission to open confrontation, and from assisting the guards in persecuting fellow inmates to cooperating with fellow inmates in passive resistance. Even an individual prisoner's behavior could change under different circumstances or in relation to different people. As seen in prison camp memoirs and fiction, the majority of inmates seemed forced to regress to being "childlike" or docile, and individual prisoners' acts of defiance were rare. However, outward docility does not automatically indicate voluntary submission and thorough obedience, but could very well be a strategy for survival. On the whole, while a few seemed to exhibit some of the characteristics pointed out by Bettelheim (including identifying with the camp authorities), many Chinese prisoners behaved more like what Des Pres explains about prisoners in concentration camps: confronting extreme hunger, they would try to survive at all cost. Nonetheless, Des Pres stresses that while making adjustments to live, concentration camp prisoners also tried hard to maintain "integrity" (202–3). Although I agree with most of Des Pres's argument, especially his rebuttal of Bettelheim's thesis mentioned above, I would not go so far as to interpret survivor behavior entirely positively. As far as laogai inmates are concerned, there were cases in which prisoners cooperated with one another, shared food, and gave gifts of food to one another (Zhang 1994, 128, 265), but there were also cases in which prisoners fought with one another for food (Zhang 1994, 263) or completely disregarded dignity, ethics, and morality. My impression from reading the memoirs is that laogai inmates, especially some of the intellectual prisoners, did not unite against the authorities as much as the Nazi concentration camp prisoners. In any case, despite their outward appearance of docility, during times of food shortage many laogai prisoners waged a constant low-key "battle" against camp personnel (such as disobeying some regulations, foraging, and going on an escapade, etc.) in order to survive. While occasionally presenting examples of relatively passive resistance, including suicides and attempted escapes, some memoirists demonstrate how certain inmates endeavor to preserve a certain measure of human dignity even during the bleakest of moments.

WUMINGSHI'S NARRATIVE OF RESISTANCE

Deeply influenced by classical Chinese canons and Western literature, Wu-mingshi (1917–2002) was determined to produce works of high philosophi-cal and aesthetic values. His pursuit of an aesthetic way of life as a free writer was brutally interrupted in 1949. He suffered under the communist regime's political pressures and was not able to leave the PRC until late 1982. Under the socialist literary system, a writer could only find employ-ment with the state. The only "public ladder of success for writers" was the Party-run "Writers' Association," which enabled the Party to monitor and control creative writing.[29] Wumingshi never worked for the authoritarian state, nor attempted to join the Writers' Association; refusing to be controlled and brainwashed, he preferred to live in isolation and poverty. When all the people were compelled to worship and eulogize Mao, and most authors were forced to adopt Maoist thought, discourse, and literary style, Wumingshi insisted on maintaining his integrity and independence as a scholar and writ-er, and continued to write—though secretly—in his own style. It was only after he settled in Taiwan in 1983 that he began to write and publish freely again.

In his second-hand memoir *Red Sharks*, narrated through the voice of Hong Xianheng, Wumingshi seeks to truthfully document the little-known aspects of life in Qinghai's laogai camps in the 1950s and 1960s. Numerous prisoners were forced to construct roads in extreme cold while living in tents; later, somewhat like pioneers, they also had to build their own barracks and cultivate farmland. Many died in the process. Intending to disclose the part of history covered up by PRC's official discourse, Wumingshi was consciously creating unofficial discourse and "literature of resistance." The first chapter, "At the Bottom of a Well," for example, recounts Hong Xianheng's solitary confinement and semi-starvation at the bottom of a covered dry well in Qinghai's Delingha Prison Farm (Delingha *jianyu nongchang*) from 1967 to 1968. It highlights Hong Xianheng's courage and endurance in surviving such prolonged severe conditions without losing sanity or hope.

Writing *Red Sharks* in Taiwan, Wumingshi did not need to worry about the CCP's censorship and retaliation, nor was he restrained by self-censor-ship. His primary objective was to reveal the hidden truth. While Wumingshi censures the inhumanity of Mao's regime, however, this work is by no means a mere anti-communist ideological tract. It is a literary narrative which he built by exercising a range of artistic skills.

Stunning narration and striking details are some of Wumingshi's strengths. He vividly depicts how hunger deprived the prisoners of human dignity, a sense of shame, as well as concern and respect for other human beings. Preoccupied with foraging for whatever was edible, inmates competed and fought with one another over food. Especially during the Great Famine from 1959 to 1961, many prisoners stooped to wretched conduct merely in order to survive, including consuming the flesh of human corpses. Some prisoners working in the irrigation squad secretly dug up the corpses of the newly dead, cut off flesh from the scrawny bodies, and sold the human flesh as beef or mutton to other prisoners. Those who ate human flesh often contracted dropsy, or died from toxicosis (Wumingshi 1994a, 346–347). Many who had nothing to barter for human flesh and had little to eat but wild plants also contracted dropsy and died (Wumingshi 1994a, 347–348).[30] Wumingshi's work is perhaps the first to reveal incidents of cannibalism in labor camps during the famine. In 2001, Yang Xianhui would also divulge, somewhat indirectly, that cannibalism occurred in a labor camp in Gansu province when many inmates were dying from starvation (Yang Xianhui 2002a, 23, 32–33). However, both writers exercised artistic restraint in their accounts of cannibalism.

Dramatic emplotment also marks the author's literary imagination. While a memoir is typically narrated in a chronological, matter-of-fact fashion, Wumingshi inverts the chronology somewhat by beginning the memoir with the chapter "At the Bottom of a Well" (an account of Hong Xianheng's solitary confinement from 1967 to 1968), rather than with the chapter that narrates Hong's arrest and imprisonment in Shanghai from 1951 to 1952, in order to highlight the extraordinarily compelling and dramatic episode about Hong's resistance to the CCP's prolonged cruel treatment.[31] Whenever possible, Wumingshi also infuses the potentially dry memoir with his aesthetic and sometimes idiosyncratic representation.

Not content with straightforward depictions alone, Wumingshi attempts to interest and inspire his readers through some unusual use of rhetoric, metaphors, paradoxes, and black humor. For example, food is what we normally assume to be the resource that brings relief to the hungry. Yet Wumingshi makes us undergo an epistemological shift, to regard how the originally positively conceived "protective resources" can become a negative concept, and how passive objects can become active weapons and agents that cause pain (Wu 2006a, 131–132). He relates that prisoners were forced to eat inedible, bitter plants which could cause stomach diseases and even ulcers. Describing how prisoners, while out in the open air at a bitterly cold work site, must hastily wolf down two small hardtack buns made of pea husks and millet, Wumingshi wrote in a black humorous way, "What we grabbed in hand seemed by no means a hardtack bun, but rather an enemy whom we hated so much that we devoured him in one gulp" (Wumingshi 1994a, 81). Eating the two tiny buns is like "throwing two stones into an empty valley," because they "hardly filled up the belly" (Wumingshi 1994a, 80). Through his uncommon representation and comments such as, "Food is a kind of pain. It is indeed what is called 'eating pain' (*chi ku*)" (Wumingshi 1994a, 79),

Wumingshi enriches the term "eating bitterness/pain," which is ordinarily used metaphorically to mean "to bear hardships or to suffer." With these surprising visceral paradoxes, the reader is jolted into recognition of truth, and is made to understand and empathize with the prisoners.[32]

Rather than narrating external events and appearances alone, Wumingshi also pays attention to describing prisoners' sensations and feelings. He captures the dread of an inmate caught in such an impasse: the prisoner's daily suffering was so extreme that even eating became painful, and while eating caused pain, not to eat anything at all hurt even more and would lead to a speedy death. The following paragraph, voiced through the narrator, demonstrates the nuanced way with which Wumingshi adumbrates the atrocious pain from severe hunger:

> The pain from hunger to death is unlike ordinary pain. . . . If you were whipped and clobbered for a prolonged period of time, you would faint at the peak of pain. Yet the kind of punishment called "hunger" is mankind's strong instinctual reflex. That kind of terrible bodily feeling far exceeds anything that can be described by language. . . . When one is at the peak of hunger, one's whole body seems to be in a state of extreme suffocation in every second, yet does not die immediately.[33]

Some of the scenes crafted by Wumingshi border on the surrealistic. Employing metaphors to show how semi-starvation brought about devolution, he creates the following grotesque picture, depicting famished prisoners as devoid of dignity and rationality, and resembling such base creatures as locusts, reptiles, rats, and mud fish (*niqiu*) in their appearance and movement:

> As mad as locusts, the hungry people crazily jostled with one another, racing to eat the seedlings of vegetables, beans, wheat, and grain in the field. . . . An extremely miserable panorama appeared. Many people became reptiles, crawling in the paddy field. Like rats, these people ceaselessly munched on rice seedlings. Yet each person grabbed a bunch of seedlings in both hands, for fear that they might be seized by someone else. At this time, the paddy fields were full of big human-shaped mud fish. All the faces turned into muddy, watery, and hideous faces. (Wumingshi 1994a, 336; translated in Wu 2006a, 147)

Wumingshi's fondness for poetic language and symbolism also surfaces in the eerie scene below, which depicts prisoners in black (on whose black front lapel or back are written the two big white Chinese characters *laogai*) laboring to build the road, against the boundless white background. In Wumingshi's representation, the prisoners have already been reduced to hungry ghosts, occupying a liminal monochrome realm, marginalized and disconnected from the human world:

These black lives were all vigorously laboring. Contrasted with skeleton-white
ice and snow, the black hats, clothes, pants, and the white characters were
particularly vivid. Added to these were one sharpened triangular face after
another, so ghostly, gloomy, and mournful. They looked like clusters of midnight black specters who suddenly appeared in the daylight. (Wumingshi
1994a, 58; translated in Wu 2006a, 143)

Repeating and interlacing the two sharply contrasted adjectives, "black" and
"white," Wumingshi weaves them into an amazingly pictorial and haunting
scene which is also pregnant with meanings. What the color symbolism
denotes or connotes depends upon the cultural and political contexts. The
black clothes signify that the incarcerated belong to a condemned group,
since the color black indicates these people's classification under the "black"
categories during the Mao era.[34] Referring specifically to the freezing ice and
snow in Qinghai, the color white symbolizes death as well, according to the
traditional Chinese cultural conception; in the West, however, the color black
is associated with death and ghosts. Wumingshi utilizes both sets of symbolic
significance to describe the prisoners as exhausted starving ghosts, the "midnight black specters," and the living dead. They are spatially and temporally
marginalized, and their whereabouts and existence are unknown to most
people. Having lost their individual identities and contacts with family and
friends, and being completely displaced and detached from the rest of the
world, they hover near the borderline of life and death. Though still "vigorously laboring," these moving black figures can easily fall down and die in
the coffin-like "skeleton-white ice and snow" (Wu 2006a, 143). Yet, the sad
truth is that this nameless horde of specters making robotic movements
against a deathly still landscape are in fact live humans capable of feeling
"gloomy" and "mournful."

Wumingshi's purpose in depicting these grotesque scenes of the prisoners
is not so much to mock them for trying to survive as to condemn the party-
state that has forced the prisoners to become so debased. Through Hong
Xianheng's voice, Wumingshi directly indicts the party-state for brutally
abusing prisoners and hiding its atrocities. The CCP's deception and hypocrisy seem to have been practiced at every level of the bureaucracy. In the
camp, if a prisoner dares to mention the word "hunger," he will be publicly
punished (Wumingshi 1994a, 73). The regime has kept secret its brutal treatment of prisoners (in blatant opposition to its proclaimed "socialist humanitarianism"), and would punish those who dare criticize the regime about the
abuse. In his preface, Wumingshi remarks that he intends the book to serve
as "further proof" of the Maoist authorities' inhumanity, in the hope that
"those who care about human rights and dignity will do something to help
break the cave's silence after they have learned its secrets" (Wumingshi
1994b, xxvii). His second-hand memoir not only bears witness to the horrors

in Mao-era prison camps but also effectively destroys the myth of the "socialist humanitarianism" constructed by the Party-state. Through his unique aesthetic strategies, he recuperates the buried memories of laogai of a specific period and place—in a sense resuscitating the ghosts of the dead souls who could not voice their grievances.

CONG WEIXI'S ART OF RESTRAINT AND INDIRECTION: LAMENTING THE LOSS OF HUMAN DIGNITY

The PRC's literary control has relied not only upon external censorship but also self-censorship. Self-censorship is generally engendered through the regime's repeated intimidation, repression, censorship, and punishment.[35] Compared with Wumingshi who resettled in Taiwan since 1983, Cong Weixi (b. 1933) and Zhang Xianliang, the two previously incarcerated writers who still reside in the PRC, would more likely be subjected to external and internalized censorship. Of course, the fact that Cong and Zhang have become successful, influential members of the Writers' Association since their "exoneration" means that they have built a strong enough supportive network within the CCP not to have to worry excessively about external censorship. Yet, they have been so accustomed to the regime's intimidation and conditioning that quite possibly some sort of self-censorship has become a habit to them, whether they are fully conscious of it or not. Nevertheless, while their memoirs reveal traces of their negotiating external and internalized censorship, I would suggest that amid their responses to censorship, there may well be some subterranean strains of protest embedded in the texts. When reading their works, informed readers would want to take this extra dimension into consideration, be ready to read between the lines, and be especially careful yet creative in interpretation.

While Cong Weixi's prison camp fictional works have been criticized for their "new false realism," they still occasionally reflect some fragments of reality garnered from Cong's own camp experiences. However, it is only in his memoir that Cong is willing to give a relatively frank, chronological, and detailed account of his past experiences in the camps. Cong claims that the publication of his *Heading into Chaos (Zou xiang hundun)* in 1989 caused a "great sensation" and was so popular as to be pirated numerous times (1998a, 1). *Heading into Chaos* would form Part One of *The Heading into Chaos Trilogy (Zou xiang hundun sanbuqu)*, published in 1998. In Part One, Cong relates how he and his wife were falsely accused of being "rightists" during the "Anti-Rightist Campaign" and sent to the labor camps. Parts Two and Three document what travails they, along with many fellow inmates, had to endure, and how, after over twenty years, they were finally exonerated.

Though the major part of the memoir focuses on Cong and his family, Cong also recounts at length the events associated with a number of his friends and notable fellow inmates.

On the whole, this memoir appears politically innocuous and Cong Weixi makes no complaint about the current PRC government. Despite narrating his personal misfortunes and grievances, he avoids openly criticizing the Mao-era regime or censuring the regime for purging and persecuting the intellectuals. Instead, the blame seems diffused. In relating how some intellectuals informed against the others, causing other innocent people to be arrested and jailed, Cong appears to fault those informers for lacking in rectitude and leading to the terrible outcome for many other intellectuals. Presenting himself as a hard-working, law-abiding model prisoner, Cong furthermore writes warmly about some of the cadres who had treated him relatively kindly in the camps. Cong also makes sure to end his memoir on a positive note, claiming that his life would have been lackluster had there been no Anti-Rightist Campaign in 1957, and that he is grateful for having been able to learn a great deal about life and China through his experiences in prison camps (1998b, 481). In other words, he implies that his decades of suffering have provided him with valuable material for his work as an author.

Cong Weixi's reluctance to condemn the regime's violation of human rights might have resulted from his ingrained fear of censorship as well as his desire to have his memoir published on the one hand, and his patriotism and loyalty to the CCP on the other. Furthermore, showing himself ready to pardon those who have done him wrong might be a way to demonstrate his tolerant and forgiving character. Artistic concerns could also have played a role: for example, Cong might have regarded vociferous attacks on the authorities as too political and repugnant to be included in his memoir, favoring instead a milder and more reserved manner in narration that continues the traditional aesthetic quality of restraint.

It is understandable if some of the readers would therefore accuse Cong Weixi of being cowardly, or find fiction and "false realism" even in Cong's memoir. Yet I would suggest that if we venture to resist the façade created under the pressure of external and internalized censorship, we might very well detect some strains of dissent hidden under the inoffensive exterior. While Cong attempts to narrate the events in a relatively calm and matter-of-fact manner, there are moments when emotions such as grief, fear, anxiety, anguish, and indignation come to the fore, and seem to belie somewhat the overall innocuous packaging of the memoir. Some of the events which Cong chooses to narrate in detail as well as the way he represents them also indirectly reveal how unjustified those innocent prisoners' sufferings were, and by extension, how inhumanely the regime treated its people.

We can detect some strains of protest in how Cong presents two fellow intellectual prisoners who committed suicide at the beginning of the Cultural

Revolution. Cong argues that while suicides are usually regarded as a "cowardly" act in books, he believes these two individuals' suicides in fact demonstrated their "bravery" and "foresight" (1998, 256). These two inmates seemed to know beforehand how much worse their tribulations would be in the years to come, and so their decision to end their lives prematurely served as a kind of wake-up call to their generation. One of them was Zheng Guangdi, a former chemist and an extremely scrawny, frail, and gentle laojiao inmate. According to Cong's narration and explanation, Zheng must have deliberately chosen a special stage on which to "act out" his death scene because he drowned himself in a famous lake in Beijing rather than in one of the many ponds in the labor camp. Cong believes that Zheng's opting to die in a spot in the capital is a calculated deed: "he wanted people to know that his suicide was a protest against that period" (1998, 256). Cong was so shaken by this tragic incident as to confess that the deceased put Cong himself and the other inmates to shame (1998, 256)—because they lacked the deceased's audacity to protest. By choosing to die in a privileged location—adjacent to the regime's headquarters—and expose his corpse for public display, Zheng succeeded in creating a spectacle to publicize his grievances and effectively indict the CCP of unjust persecutions. Cong's representation of this tragedy as well as the responses from him and the others reveals the immense affective power this suicide-as-protest exerts. While by no means rebellious, Zheng set an example for those who dare not disobey the authorities or publicly commit suicide, and his independent act of passive resistance becomes, relatively speaking, a symbolic gesture of active resistance.[36] Cong's representation makes Zheng an almost martyr-like figure, whose suicide not only demonstrated his extraordinary courage but also drew attention to personal and collective sufferings.

Furthermore, presenting himself as being too intimidated to contemplate an escape, Cong narrates at length the adventures of two audacious inmates who escaped and earned freedom for a while before being re-arrested (1998, 204–9, 424–30). Cong seems to express both awe and envy when describing their adventures as dangerous but also exciting, impressive, and even romantic at times. Instead of taking the side of the laogai cadres in condemning the escapees, Cong writes about these two inmates in an approving tone, depicting them as heroes of moral integrity, thereby expressing a high regard for them. Interestingly, even from a Bettelheimian perspective, both the inmate who took the initiative to commit suicide publicly to protest against injustice and the escapees who actively resisted the authorities seemed portrayed in varying degrees as triumphant representatives for "human dignity and freedom."

Cong Weixi's preface (1998a, 1–3) to the memoir further discloses an intertwining of surface self-control and some subterranean strains of unease. Though written with considerable restraint, Cong's preface occasionally reveals his mixed feelings. Cong defends the writing of the memoir, using intellectual justifications. He claims that he takes the memoir very seriously because he is "recounting the spiritual history of a whole generation's intellectuals," and his memoir mirrors "the group portrait of the intellectuals" of his generation (1998a, 2). His memoir not only consists of self-portrayals but also biographical vignettes of many other noteworthy intellectual inmates and some non-intellectual prisoners. He seems to adopt the stance of a detached, cautious historian, who strives to collect facts and record them as accurately as possible. He declares that although the publication of Part One of the memoir was a success, he delayed publishing the last two parts immediately, because he had to straighten out his blurred memories, revisit those labor camps in which he had done time, obtain verification for some of his remembrances, and reflect on the past rationally. While emphasizing the "authenticity" of the events recorded in his memoir, he confesses to feeling sad in remembering the desolation of the past (1998a, 2). Still, Cong refrains from directly criticizing the regime, nor does he seem to hold Mao responsible for his and many others' unjustified sufferings. His more personal, unhappy emotions thus coexist—albeit inconspicuously—with the intellectual justifications and self-censorship.

Nonetheless, Cong's references to two canonic literati-officials of integrity in his preface (1998a, 1) serve as significant signposts and give readers the key to a hidden subtext. Cong alludes to Qu Yuan (340?–278 B.C.) and Sima Qian (c. 145–c. 85 B.C.), who loyally remonstrated with their rulers, yet lost the rulers' favor and were punished as a result. Slandered by treacherous fellow officials and banished by the king to the far south, Qu Yuan, the minister and poet, eventually committed suicide by drowning himself in a river. The great Han historian Sima Qian was wrongfully charged because he enraged the emperor when defending a general he admired. Cong Weixi could certainly identify himself with both literary figures—especially Qu Yuan—since he had been loyal to Mao and the CCP, his undeserved punishment was triggered by some other colleagues' false accusation that he was a "rightist," and his serving in labor camps located in remote areas was a form of internal exile. Cong seems to be encoding some criticism of the regime with his allusion to Qu Yuan and Sima Qian. Subtextually, he invokes his own undeserved suffering, and draws a parallel (and contrast) between the rulers who mistreated these two canonic figures and Mao, who, along with his regime, brought disasters upon millions.

We can uncover additional deeper meanings and resistance subtly embedded in Cong's allusion to these two figures. Qu Yuan reputedly composed such great lyrics as *Encountering Sorrow* (*Li sao*) only after he was banished, while Sima Qian completed his monumental work, *Historical Records* (*Shi ji*), after he had suffered unjustified punishment. Their works have been interpreted as containing political protest or allegory. By alluding to the two figures, Cong may be hoping that his memoir—composed after his suffering and focusing on the experience—would also become a masterpiece with embedded political significance. Moreover, instead of committing suicide like Qu Yuan in order to retain his dignity, Sima Qian accepted the ignominious sentence—castration. In his famous "Letter in Reply to Ren An" ("*Bao Ren Shaoqing shu*"), Sima Qian revealed the reason for his choice: he decided to bear the humiliation and survive because he wanted to finish his work, in hopes of earning later generations' recognition of his writings.[37] Consciously adopting the role of a historian, Cong appears to be taking Sima Qian as an inspirational role model. Cong's aspiration to identify with the grand historian is especially poignant, since he himself was not only falsely accused and punished, but, according to his valiant admission in this memoir, suffered from trauma-related impotence from 1970 to the early 1990s (1998b, 406).[38] And while Cong may have praised some of his fellow inmates who committed suicide, he chose to survive even if in disgrace. I believe his decision resulted not so much from cowardice as from other calculations. He had a strong sense of commitment and responsibility toward his elderly mother, little son, and his wife—who had attempted suicide twice during the period of her incarceration. Furthermore, though his hopes of being a writer were dashed during his imprisonment, he had probably chosen to emulate Sima Qian, and to survive the humiliation (including his impotence) and hardships so that someday he could record part of this history for later generations and for his vindication.

Of the various depictions of traumatic events in Cong Weixi's memoir, what stands out are the extended portrayals of camp inmates' severe hunger. Whether intentionally or unintentionally, Cong's representation of these scenes particularly serve to implicitly reflect the regime's cruelty. Originally equipped with high self-esteem as a well-educated writer, Cong laments, above all, the loss of identity and dignity he and his fellow intellectual prisoners had to endure in the camps. Prolonged severe hunger made him feel he had degenerated to the status of a beast; in fact, he even envied a workhorse because it enjoyed plentiful food and was free from human suffering (Cong 1989, 107). In addition to writing down his own pain, Cong serves as a scribe of a collective testimony. He witnessed how semi-starvation drove originally highly civilized intellectuals to devolve to barbaric primitives or worse: in desperation they ate all sorts of creatures they could find, including such poisonous animals as toads, and would even eat such items as "toothpaste, tooth powder, shoe soles, and cotton wadding" (Cong 1998b, 161, 163). According to his observation, hunger had been so widespread among inmates and so severe as to frequently cause "psychological pathology" (Cong 1989, 152–153). Cong also coins the term, "the disease of hunger" (*ji'e zheng*), noting how inmates suffering from it often fought with other prisoners over the little bit of gruel left at the bottom of the vat, and scavenged among garbage heaps (Cong 1998b, 194). Cong admits that at first he despised such behavior, but later, because he had witnessed the pathological behavior so often, he no longer found it strange (Cong 1998b, 130–31).

Cong Weixi is one of the earlier laogai memoir writers to point out the lingering pathological effect of semi-starvation. According to Judith Herman, "People subjected to prolonged, repeated trauma develop an insidious, progressive form of post-traumatic stress disorder that invades and erodes the personality," and while the intrusive symptoms of post-traumatic stress disorder "tend to abate in weeks or months" in survivors of "a single acute trauma," these symptoms often persist in survivors of "prolonged, repeated trauma" (Herman 86–87). What Cong Weixi witnessed in the camps also includes the continual pathological symptoms in some of the survivors of the "prolonged, repeated trauma" of severe hunger. He sadly observes that many in the camps exhibited what he terms "the post-famishment syndrome" (*ji'e houyizheng*) (Cong 1998b, 197, 222): after having endured severe hunger, they habitually felt starved (even after the daily ration had increased) and would crave to eat anything, even unclean scavenged things (194, 197, 221–223; Williams and Wu 2004, 167). The "post-famishment syndrome" is one kind of the "post-laogai syndrome" (*laogai houyizheng*) which many inmates continued to suffer from even after their release.[39]

While Cong Weixi's memoir may be as "authentic" and true as he claims, the reader can well imagine that Cong would probably not wish to be comprehensive in documenting his experiences. Some of the more politically controversial details, for example, would most likely not be recorded. Instead of openly blaming or criticizing the Mao-era regime, he focuses on events that illustrate either the strengths or the weaknesses of the intellectuals whose story he follows. Playing the role of a historian, Cong seems to make an attempt at documenting events objectively and calmly. Referring to one of the Eight Daoist (Taoist) Immortals in Chinese mythology who reputedly sits backward on his donkey and "looks backward," Cong reminds his reader of the importance of learning from the past, or, "reviewing the old in order to learn the new," as in one of Confucius' sayings (1998a, 2). Cong's memoir may not depict examples of heroic defiance or horrible extremity as exhaustively as does Wumingshi's text, nor does it adopt an oppositionist stance and accusatory tone, yet it vividly portrays inmates' suffering and their attempts at survival. In Cong's representation, some of these efforts to survive as well as the suicides and escapes can be interpreted as passive or even active resistance. As a memoirist who also intends to write a "collective biography" of his fellow sufferers, Cong seems able to eventually transcend his personal grievances to some extent. His restrained style notwithstanding, Cong occasionally embeds subtextual messages in his narration. No doubt the inspiration from historical canonical figures such as Sima Qian gave Cong Weixi the courage to reassert the dignity and rectitude of a responsible intellectual and to record his camp experiences truthfully—to the extent that this would not land him in jail once more.

MULTIVALENCE IN ZHANG XIANLIANG'S MEMOIR *MY BODHI TREE (WODE PUTISHU)*

A great irony in the cases of Cong Weixi and Zhang Xianliang (along with many intellectuals of their period) is that they were in fact loyal to Mao and the CCP when they were mislabeled "rightists." Despite being wrongfully imprisoned for two decades, these two writers have both served the PRC government since their release. Nevertheless, the long period of intimidation seems to have left behind a strong fear and self-censorship palpable in their writings. Compared with Cong Weixi's memoir, however, Zhang Xianliang's memoir *My Bodhi Tree* (*Wode putishu*, 1994) exhibits even more multivalence and irony, partly resulting from the interaction of his emotional responses and his heightened consciousness of both external and internalized censorship. Unlike Cong, Zhang hardly feels grateful for learning lessons about life through his two decades of incarceration, and he includes more criticism of Mao and the labor camp—often indirect and ironic—in his memoir.

Unlike Cong Weixi's memoir (1998), which covers over twenty years' laogai life and various prison camps and locales, *My Bodhi Tree* focuses on only six months—or about 2 percent of Zhang Xianliang's entire prison time—and one single camp.[40] Despite the limitation of its coverage, Zhang's memoir provides rich materials and philosophical reflections (some of which extend well beyond the six months), and is an especially valuable document of "prolonged, repeated trauma." Reportedly written on the basis of a diary secretly kept between July 11 and December 20, 1960, this memoir has an unusual format which consists mostly of repetitions of a pattern: first, there would be four or five days' brief diary entries from 1960; then, these would be followed by lengthy remembrances and explanations (presumably written in the early 1990s) about some of the activities and events recorded in (or omitted from) those entries. The diary entries are deliberately terse and innocuous. Keeping a diary in labor camps was in general forbidden, and if anything he wrote was found to be "counterrevolutionary" or "reactionary," Zhang would have had to spend even more years in prison. By his own admission, he took care to write mostly about mundane activities that were unlikely to arouse suspicion, and placed special emphasis on paraphrasing the "reports" (which were in fact "curses") of camp cadres (1994, 130). In other words, Zhang's diary avoided any mention of controversial subjects such as ideologically incorrect remarks, yet included camp cadres' castigation of prisoners for their foraging, escape attempts, theft, and malingering. It is mostly in Zhang's ample annotations that we find a wealth of information and fleshed-out meaning.

Many of Zhang Xianliang's annotations of the diary entries, as well as his reflections and comments, describe different aspects of the prolonged trauma of hunger. For example, camp cadres typically forbade prisoners to share food so as to keep prisoners from bonding with one another, and to keep them isolated and disconnected. Because hungry prisoners were so intent on obtaining something to eat, they constantly quarreled or fought over even a small bite of food (1994, 220). Eventually, they regarded one another as enemies in the struggle for survival. Therefore, the conflict among prisoners over food could weaken any solidarity they might have established while strengthening the camp personnel's power over them.

Yet Zhang's diary also reveals that some prisoners actually cooperated with one another to obtain food, often violating camp regulations: they engaged in bartering, helped one another in foraging, stealing, and smuggling contraband back to the barracks, and shared food. Zhang even compares the unusual gratification of eating one's fill of foraged foodstuffs together with a cellmate during famine times to sexual gratification (189–90). Through secretly sharing and exchanging food and other resources, thereby going against camp authorities' injunctions, these inmates bonded with one another to ensure group survival while also engaging in a passive form of collective resistance.

The unique format of Zhang Xianliang's memoir provides multiple perspectives upon the recorded events. The older narrator (hereafter also "Old Zhang") of the "annotations" is trying to remember the background of some of the diary entries of over thirty years ago, and to recapture what the youthful narrator (hereafter also "Young Zhang") of the diary had seen, heard, experienced, and felt. The immense gap in time, combined with two narrators and other speakers, occasionally permits relatively open-ended interpretations on certain events. Though sympathizing with the suffering of his younger self, the more mature narrator does not portray him as someone possessing "heroic" defiance, but instead, somewhat self-deprecatingly (even humorously) presents him as naïve, quite famished, and merely trying to survive: obsessed with acquiring food, Young Zhang sometimes resorted to despicable or deceptive patterns of behavior; he had lost his sense of honor and felt almost no shame when punished or disgraced by camp personnel. Seeing how other starving inmates had developed edema or eventually died one after another, Young Zhang stooped so low as to beg for leftover food from those prisoners who had lost their appetite and were about to die (217–20, 246). Once he even devised a trick to fool the cook, though he failed, and the cook cursed and humiliated him (247–49). The events and views of Young Zhang are mediated through Old Zhang with mixed emotions, including self-approval, occasional self-denigration, self-justification, a tinge of pity, sadness, and wry humor.

Since the narrative can be ambiguous enough that no one single judgment of a character or one simple interpretation of an event is possible, it sometimes invites the reader to read resistantly.[41] The early part of the diary explains how Young Zhang became one of the "favored" prisoners: admiring the Old Commissar who was in charge of his camp, he made it known to the commissar that he wanted to write an article singing his praises; soon afterward, Zhang was somehow transferred to do lighter labor, becoming a prisoner who was "looked after." It is not completely clear whether the youthful Zhang truly admired the commissar and became a favored prisoner due to a happy coincidence, or whether Zhang intended to ingratiate himself with the commissar by letting him know that he planned to write a eulogy of him, thereby using this as a tactic to earn favored status. In either case, it is clear that the commissar loved flattery and eulogy, secretly rewarded Zhang, and so was a leader that could be "corrupted." There is also a certain co-mixture of self-deprecation, self-congratulation, and boasting implied in narrating how the hungry Zhang obtained his new status and earned a lighter workload and a little extra food.

The memoir's depictions of the old commissar—who was originally a farmer with hardly any education—are indeed more complex than they appear to be at first. While praising the commissar's ability to lecture and control the prisoners (many of whom were far better educated than he), the mature narrator relates how Young Zhang accidentally discovered that the commissar actually ate one duck a day in secret. Zhang was shocked because he could not believe that the well-respected, "paternalistic" leader would not share the suffering with his people while the country was plagued with famine. The surprising discovery affords the reader a metaphorical reading, especially when placed in the context of the mature narrator's comments on Mao Zedong, which often mask criticism as accolade. At one point, Zhang Xianliang wrote sarcastically, "Everything in China was illuminated by the shining glory of the person of Chairman. Without the radiant light emanating from Mao Zedong, the country would soon have been revealed as nothing more than a pile of rotten garbage" (1994, 275; 1996, 185). The hint of Mao as authoritarian and tyrannical can hardly be missed in the manner Zhang praises Mao as an almost godlike figure who alone could claim to represent "the country" (1994, 275), and as the only ruler in China's long history to actuate a national shortage of salt (281). Just as Mao Zedong lived in affluence amid a sea of poverty created by him, so the commissar secretly devoured ducks while others ate grass. We can especially appreciate the poignant irony in this remark when placing it in the context of the CCP's propaganda about a "classless," "proletarian," "egalitarian" society.

Indeed, irony is Zhang Xianliang's secret weapon, while overt condemnation and protest are not. Claiming that Young Zhang was mindful of censorship when writing his diary, the mature narrator may still engage in a little self-censorship himself. When recounting past events, Old Zhang would underscore the fact that Young Zhang never entertained any "counterrevolutionary" ideas or intended to do anything subversive: Young Zhang did not deliberately seek out the commissar's weaknesses; he just happened to hear about the latter's duck-eating from a camp employee who cooked the ducks for the commissar. Neither Young Zhang nor Old Zhang would bluntly characterize the commissar as hypocritical or Mao as cruel and sanctimonious, for example.

Zhang Xianliang also puts the "counterrevolutionary speech" in the mouths of privileged prisoners or ordinary criminals, while letting Young Zhang serve as a passive audience, thereby remaining ostensibly blameless. On another occasion, for example, Young Zhang would hear a criminal convict complain bitterly that the prison cadres "kill people with a wooden knife" (*yong mu daozi sha ren*), which means that the authorities slowly destroy the prisoners by keeping them hungry and exhausted from hard labor (1994, 70). On yet another occasion, Young Zhang hears a Muslim candidly claim that the regime is remolding the people by making them starve, and that is the only effective way to force them to submit to Chairman Mao and worship him (100). As an exceptional, privileged prisoner who receives plentiful food aid from his kinsmen, this Muslim proudly proclaims that he will never be remolded because the authorities cannot force him to go hungry. In Zhang Xianliang's representation, Young Zhang is merely the passive and surprised listener, and not responsible for the Muslim's "reactionary" speech. Yet for the reader this Muslim stands out almost as a hero, and his analysis of the regime's appalling tactics is brilliant and penetrating. He can afford to be relatively independent and free in thought, and not to prostrate himself to the authorities, because he does not need to beg for food from them. While this Muslim might have indeed been a real-life figure who saw through the regime's scheme of starving people into submission, it is equally likely that Zhang Xianliang has skillfully created a defiant character to serve as a mouthpiece for some of Zhang's own "reactionary" insights, while relieving both Young Zhang and the author of any possible blame.

In addition to recollecting how Young Zhang and his fellow inmates tried to survive, the mature narrator psychoanalyzes them occasionally, in an attempt to understand and recapture their feelings. Through retrospective narrative and analysis, Zhang Xianliang invites the reader to sympathize with Young Zhang (however unheroic he may appear), who endured both "prolonged trauma" and a few "single traumatic events" associated with near starvation. The mature narrator recalls that once his younger self tried to steal food from a horse cart and grabbed something that felt like a big turnip; he was then horrified to discover that what he pulled out was in fact a frozen human arm, and the cart was laden with corpses. This gruesome event was so traumatizing that after his release, he would feel nauseated upon seeing butchered chickens or ducks, and became almost a vegetarian (154–56). Zhang's uncontrollable nausea is clearly one form of hunger-related pathology.

Laogai prisoners would routinely be stripped of most of their personal belongings. Food was usually the last item prisoners would give up, and certainly the most difficult for them to part with during famine. Zhang Xianliang masterfully represents the extreme difficulty for the inmates to preserve even a little bit of food for themselves, and how that situation damaged not only inmates' health but also their dignity, identity, and whole well-being. On one occasion, when the two beets Young Zhang had stolen and carefully hidden away were discovered and confiscated, he wept and begged the confiscator, "Leave them for me! Leave them for me!" (294). The author describes the beets as aesthetically and sensually appealing, relating how much care Young Zhang took to clean and peel them, how dear he held them, and that he treasured them so much as to save them for enjoyment later. What the confiscator seized, therefore, was not just foodstuff essential for Zhang's survival. Those two beets represent something resembling the most beloved creation of an artist; close to the young man's heart, they constitute part of his integrity.

Remembering this event in the context of his entire life, Old Zhang claims that he had never shed a tear when he was arrested and sentenced (a total of five times in his life) and even when he was taken to the execution ground, yet he could not help weeping out loud when the beets were confiscated (294). In retrospect, he realizes that it was not only his younger self's empty stomach, but rather his "entire person," that was "traumatized" at that time: "Under the irresistible threat, all my personality, my goal in life, my defense system, my self-respect, and my self-realization have completely collapsed!" (295). Comparing this event with his near-execution experience, the older narrator in fact judges the moment of his younger self's beloved beets' being snatched away to be the breaking point of his will to live. Looking back pitifully on this event thirty years later, Zhang obviously finds it to be perhaps the most devastating "single traumatic event" in his life.

Examining the various hunger-related traumas endured in the camps, the mature narrator declares that hunger debilitates prisoners not only physically but also psychologically and emotionally. It could remold prisoners' emotions by eroding their feelings for anybody else, including their family members. He describes how prisoners had "turned into wolves or machines that could only devour food," and that they would insistently demand food from their family for whom they no longer had any love (129–30). The diary entry of September 5, 1960, briefly records that Young Zhang had a nightmare, in which he was hitting his mother with a shoe. Upon awakening, he felt that the dream mirrored the real-life situation because he had been hurting his mother by pestering her constantly for food and clothing (128). Old Zhang recalls that in those days his letters to his mother expressed no affection, consisting merely of itemized lists of the supplies he wanted (130). We can interpret the dream as a figural reflection of the reality and Zhang's feelings about his mother and himself. According to Old Zhang's analysis, the nightmare served as a reproach, while indicating that his younger self felt compunction about tormenting his mother. But what might have triggered this sudden sense of guilt that night? The mature narrator then reveals a tragic event Young Zhang witnessed during the afternoon of September 4, but dared not record. It is worthwhile to examine this episode extensively so that we can see how some of the subtexts and multiple perspectives are woven into the text.

As recollected by Old Zhang, a prisoner's wife and little daughter traveled a long way to visit him, yet the prisoner not only did not express any affection for them, but quickly snatched the small bag of food from his wife's hand, walked up to the bank of the canal to sit down by himself, and devoured all the food. Then he killed himself by slitting the veins on his wrists (1994, 132–41; 1995, 231–45). Instead of retelling this event in a straightforward, matter-of-fact manner, Zhang Xianliang augments and embellishes it and includes multiple points of view. At first, all the prisoners' voyeuristic interest was focused on the tiny bag of food brought by the wife, and they were envious of this prisoner for being able to enjoy it. Watching this prisoner eat flatbread and even an egg, some of the prisoners started to drool, and feel frustrated and angry. No doubt this man was regarded as the most fortunate one of the day, and the object of everybody's envy.

Old Zhang remembers his younger self to be perhaps the only one present at the scene who had a voyeuristic interest also in the aesthetic and romantic potentials of the reunion of the couple. Because his team were cutting grass close to the canal, and he had already stolen two beets and hidden them safely away, Young Zhang had both the proximity and the ease of mind to observe the wife, the daughter, and the husband. He was expecting to watch a sentimental drama, to see the couple embracing. Touched by the woman's beauty, elegance, and especially her dedication to the husband, he was jealous of the husband (whom he found undeserving of this woman) and disappointed by the husband's loveless behavior. He could well imagine how long it must have taken the woman to save enough from her small daily food rations to be able to bring a little bag of food to her husband, and he noticed that the woman was silently weeping while holding back her finger-sucking hungry daughter from the husband who was eating by himself. Joined in frustration were the wife who originally expected some affection from her husband, the child who originally expected some love from her father, and

Young Zhang, who originally expected to see a tender scene. Young Zhang's frustrated voyeuristic desire and his pity for the woman and child then gave way to horror when he heard a "piercing, heart-rending scream" from the woman: when she went up to the bank of the canal and found her husband dead, she screamed and fainted. The woman was at first presented as a symbol of beauty and elegance, then as a virtuous, self-sacrificing wife, and finally as an object of pity. Yet crowning all these was her heart-rending scream, which traumatized Zhang for the rest of his life. The mature narrator is also concerned with how shocking and traumatic it must have been for the little girl: "she had hoped her Dad would give her a little something to eat, or some warmth or fatherly love, yet what she saw in the end was her father's blood flowing as if in a great ocean" (1994, 142).

Why would a "fortunate" prisoner kill himself immediately after he has eaten his fill? Presenting various perspectives and explanations for the suicide's motivation from fellow inmates, the narrator insists, nevertheless, that he found only one explanation most plausible—that the prisoner, worried about dying as a hungry ghost, chose to end his own life only after having had the opportunity to eat his fill (139–40). The prisoner's behavior illustrated that he had no more affection for his wife and daughter, and all he was obsessed with was getting food to fill up his empty stomach. Pondering this, Old Zhang shares a sudden insight into the metaphor, "kill people with a wooden knife": the wooden knife was not aimed at "a person's throat, chest, or belly," but rather at the "invisible emotional bonds which tied a person to the world around him." He claims that this prisoner "had not lost his reason, but instead had lost his feelings" (141). This section thus seems like a well-argued essay beginning with an initial thesis the narrator puts forth, followed by the suicide which illustrates the thesis, and concluding with an explanation that supports the thesis.

The mature narrator attempts to create a sense of closure by privileging his own explanation while dismissing several other possible reasons for the prisoner's motivation in committing suicide. The closure is also a "safe" one: according to Old Zhang's interpretation, the prisoner committed suicide right after eating his fill in order to avoid becoming a hungry ghost and suffering excruciating pain in the next life. In other words, it was this prisoner's selfish fear of potentially endless, extreme suffering in the next existence that made him so unconcerned about his wife and daughter as to commit suicide. Such an interpretation implies that his death was not the fault of the camp cadres or the regime. Yet, plausible as this explanation may be, it does not foreclose other readings of the suicide, be they mentioned in this memoir or not. One of the interpretations proffered by fellow inmates (though dismissed by the narrator) seems very possible: the man committed suicide out of shame after he had eaten his fill and remembered that his wife and child had also been suffering from hunger.

Despite offering an apparent closure to this tragic anecdote, Zhang Xian-liang in fact provides the reader with enough clues to construct alternative explanations. The interpretation channel is still kept open, though the open-ness cannot be endless. The mature narrator goes out of his way to inform the reader that this prisoner was originally a model member of the Communist Youth League and a middle school teacher of political ideology. Because he became fascinated with Buddhist philosophy at one point, and once inadver-tently announced, "There is no clear boundary between idealism and materi-alism," he was denounced by other intellectuals of his district, accused of being a rightist, and sent to the labor camp. In the camp he had all along appeared normal and was regarded as a hard-working model prisoner (140–41). In other words, this man had been wrongfully charged and perse-cuted, and was a model prisoner somewhat favored by camp cadres. The extensive information provided by Old Zhang makes the reader even more curious about why such a prisoner would commit suicide. Just as Cong Weixi wonders about a certain suicide's choice of location, so Zhang Xianliang is intrigued about the timing: why would this inmate choose to kill himself right at that moment and in the presence of his wife and daughter, rather than before their arrival or after their departure (139)? There are enough details and questions about the inmate that compel the reader to resist one single interpretation of the event.

The representations of the camp cadres and their reaction to the suicide further complicate the issue. For example, why had camp cadres been so kind and solicitous toward the prisoner's wife? In addition to their favoring the submissive prisoner to some extent, a major reason we might infer is prob-ably their plan to utilize the opportunity of a rare visit from an educated woman like her to broadcast their camp's "humane" treatment of prisoners. The prisoner's suicide must have frustrated their design. The fact that their model prisoner committed suicide in public must have been like a slap in their faces, and certainly diminished their authority. As Old Zhang recalls, camp cadres became flustered and angry upon finding out about the suicide, and after ordering eight prisoners to carry away the bodies of the couple, forbade the other prisoners to look at the site of suicide. A camp cadre transferred his rage onto the prisoners by cursing them and whipping them with a rope, and punished Young Zhang's group by making them work an additional hour after the other prisoners had returned to the barracks. Obvi-ously camp cadres worried about the suicide's negative impact on their own performance evaluation, prisoners' morale, and the camp's reputation, and so tried to cover up the tragic event as best as they could. Yet they could not suppress the event's reverberations, such as prisoners' private discussions about the dead man and speculations about his motives in committing sui-cide.

Given the intricate dynamics between camp cadres and prisoners, I would suggest that it seems likely that the prisoner committed suicide because he had long suffered injustice and pent-up grievances, and could no longer endure his horrible life. Possibly he chose to die in front of his wife and child because he wanted them to know about his anguish in the camp and send a message to the outside world. By committing suicide in public, he created a spectacle, made himself conspicuous, and made a point about his repressed grievances. In other words, his suicide could be viewed as a testimony to his suffering as well as a gesture of revolt against the authorities. Such an interpretation does not exclude the other possible explanations mentioned above. The suicide itself is like a fluid symbol or cipher, which has value and becomes meaningful when plausible explanations are attached to it. Zhang Xianliang's representation of the event is resilient enough to suggest that the suicide might have been motivated by a number of reasons—impulsive or premeditated—that are not necessarily mutually exclusive.

In fact, even the seemingly convincing conclusion drawn from the mature narrator's musings over inmate psychology becomes ambivalent. In conjunction with this tragic event, for example, Old Zhang proclaims, "what makes people lose normal feelings is not 'remolding through labor,' but hunger" (129). Insisting on regarding hunger as the culprit, he diverts readers' attention and seems to absolve "remolding through labor" from blame. Such an assertion is "safe," because it frees him from criticizing the laogai system, camp cadres, or the regime's leaders. At first glance, this assertion seems to make sense, and appears to be a logical conclusion. However, a knowledgeable reader would most likely resist the temptation to take the narrator's assertion at face value. In reality, semi-starvation's trauma is far less severe when one can stay with one's beloved family instead of being imprisoned and living in fear, and is not forced to perform hard labor. Despite the narrator's claim, a thoughtful reader would understand that it was actually the labor camp, the "remolding through labor," that made inmates' hunger so extreme and unbearable, that turned inmates into "wolves or machines" and made them "lose normal feelings" and affection for their families outside the camp; it was the party-state's "remolding through labor," in which hunger was but one of its means of control, that broke the prisoners both physically and psychologically.

Zhang Xianliang's "eyewitness" account of the anonymous inmate's suicide is far more dramatic, compelling, detailed, and nuanced than Cong Weixi's recounting of Zheng Guangdi's suicide. Zhang's narration makes readers wonder why a law-abiding school teacher and Communist Youth League member would have been thrown into jail. The readers would also be moved to pity this man—witnessing how he had been reduced to a walking skeleton in the camp and how grotesque his suicide was—and feel compassion for his innocent family, who had to endure undeserved suffering and trauma. Furthermore, Zhang's representation occasionally invites readers to adopt variant viewpoints and resist the narrator's "dogmatic" assertion. As exemplified by this tale of suicide, Zhang's richly textured memoir offers multiple perspectives, allows readers to bring in their own feelings and interpretations, and enables readers to recognize an aesthetics of resistance and multivalence that occasionally approaches the levels of "sublime pathos."

CONCLUSION

These laogai memoirs serve various functions—informational, historical, affective, aesthetic, political, and educational. This "testimonial" literature contains a wealth of information on many Mao-era prison camps along with the disastrous "Anti-Rightist Campaign" and famine. It exposes the regime's inhumane deprivation of many people's basic human rights and enlightens us on the tactics of state control. In one way or another, the laogai memoir can be informative and instructive since it reveals not only the harsh realities of labor camps but also different forms of resistance as well as the resourcefulness of some of those inmates who managed to survive extreme conditions such as semi-starvation.

To some degree, these memoirs are a kind of "trauma" narratives that can be cathartic to both writers and readers. Writing laogai memoirs could function as a form of purgation and healing for the authors, who could work through their harrowing memories and release part of their pent-up grievances through recounting, recollecting, discussing, and even analyzing their laogai experiences and psychology. While confessing how they continue to suffer from a sort of PTSD-like "post-laogai syndrome" even after their release, some of the formerly incarcerated writers believe that they have acquired wisdom through their experience of traumatic captivity. Both the initial Chinese title of the first part of Zhang Xianliang's memoir, *Fannao jiu shi zhihui* (Vexation Is Wisdom, 1992), and the title of his complete memoir, *Wode putishu* (My Bodhi Tree), for example, suggest an attainment of Buddhist enlightenment through affliction. Expressing the writers' profound reflections on their sufferings, the memoirs can even be cathartic, recuperative, and inspiring for their readership.

As illustrated by the three representative memoirs I focused upon in this chapter, this testimonial literature certainly goes beyond being expository, self-expressive, or cathartic. I highlighted some aspects of these authors' artistic treatment of their materials, such as Wumingshi's use of metaphors, paradoxes, and visceral surrealism; Cong Weixi's art of restraint and encoded challenge; and Zhang Xianliang's skill in irony and generating multivalence. These aesthetic elements help enhance the memoirs' affective power, moving the reader to empathy while raising the reader's consciousness and understanding of the various dimensions of suffering. I argued for the special need to search carefully for the subterranean strains of protest embedded in the memoirs of Cong Weixi and Zhang Xianliang, who had to negotiate external and internalized censorship during the process of their writing. Overall, through its rhetoric and discourse, this literature manifests an aesthetics of resistance in various forms and degrees.

The CCP regime has all along asserted its authority and legitimacy to rule by forcing people to take its official version of past historical events as true. The individual memories and histories in these "trauma" narratives to some extent resist the monopoly of official discourse and perspective, and serve to reverse (or at least crack) the "grand" narrative of history fabricated by the party-state. More importantly, some of these narratives have found resonance with large groups of readers in China and abroad, including a number of the relatives and friends of those who have or have not survived the laogai. The emerging collective memory of the prison camp system and the "Anti-Rightist Campaign" will likely become powerful enough to help counter the amnesia and political apathy encouraged by the current regime. These laogai memoirs thus play a crucial role in this transformational process through their power to educate and influence readers cognitively, emotionally, and aesthetically.

NOTES

1. For example, Vera Schwarcz (109–110) points out that while many museums have been erected to remember the Holocaust, the Chinese government refused the request from Ba Jin, a much-venerated writer, to build a Cultural Revolution Museum to commemorate the victims of the Cultural Revolution (1966–76).

2. Fang Lizhi mentions how he and his colleagues had to abort a planned "Scholarly Conference on the Thirtieth Anniversary of the Anti-Rightist Rectification" for 1987 due to severe pressure from the authorities (1990, 31). Public discussions and meetings about the "Anti-Rightist Campaign" usually can only take place outside of the PRC and in the countries which permit freedom of speech and peaceful assembly. One such conference, "The Course of Contemporary Chinese Intellectuals: An International Symposium Commemorating the Fiftieth Anniversary of the Anti-Rightist Campaign," was held at Univ. of California, Irvine, and Monterey Park Bruggemeyer Library, CA, on June 29–30, 2007.

3. For example, Chen Kuide, the editor of *Guancha* (observechina.net), and a few others, have noted that the CCP would never admit any of its mistakes because it fears that such an admission would "shake" its "legitimacy in ruling" (Ji 2007).

4. Laogai is the abbreviation of *laodong gaizao* ("remolding through [forced] labor").

5. It is instructive to listen to NPR's Steve Inskeep (2008) interviewing the PRC's Ambassador to the United States, Zhou Wenzhong, about the violence in Tibet. Zhou insisted that it was not a religious or ethnic issue, but a "law and order" issue. Repeatedly evading Inskeep's questions about whether the Tibetans have "legitimate grievances" against the Chinese government, Zhou continued to parrot the official version and accuse the demonstrators of "violent crimes," "disrupting social order," and attempting to "sabotage" the Beijing Olympics.

6. Fang Lizhi points out communist "Techniques of Forgetting History" and criticizes such China experts as Edgar Snow for helping the CCP in their "techniques of forgetting" and propaganda (1990, 30–31). Discussing the regime's "tactics of amnesia" following the 1989 Tiananmen Square Massacre, Perry Link mentions that the first step of the CCP's tactics is "truth-inversion": the army units using tanks and guns to slaughter unarmed citizens were "officially described . . . as 'heroes of the people' controlling 'rioters' and pacifying 'dregs of society.'" The second step is "diminution": "over the course of a decade the massacre became a mere 'incident' . . . then petered into a wisp of practically nothing" (2004, 41).

7. In 1978, the CCP regime still concluded that "the Anti-Rightist Campaign was necessary" (Ji 2007).

8. This figure does not take into account numerous rightists' family members and relatives whose lives were negatively impacted.

9. Jeremy Murray (2005) argues that "the formerly polarized official and nonofficial perspectives within China have moved closer together than they have been since perhaps the first decade of the PRC's existence." On this point Murray refers to three essays in Jeremy Brown and Paul G. Pickowicz, eds., *Dilemmas of Victory* (2007). Murray mentions how the 1980s "saw an outpouring of nonofficial voices from Chinese emigrants and from dissidents within the PRC that criticized the excesses of the party-state, especially the recent destruction and chaos of the Cultural Revolution."

10. Naomi Klein (2008) also refers to this assumption in her essay, "China's All-Seeing Eye." I thank Simone W. Davis for calling my attention to this interesting essay.

11. See the AP report, "China blocks access to *New York Times* Web site," December 20, 2008, http://biz.yahoo.com/ap/081220/as_china_internet.html?.v=6 (accessed December 21, 2008).

12. See Jeremy Murray 2005. On this point Murray refers to Peter Hays Gries, *China's New Nationalism: Pride, Politics, and Diplomacy* (Berkeley: Univ. of California Press, 2004).

13. See, for example, Rey Chow 2000, 4.

14. The Republic of China (ROC) government under the Nationalist Party (KMT, Kuomintang, a.k.a. Guomindang) withdrew to Taiwan after losing mainland China to the CCP in 1949. A genuinely democratic, multi-party system has developed in Taiwan, ROC, since the late 1980s.

15. Economically the United States is overly indebted to China. As accurately pointed out by Hillary Clinton recently, the United States is putting the "nation's security and our leadership of the world at risk because of this indebtedness" (Mason 2008). The United States has also become dependent on China's help politically, as in its negotiations with North Korea, for example. Moreover, scandals such as the U.S. military's torture of Iraqi detainees in Abu Ghraib prison have damaged the moral stature and credibility of the United States.

16. See also the discussion in Williams and Wu 2004, 155–158.

17. See brief descriptions of the new publications on the website of the Laogai Research Foundation, http://www.laogai.org/news/index.php.

18. Wumingshi ("Anonymous" or "Man Without a Name") has been the preferred pseudonym of Bu Naifu (Pu Nai-fu), alias Bu Ning (Pu Ning). Wumingshi's *Hongsha* (Red Sharks) was first published in 1989. The edition used in this chapter was published in 1994. The condensed English version of this work is Pu Ning (pseud. Wumingshi), *Red in Tooth and Claw: Twenty-six Years in Communist Chinese Prisons*, trans. Tung Chung-hsuan (New York: Grove Press, 1994).

19. The PRC instituted the "Down to the Countryside Movement" in the 1960s and 1970s, forcibly sending millions of the educated urban youth to remote mountainous areas or farming villages. One of the ostensible reasons was that the privileged youth would then rid themselves of bourgeois thinking and learn from the farmers and workers. A "sent-down youth" refers to an urban student who was thus "exiled" to remote areas.

20. Cong Weixi published *Zou xiang hundun* (Heading into Chaos) in 1989. Nine years later, this became Part One of his trilogy, *Zou xiang hundun sanbuqu* (The Heading into Chaos Trilogy), published in 1998. Zhang Xianliang's *Wode putishu* (My Bodhi Tree) was published in 1994. The first half of this work has been translated into English by Martha Avery as *Grass Soup* (1995), and the second half has been translated by Avery as *My Bodhi Tree* (1996).

21. For more information, see Harry Wu 1992, Seymour and Anderson 1998, and Williams and Wu 2004.

22. See the report, "Laojiao zhidu bu he shiyi shangwan ming Zhongguo xuezhe yu feichu," in *Da ji yuan*, July 9, 2008, http://www.epochtimes.com/b5/8/7/9/n2184852.htm (accessed December 8, 2008).

23. Of course, prisoners could also use hunger strikes as a form of resistance. For example, in his memoir Harry Wu describes his hunger strike when caged in an isolation cell, as well as the subsequent brutal force-feeding (1994, 183–84). However, the focus of this chapter is the CCP's use of semi-starvation to control inmates, rather than desperate prisoners' hunger strikes. During periods of extreme starvation, it was understandably much less likely for prisoners to resort to hunger strikes, since most of them would be preoccupied with trying their best to survive.

24. The weight of the food parcels was usually limited to ten catties (around 11 pounds) each, though regulations varied from camp to camp.

25. One catty is a little more than a pound, and about half a kilogram.

26. See Williams and Wu 2004, 90; Cong Weixi 1989, 217–218; Bao and Chelminski 1976, 227–228, 253.

27. See Williams and Wu 2004, 90; Cong Weixi 1987, 367, 393; 1989, 107; Bao and Chelminski 1976, 242.

28. See Terrence Des Pres 1976, 158–167, especially 161–62. See also Kalí Tal's discussion of the debate between Bettelheim and Des Pres (1996, 32–38).

29. See Link 2000, 119–121.

30. See also Wu 2006a, 132–33.

31. Ironically, the English translator and editor shifted the sequence of the first two chapters to make the presentation of the story more chronological, thereby defeating Wumingshi's original purpose.

32. Cf. Wu 2006a, 132.

33. See Wumingshi 1994a, 354; the full paragraph is translated in Wu 2006a, 148.

34. Class discrimination during the Mao era was based on class origins. Those classified under the Red Categories (such as poor peasants, workers, revolutionaries, cadres, etc.) were considered good and superior, while those classified under the Black Categories were regarded as bad and inferior. A person whose parents were classified as Red would automatically belong to the Red Categories. During the Cultural Revolution (1966–76) when class discrimination became extreme, the Five Black Categories referred to landlords, rich farmers, counterrevolutionaries, bad elements, and rightists.

35. As Perry Link indicated, "The major incentive for self-censorship was a vague but omnipresent fear of criticism and punishment" (2000, 82–83).

36. There have been historical and fictional examples of such acts of defiance in traditional China. One of the earliest inspirational examples for this type of suicide as public protest is that of Qu Yuan (340?–278 B.C.)—a loyal minister banished by his king, Qu Yuan drowned himself in a river as a protest. A famous literary example can be found in the story of Du Shiniang: a beautiful and virtuous courtesan, Du is betrayed by her lover who sells her to a salt merchant; before committing suicide by throwing herself into a river, Du creates a spectacle and publicly denounces her lover and the merchant; and after her death, Du's ghost seeks vengeance and justice (Feng 1981, 498–99). See Story 32 ("Du Shiniang nu chen baibao xiang") in Feng Menglong's (1574–1645) collection of stories, *Jingshi tongyan*. Furthermore, Story 34 ("Yiwenqian xiaoxi zao qiyuan") in *Xingshi hengyan*, another collection compiled and edited by Feng, features a woman who, feeling unjustly disgraced in a quarrel, tries to hang herself on the door frame of her abuser's house (Feng 1979, 716). In chapter 9 of the seventeenth-century novel *Xingshi yinyuan zhuan*, the mistreated wife hangs herself on the door frame of her husband and his concubine's quarters as a public protest (Xi Zhou Sheng 1981, vol. 1, p. 130). In folk belief, the ghost of such an aggrieved person would take revenge upon those who have unjustly inflicted harm or pain on her.

37. Sima Qian explained about enduring the dishonor of being castrated in his "Letter in Reply to Ren An": "The reason I bore through it in silence and chose to live at any cost . . .

was . . . because I despised perishing without letting the glory of my writings be shown to posterity" (140–41).

38. The immediate catalyst was the traumatic experience of his wife's second attempted suicide and his own handcuffing and confinement in a tiny punishment cell in 1970 (Cong 1998b, 357–60, 406).

39. In his *Jiabiangou jishi* (2002a, 134), Yang Xianhui also records how an ex-inmate suffers from the "post-famishment syndrome." For the "post-laogai syndrome" (*laogai houyizheng*), see Cong Weixi 1986, 253, as well as Williams and Wu 2004, 122.

40. As mentioned previously, the Chinese version of Zhang's memoir, *Wode putishu* (My Bodhi Tree), has been translated into English by Martha Avery as *Grass Soup* and *My Bodhi Tree*. See also Kinkley's (2006) interesting discussion on this work as well as my analysis of three of Zhang Xianliang's novels (2006b).

41. For an earlier suggestion for readers to read resistantly, see Judith Fetterley's *The Resisting Reader: A Feminist Approach to American Fiction* (1977). Fetterley argues forcefully that the feminist critic has to exorcize the "male mind," refuse to "assent," and read an old text "from a new critical direction" (xxii).

REFERENCES

Associated Press. 2008. "China blocks access to *New York Times* Web site." December 20. http://biz.yahoo.com/ap/081220/as_china_internet.html?.v=6 (accessed December 21, 2008).

Bao Ruo-wang, and Rudolph Chelminski. [1973] 1976. *Prisoner of Mao*. Harmondsworth: Penguin.

Bettelheim, Bruno. 1979a. "Individual and Mass Behavior in Extreme Situations" (1943). In *Surviving and Other Essays*, by Bruno Bettelheim, 48–83. New York: Knopf.

_____. 1979b. "Surviving." In *Surviving and Other Essays*, by Bruno Bettelheim, 274–314. New York: Knopf.

Chow, Rey. 2000. "Introduction: On Chineseness as a Theoretical Problem." In *Modern Chinese Literary and Cultural Studies in the Age of Theory: Reimagining a Field*, ed. Rey Chow. Durham: Duke Univ. Press.

Cong Weixi. 1986. *Duan qiao*. Beijing: Zuojia chubanshe.

_____. 1989. *Zou xiang hundun* (Heading into Chaos). Beijing: Zuojia chubanshe.

_____. 1998a. "Qiuduzhe yan." In Cong Weixi, *Zou xiang hundun sanbuqu*, 1–3. Beijing: Zhongguo shehui kexue chubanshe.

_____. 1998b. *Zou xiang hundun sanbuqu* (The Heading into Chaos Trilogy). Beijing: Zhongguo shehui kexue chubanshe.

Davis, Matthew. 2008. "China cracks down on protest news." BBC News, March 18, http://news.bbc.co.uk/2/hi/asia-pacific/7302625.stm.

Des Pres, Terrence. 1976. *The Survivor: An Anatomy of Life in the Death Camp*. New York: Oxford Univ. Press.

Fang Lizhi. 1990. "The Chinese Amnesia." Trans. Perry Link. *The New York Review of Books* 37.14 (September 27): 30–31.

Feng Menglong (attribution). 1979. "Yiwenqian xiaoxi zao qiyuan." In *Xingshi hengyan*, comp. and ed. Feng Menglong, 708–37. Beijing: Renmin wenxue chubanshe.

_____. 1981. "Du Shiniang nu chen baibao xiang." In *Jingshi tongyan*, comp. and ed. Feng Menglong, 485–500. Beijing: Renmin wenxue chubanshe.

Fetterley, Judith. 1977. *The Resisting Reader: A Feminist Approach to American Fiction*. Bloomington: Indiana Univ. Press.

Gries, Peter Hays. 2004. *China's New Nationalism: Pride, Politics, and Diplomacy*. Berkeley: Univ. of California Press.

Herman, Judith Lewis. 1992. *Trauma and Recovery*. New York: Basic Books.

Huang Wenfan. 1990. "Zhongguo de Suoren Nixin—*Gulage qundao* yu *Hongsha* bijiao chutan." In *Hongsha*, by Wumingshi, 445–68. Taipei: Liming wenhua shiye gongsi.

Inskeep, Steve. 2008. Interview with Zhou Wenzhong. National Public Radio, March 27, http://www.npr.org/templates/story/story.php?storyId=89140776 (accessed March 28, 2008).

Ji Wei. 2007. "Fanyou wushi zhounian: Zhonggong de jihui yu jiaoxun." In BBC Chinese.com, October 11, http://news.bbc.co.uk/chinese/simp/hi/newsid_7030000/newsid_7039800/7039829.stm (accessed April 6, 2008).

_____. 2008. "Fanyou yundong wushi zhounian: fengbao lailin." In BBC Chinese.com, February 6, http://news.bbc.co.uk/chinese/simp/hi/newsid_7030000/newsid_7039700/7039748.stm (accessed April 3, 2008).

Kinkley, Jeffrey C. 1991. "A Bettelheimian Interpretation of Chang Hsien-liang's Concentration-Camp Novels." *Asia Major*, 3rd ser., 4.2: 83–113.

_____. 2000. *Chinese Justice, the Fiction: Law and Literature in Modern China*. Stanford: Stanford Univ. Press.

_____. 2006. "Labor-camp Fiction as Conversion Literature: Zhang Xianliang and Ōoka Shōhei." In *Remolding and Resistance among Writers of the Chinese Prison Camp: Disciplined and Published*, ed. by Philip F. Williams and Yenna Wu, 68–100. London: Routledge.

Klein, Naomi. 2008. "China's All-Seeing Eye." May 29, http://www.rollingstone.com/politics/story/20797485/chinas_allseeing_eye (accessed August 10, 2008).

Lai Ying. 1969. *The Thirty-Sixth Way*. Trans. Edward Behr and Sidney Liu. Garden City, NJ: Doubleday.

"Laojiao zhidu bu he shiyi shangwan ming Zhongguo xuezhe yu feichu." 2008. *Da ji yuan*, July 9, http://www.epochtimes.com/b5/8/7/9/n2184852.htm (accessed December 8, 2008).

Link, Perry. 2000. *The Uses of Literature: Life in the Socialist Chinese Literary System*. Princeton: Princeton Univ. Press.

_____. 2004. "What the Tiananmen Mothers Offer China." *China Rights Forum* 2: 41–43.

Mason, Jeff. 2008. "Clinton says China holdings threaten U.S. security." Reuters, March 29, http://news.yahoo.com/s/nm/20080329/pl_nm/usa_politics_clinton_china_dc_1.

Murray, Jeremy. 2005. "China in the International Spotlight: Some Problems in the Analysis of PRC Narratives by Foreign Scholars." http://orpheus.ucsd.edu/chinesehistory/pgp/jmurrayprcessay.htm.

Peng Yinhan. 1984. *Dalu jizhongying*. Taipei: Shibao wenhua chuban.

Schwarcz, Vera. 1998. *Bridge Across Broken Time: Chinese and Jewish Cultural Memory*. New Haven and London: Yale Univ. Press.

Seymour, James D., and Richard Anderson. 1998. *New Ghosts, Old Ghosts: Prisons and Labor Reform Camps in China*. Armonk: M. E. Sharpe.

Sima Qian. 1996. "Letter in Reply to Ren An." In *An Anthology of Chinese Literature: Beginnings to 1911*, ed. and trans. Stephen Owen, 136–42. New York: W.W. Norton.

Tal, Kalí. 1996. *Worlds of Hurt: Reading the Literatures of Trauma*. Cambridge: Cambridge Univ. Press.

White, Lynn T., III. 1987. "Thought Workers in Deng's Time." In *China's Intellectuals and the State: In Search of a New Relationship*, ed. Merle Goldman with Timothy Cheek and Carol Lee Hamrin, 253–74. Cambridge, MA: The Council on East Asian Studies at Harvard University.

Williams, Philip F., and Yenna Wu. 2004. *The Great Wall of Confinement: The Chinese Prison Camp Through Contemporary Fiction and Reportage*. Berkeley: Univ. of California Press.

_____, eds. 2006. *Remolding and Resistance among Writers of the Chinese Prison Camp: Disciplined and Published*. London: Routledge.

Wu, Hongda Harry. 1992. *Laogai—The Chinese Gulag*. Trans. Ted Slingerland. Boulder, CO: Westview.

_____ [Wu, Harry], and Carolyn Wakeman. 1994. *Bitter Winds: A Memoir of My Years in China's Gulag*. New York: John Wiley and Sons.

Wu, Yenna. 2006a. "Expressing the 'Inexpressible': Pain and Suffering in Wumingshi's *Hongsha (Red Sharks)*." In *Remolding and Resistance among Writers of the Chinese Prison Camp: Disciplined and Published*, ed. Philip F. Williams and Yenna Wu, 123–156. London: Routledge.

_____. 2006b. "Traumatic 'Remolding' and Its Ethical Implications in Three of Zhang Xianliang's Novels." In *Remolding and Resistance among Writers of the Chinese Prison Camp: Disciplined and Published*, ed. Philip F. Williams and Yenna Wu, 27–67. London: Routledge.

Wumingshi (pseud. of Bu Naifu, alias Bu Ning). [1989] 1994a. *Hongsha* (Red Sharks). Taipei: Liming wenhua shiye gongsi.

_____ (Pu Ning). 1994b. "Prologue: The Secret of the Cave." In Pu Ning, *Red in Tooth and Claw: Twenty-six Years in Communist Chinese Prisons*. Trans. Tung Chung-hsuan. New York: Grove Press. xxv–xxvii.

_____ (Pu Ning). 1994c. *Red in Tooth and Claw: Twenty-six Years in Communist Chinese Prisons*. Trans. Tung Chung-hsuan. New York: Grove Press.

Xi Zhou Sheng (pseud.). 1981. *Xingshi yinyuan zhuan*. 3 vols. Shanghai: Shanghai guji chubanshe.

Yang Diansheng, and Zhang Jinsang, eds. 1999. *Zhongguo tese jianyu zhidu yanjiu*. Beijing: Falü chubanshe.

Yang Xianhui. 2002a. *Jiabiangou jishi: Yang Xianhui zhong duan pian xiaoshuo ji*. Tianjin: Tianjin guji chubanshe.

_____. 2002b. "Xiezuo shouji (dai ba)." *Jiabiangou jishi: Yang Xianhui zhong duan pian xiaoshuo ji*. Tianjin: Tianjin guji chubanshe. 355–56.

Zhang Xianliang. 1994. *Wode putishu* (My Bodhi Tree). Beijing: Zuojia chubanshe.

_____. 1995. *Grass Soup*. Trans. Martha Avery. Boston: David R. Godine.

_____. 1996. *My Bodhi Tree*. Trans. Martha Avery. London: Secker and Warburg.

Chapter Four

The Argument from Silence

Morocco's Truth Commission and Women Political Prisoners

Susan Slyomovics

On April 16, 1996, the first witness to appear at the first hearing on the first day of South Africa's Truth and Reconciliation Commission (TRC) was a woman. Mrs. Nohle Mohape described how her husband Mapetla, a supporter of Steve Biko and the black consciousness movement, was killed in police custody in 1976. His death was not a suicide, as the official verdict claimed. On the second day, Nomonde Calata, widow of Fort Calata (one of the "Craddock Four" African National Congress activists killed in 1984), broke down, wailing in anguish. Listeners described her screams as unbearable and switched them off when played repeatedly over South Africa's television and radio stations (Boraine 2000, 103). Antjie Krog, a journalist covering the hearing, declared:

> For me, this crying is the beginning of the Truth Commission—the signature tune, the definitive moment, the ultimate sound of what the process is about. She was wearing this vivid orange dress and she threw herself backwards and that sound, that sound, it will haunt me forever and ever. (Krog 1998, 42)

In Casablanca, Morocco, on Sunday November 14, 1999, Maria Charaf's wrenching screams carried through the packed hall of the Complexe Anoual during the first public service to commemorate the fourteenth anniversary of the death of her husband Amine Tahani (which was combined with the twenty-fifth anniversary commemoration of the death of Abdellatif Zeroual). The gathering celebrated the lives and achievements of two successive generations of young Marxist activists united by political convictions but also by

87

the status of each as *shahid,* a martyr to torture during police custody. Before 1999, annual private ceremonies were held in various family homes always subject to intense police surveillance. After the death of King Hassan II on July 23, 1999, the aforementioned November 14, 1999, Casablanca commemoration became a public occasion to highlight political and juridical demands that are part of contemporary public events: the moderator Abdelhak Moussadak (Marxist political prisoner, 1984–91) reviewed the political trajectories of the two activists' lives in order to call for trials of torturers at Derb Moulay Cherif, Casablanca's secret detention center, especially a trial for the head of operations, Youssfi Kaddour, considered responsible for their deaths (Moussadak 1999, np).

Although the Moroccan state has imprisoned tens of thousands of dissidents and political opponents since independence in 1956 from France, the death of King Hassan II on July 23, 1999, was a watershed moment. During decades known to Moroccans as the "years of lead" (*les années de plomb* in French) and "the black years" (in Arabic, *sanawāt al-sawda'*), political opponents of Hassan II's regime (1961–99) often "disappeared" in the manner of dictatorships in Chile and Argentina. These opponents—many of them leftists, feminists, Berber/Amazigh activists, or Islamists—were tortured or killed while in state custody. In 1990, King Hassan II established the Advisory Council on Human Rights (in Arabic, *al-Majlis al-Istishari li-Huqūq al-Insān* or in French, *Conseil Consultative des Droits de l'Homme*), modeled on a similar French institution, to rehabilitate the regime's reputation for repression. These official efforts intensified after the king's death.

Funded by Fulbright and AIMS awards for one year of research, I arrived in Morocco on August 1, 1999, a week after the death of King Hassan II, the ascension of his son and heir, King Muhammad VI, to the throne, and a day after the new king's first throne speech televised to his subjects, in which he confirmed his commitment to establish the rule of law and to safeguard human rights (Muhammad VI 1999, 1). I was swept into the study of public events heralding a different Morocco that was willing to address, after thirty-eight years, the issue of a state's acknowledged crimes against its own citizens: illegal detention, forcible disappearance, and torture.

My fieldwork and interviews were principally undertaken in the newly opened public spaces where the performance of human rights is enacted in Morocco: meetings, reunions, commemorations, sit-ins, demonstrations, and vigils that occur at the Casablanca courthouse, in front of the Rabat Parliament building, at the headquarters of various human rights organizations and union offices, and even in the cemetery during funerals (Slyomovics 2005). I was present in the audience during the November 14, 1999, Casablanca commemoration, when Maria Charaf, wife of Amine Tahani, and Abdelkader Zeroual, the father of Abdellatif Zeroual, recounted that they too had passed through the Derb Moulay Cherif secret detention center, as did many family members of political prisoners. Each speaker testified to his or her personal experience, placing narratives in the context of remedies for disappearance and political imprisonment.

As early as 1997, Maria Charaf had published in Morocco a French-language memoir entitled *Être au feminine,* excerpts of which were translated into Arabic for her public testimony. She spoke about her life and education; she is a graduate of Morocco's elite engineering school, where she met her husband, Amine Tahani, a fellow engineer. Active in the leftist student movement, they were arrested at the same time during waves of police roundups that swept through the student and intellectual milieu beginning October 1985. At Derb Moulay Cherif, she and her husband were blindfolded and found themselves among the overflow of prisoners confined in the corridors. Unlike her husband, Charaf labels herself a third category of detainee, the rare one eventually released yet condemned to perpetual "political widowhood" (Ramphele 1996, 99):

> I have no idea about the duration of my detention: a day? A week? A month? A year? Really, I had no idea, all is so conjectural in these matters! This uncertainty caused me anguish, and I began to lose all notion of time by the third day. My uncertainty was already of the order of twenty-four hours. So, I pulled a rather thick thread from one of the covers and I knotted it three times. From then on, each time the guard gave me my daily bread in the morning I would add a knot. That was already something won, because this mastery over time, though relative, brought me a certain calm. Amine was frequently called for interrogation, he returned from it each time held up by two guards, his head falling on his shoulder as if he had fainted. Despite these conditions, I was able to keep my morale high, refusing to think about my son, in any case he could only be in good hands. . . . Beginning 4 November, I could no longer sense the presence of Amine. I no longer heard him coughing, they no longer called his number for interrogation. Anxious, I questioned one of the guards, but he would tell me nothing. I finished by understanding that he was transferred to the hospital. I learned later that medical personnel refused to admit him at first given his desperate state. Finally, they admitted him and registered him under a false name. (Charaf 1997, 73–74)

As part of the November 14, 1999, ceremony, an audiocassette of Tahani speaking publicly, recorded shortly before his death, was played to the audience. Maria Charaf screamed uncontrollably; Tahani's disembodied voice was halted. The reaction of listeners in the hall, as I recall, was a mixture of shock, silence, and sympathy but also disbelief. Charaf was informed, the organizers noted, about the existence and plans to broadcast the tape. But hearing the actual voice of her dead husband, as if still alive and politically active, bore little resemblance to the sober, familiar, contained, and formulaic speech acts of public commemoration, witnessing, and testifying. While taping the ceremonies, I too experienced listening to Charaf's agony as a trans-

gression, instinctively pressing the stop button of my tape recorder. Therefore, I have only a fragment of Tahani's taped voice and her screams.

The screams of victims are silent about facts but not emotions, given
public breakdowns by surviving family members decades later. Screams convey a silence, in the sense of inarticulate speechlessness, and are characterized by an opposition to the human word. Nonetheless, silence is informative. For historians, a common methodology is the "argument from silence,"
(in Latin *argumentum ex silentio*), a mode of reasoning that also cautions
against the logical fallacy of assuming that someone's silence is necessarily
proof of ignorance. Therefore, if one looks at written sources or oral testimony for confirmation that events did or did not happen, and there is only
"silence" in the materials, this silence does not signify that the events did not
occur or that information about these events does not exist. Lack of knowledge about something says nothing about its existence or nonexistence. All
we have is information about a silence. Although the sequence of witness
testimonies narrated on November 14, 1999, include details pertinent to the
workings of Morocco's secret detention center of Derb Moulay Cherif in
Casablanca, the spaces of incarceration, the torturers' tools, and even the
torturers' name, there is silence emanating from the archives and the state
apparatus.

COMPARING TRUTH COMMISSIONS: SOUTH AFRICA AND MOROCCO

On January 7, 2004, endeavoring to fulfill his father's 1994 promise to "turn
the page definitively" on the rampant abuses of the past, King Muhammad
VI appointed Driss Benzekri to head a newly formed Justice and Reconciliation Commission (*Hay'āt al-Insāf wa-al-Musālaha*). Benzekri, himself a former political prisoner (1974–91) from the outlawed Marxist-Leninist group
Ila al-Amam, presides over sixteen commissioners, eight of whom are drawn
from the Advisory Council on Human Rights plus eight nationally recognized experts in law, medicine, and women's rights. Among them are other
former political prisoners and victims of torture and disappearance. The commission's mandate to investigate human rights violations begins with independence and ends with the establishment of the 1999 Indemnity Commission, an earlier attempt to redress forty-three years of the regime's war
against its own citizens. The competence of the commission is non-judicial
(*dhāt ikhtisasāt ghayr qadā'iyya*): both a short-lived 1999 Indemnity Commission and the 2004–5 Justice and Reconciliation Commission accord blanket immunity from criminal prosecution to perpetrators and victims alike
(Slyomovics 2001, 2003, 2005a). Since its establishment by royal decree on

January 2004, the commission received over 22,000 claims by victims of the regime, requesting reparations for human rights abuses between 1956–99 by the deadline date February 13, 2004.

South Africa's Truth and Reconciliation Commission (TRC) heard and reported on victim testimonies about human rights violations occurring between 1960 and 1994, the years of apartheid. Critics of the South African TRC complain there is little history and context in the final five-volume report issued in 1998. Description prevails over analysis of national patterns of apartheid, and violations are not embedded in specific historical backgrounds and contexts (Posel 2002). In Morocco, the story of forcible disappearance, secret torture, and deaths during police custody or in secret prisons is also told about the past from the perspective of the present and entirely in the victims' voices. The Moroccan Justice and Reconciliation Commission is not the South African TRC. Like Chile and Argentina before it, but in striking contrast to South Africa, Morocco chooses to circumscribe justice, eschewing punishment to concentrate on identifying, verifying, and reporting the process of uncovering the truth about arbitrary detention and secret torture sites. What appears as a minimal commission accomplishment will prove to be its most powerful legacy—to collect and tabulate witness testimonies narrated by the enormous number of Moroccans eligible for reparations. Such descriptively ahistorical yet powerful accumulations of testimony are advocated by José Zalaquett, a lawyer and member of the Chilean Truth Commission:

> I would like to draw the distinction between revealing the truth about secret crimes and interpreting the political processes that led to such situations. The distinction between fact and interpretation has become very important in the working of truth commissions. They should largely concentrate on facts, which may be proved, whereas differences about historical interpretations will always exist. The report can make recommendations by pointing to the immediate context of the atrocities, but not to the remote context. This is not the place for an historical analysis of class struggles. (Truth Commissions 1997, 15)

Zalaquett argues for a legal, positivist approach anchored by the research imperative of hearing testimony combined with additional empirical evidence in government archives, when made available. Let historians take over later, he seems to say, and let them talk to each other.

As more truth commissions form and publish reports, the distinction blurs between Zalaquett's recommended methodology (descriptions plus quantitative categorizations couched in vocabularies for the database) and the expansive, emotion-laden victim narrative. Both quantitative and qualitative processes fail to address the "argument from silence," the nonexistence of information that points to silences surrounding my related topics: the fact of disappearance, the world of the perpetrators, and the silence of rape victims. While disappearance, torture, and rape affected a significant population of Moroccans regardless of their politics or sex, in this chapter I explore the intersection of gender and silences and, in particular, women's experience of disappearance and rape, along with its articulation (or lack of expression) in language.

THE SILENCE OF DISAPPEARANCE VERSUS SCHEHERAZADE OF MOROCCO

Using testimony to document absence due to disappearance, kidnapping, and arbitrary detention is not always successful. Courts and lawyers prefer to deal with texts and documents generated by witnesses but less so with deeper levels of feelings and the experience of everyday life. Testimonies about absence raise problems of context and memory, of firsthand versus second-hand witness, and of witness versus hearsay: how to number the people arbitrarily detained, disappeared, raped, tortured, and killed (Brysk 1994, 676–692). There are those who disappeared and never reappeared, and to this day it is not certain if they are alive or dead. Some who disappeared have returned; the price to reinhabit the world of the living is silence, silence from the victim and silence from the extended family. Most disappeared never reappear. Even modest attempts by families to locate missing members expose family members to charges of political subversion. Family members and neighbors of the disappeared become targets of disappearance. In my fieldwork conducting interviews over the years, it is uncommon to meet a Moroccan activist and his or her family who do not qualify for indemnities as victims of human rights abuses (Slyomovics 2005, 43–66).

To uncover the lineaments of a different kind of depopulation and population, not only the numbers of disappeared but also those terrorized by direct and indirect means into silence has become a major difficulty for Moroccans. Within these populations of disappeared and silenced, women as a subgroup offer particular challenges. In other words, what have been the ways women express in writing and oral testimony the variety of forms of violence perpetrated against women? Why is the figure of Scheherazade from *A Thousand and One Nights* in the foreground for Moroccans who testify to torture and disappearance—what aspects of her plight, her fate, and her narrative strategies resonate for them? Moroccan sociologist Fatema Mernissi provides one insight into Scheherazade's current prominence. Mernissi notes in her book *Scheherazade Goes West* that Scheherazade is evoked as a liberator for the Muslim world, as a political heroine who keeps a tyrant at bay through the power of her intellect and wordplay, and finally, as the truth-telling taleteller and, consequently, the standard bearer for the human rights movement (Mernissi 2001, 55). According to this reading, the figure of Scheherazade represents one way to understand testimony and witnessing as the creation of a forceful and oppositional gendered subject emerging through the act of speech.

Abdellatif Laabi, a francophone Moroccan writer incarcerated from 1972–80, acknowledges Scheherazade as an inspiration for his 1982 French-language novel, *Le chemin des ordalies*, a memoir of his imprisonment and torture. Laabi describes a compelling Scheherazade:

> She who was the greatest storyteller (*romancière*) of your traditional culture was only so because she lived permanently under the oriental sword of Damocles. "You write or you are killed . . . " You will know that this is the voice of history speaking. It refers to one of its most brutal laws: all silence is death by default. (Laabi 1982, 61)

Scheherazade and her tale must be retold—in Laabi's phrase, "you write or you are killed"—and these retellings are elastically accommodating. Laabi's memoir goes on to deploy the frame of a seemingly traditional folktale, the story of a girl named Saida kidnapped by the king. His tale was inspired by details from the real-life story of a real-life Moroccan heroine, Saida Menebhi, a Marxist woman political prisoner who died in Casablanca during a mass political prisoner hunger strike in 1978 fighting for the right to trial after eight months of secret detention (Menebhi 1999, 121–127).

These two aspects of Scheherazade—both Mernissi's feminine narrator as well as Laabi's tale of the abducted female—figure greatly in the life and works of Moroccan activist Fatna El Bouih (Marxist political prisoner, 1977–1982). El Bouih calls forth Scheherazade as the feminine and female teller of truth to arbitrary power and as the emblematic figure for women political prisoners in Morocco. Her book, *Hadith al-'atama* (Talk of Darkness), published in Arabic in 2001, opens to dream-like premonitions in which she compares her fate to the tales of *A Thousand and One Nights*. El Bouih stands on the banks of the Bou Regreg River summoning memories of her travails decades before:

> At that moment I recalled whenever I awoke my father would tell me, a little girl terrified by nightmares, about the many tales of *A Thousand and One Nights,* that he recounted good-humoredly at night. Stories of kidnap, of abducted women and girls. My father said: "These stories happened in past centuries." It never crossed his mind—may God rest his soul—this could happen again in our time. (El Bouih 2001, 10)[1]

El Bouih's prison memoir begins in 1977 with her kidnapping and disappearance for seven months with other women political prisoners. *Rani nimhik* (I will erase you) was the brutal phrase uttered by Youssfi Kaddour, named as chief torturer by El Bouih in her account of secret detention and torture. Despite the fact she knew she had disappeared somewhere into Morocco, El Bouih's abduction is intensified by perpetrator's words to efface her from the record, the written page, the very map of her country. To account for the experiences of generations of Moroccan women as voiceless and powerless, author El Bouih constructs a first-person narrator to stand for the collective experience of her intellectual and activist women comrades, many too traumatized to tell their stories. El Bouih's prison memoirs include her own experiences and extend to collective experiences. To her own chapters in her published account, *Hadith al-atama*, are added oral histories she undertook with two other women political prisoners from the same Meknes Group, Widad Bouab and Latifa Jbabdi, drawn from articles first published in 1994 in *Ittihad Ichtiraki*, Morocco's large circulation arabophone newspaper (El Bouih 1994, 5–6). The impression of a collective authorship and the origins of one's own writing in collecting other women's oral histories clearly point to the imposition of powerful restraints shaped by history and gender. El Bouih spoke of her initial sense of shame that impeded writing about her own experiences:

> Remember that the model for all Moroccan females is the woman who lowers her eyes, never raises her voice, whose tongue "does not go out of her mouth," as in the Moroccan proverb "ilfum mesdūd ma dukhuh dbana" (into a closed mouth no flies can enter). Girls are raised with: "Samt hikma u-mennū tfarraq ilhikayem" (silence is wisdom and from it comes even greater wisdom). It is part of my society. This was the way I, my colleagues and friends were raised and I revolted against this situation. I was interviewed in 1994 by Malika Malek for Moroccan television. A half hour interview about my experiences as a former political prisoner was cut and only two minutes broadcasted. So I began writing about other women political prisoners and their amazing courage that should be part of Moroccan history. At first, I could not write about myself because that was *hshumah* (shame). (El Bouih 2001a, 42–43)

El Bouih employs the collective testimonial self (Summer 1988, 107–130) to avert "shame" by speaking out as if from within a throng of Moroccan women political prisoners. Intentionally, she allies her individual voice, one that she hopes exemplifies a constructed female collectivity, to national and universal struggles for human rights. When she addressed a non-Arab, English-speaking public during her 2001 American tour, she observed: "I do not speak only in my name, but also in the name of thousands of Moroccans before me, victims of this wound, and for those who remain so to this day throughout the world, at the very moment when we meet here in safety" (El Bouih 2001b). She called upon audiences to rethink female stereotypes of the Arab-Muslim world by explicitly invoking its most famous storyteller who so charmed her royal spouse with endless tales that she talked her way out of death and into his heart:

> Listen to the voice of the south wind, the south as the voices of peoples and social movements of liberation, the voices of women, the south as Morocco. A new voice comes from the harem, a new voice, a new harem, a new Scheherazade, who emerges from silence to go beyond history to where women are deprived of all power, to dig to the bottom of this harem to change the current of history. Scheherazade has spoken and a miracle has been produced.

El Bouih proposes a female voice rooted in the legendary seductive verbal prowess of Scheherazade but also a voice that narrates the singular experience of feminist women political prisoners in Morocco who, like El Bouih were re-gendered men by their torturers. So central is the theme of a woman forced to become a man that her book, *Talk of Darkness*, was published in French under the title, *Une Femme Nommée Rachid* (A Woman Called Rashid):

> They gave me a number and a name: "From now on your name is Rashid." "You cannot move or speak unless you hear your name, which is 'Rashid.'" It was the beginning of the destruction of my identity. My kidnapping and my arbitrary imprisonment, and now it was the turn of my femininity in making me into a man. For them I was a man called Rashid. (El Bouih 2001, 14–15)

A fellow detainee Widad Bouab, was renamed Hamid: "Guards represented a separate category of humanity. One day one of them said to his colleague, 'You see these girls that want to enter the world of politics and to perform men's jobs. Select . . . for them men's names.' In this way they chose a man's name for each one of us" (Bouab 1994, 5; repr. El Bouih 2001, 115). When a guard handcuffed El Bouih as she was being transported to trial, she asked why she was being treated differently from the non-political women prisoners. Her prison guard replied, "For me you are not a woman. You are a man. Women are in the harem" (Alqoh 2000, 48–49). Seventeen years after her disappearance, Latifa Jbabdi writes in her published testimony, "To hide the feminine presence inside detention they called us by masculine names. They called me Sa'id or Tawil [the tall one] or the Doukkali. Only during interrogation was my name feminized to summon me as the Coach or La Pasionaria" (Jbabdi 1994, 6; repr. El Bouih 2001, 123). Jbabdi, Bouab, and El Bouih doubly disappear—first as activists, then as female voices in the political sphere. Calling women political prisoners by men's names did not deter the more commonplace insults and violations directed specifically at women. When arrested in her house, for example, El Bouih was called a whore, and in the police station she witnessed as routine police behavior the rape of arrested prostitutes and the sexual traffic in women detainees. The male

torturer demands absolute domination, achieving control over female prisoners through threats of rape or rape, strategies that transform the feminine
body into a political one that is subsequently available for physical punishment (Scarry 1985).

Added to political repression, El Bouih reports, is a repression specific to
women: "Torture, interrogations, wounds, cries, and moans. . . . We used to
suffer a great deal, we women, for example, during our period, because we
couldn't change" (interview October 3, 1999). Widad Bouab, who was with
El Bouih in the Derb Moulay Cherif secret detention center, maintains that
long delays in delivering sanitary napkins to the women prisoners was deliberate prison policy (interview December 11, 1999; Bouab 2001, 4). Allowing
the women to soil themselves with their menstrual blood was a part of a
system of humiliations, and worse, specific to women detainees, that included being treated as prostitutes, forced nakedness, rape threats, and rape:
"I was blindfolded, hands manacled behind me, and thrown into a van with
no place to sit. I vomited, I had my period and bled heavily, I was bathed in
blood. Fortunately I was wearing black pants. . . . I wore red and black for
seven months, a red sweater and black pants—the red and the black" (interview October 3, 1999).

SILENCE AND RAPE

A dilemma is faced by truth commissions that rely on the testimony of
survivors and Scheherazade-like witnesses able and willing to tell tales of
tyrants: the perpetrators recede into the background. From the silence surrounding torturers, a barely discernible chain of command seems to emerge
from the top downward in which specific bureaucratic steps must occur in
order for disappearance and torture to take place. Bureaucratic decision-
making processes evolve over time: decisions become written orders, then
directives in writing disappear and are replaced by oral orders, and finally no
orders at all. A colonial French-built district jail, for example Derb Moulay
Cherif in Casablanca, is transformed into a secret detention center and then
enlarged into a holding pen with the capacity for mass torture of large numbers of inmates. Police and jailers come to understand that the purpose of
disappearance and torture is to make the fact of torture disappear.

The descent from written bureaucratic orders to oral commands to
screams must be deliberately reversed. To grapple with the silence of torture,
Morocco's Justice and Reconciliation Commission held a series of public
hearings featuring victims' oral testimonies that were broadcast on Moroccan
television and subsequently posted on the commission website
(www.ier.ma). During the televised hearings, although speakers acquiesced

to commission directives not to pronounce the name of their torturers, newspapers transcribed testimonies and reported the profound emotional impact of spoken revelations on the viewing public. As an honored member of the audience, El Bouih attended the first public televised hearings held in Rabat on December 21–22, 2004. She chose not to testify in the commission hearings yet to be present and listen. Although commission hearings ostensibly granted a voice to her and other women political prisoners, she could not initiate retribution by naming torturers who had renamed and numbered her; she could only recount her victimization. Moreover, unlike other speakers, El Bouih's story has been widely disseminated in newspaper articles since 1994, satellite television interviews, and multiple translations. Media revelations about torture and disappearance are evidence of a powerful desire to transform, albeit to contain, the political culture of Morocco. Staging public truth commission hearings for the world to see made the visual as important as the testimonies narrated. Twenty-eight years after her release from prison, El Bouih entered the hall for the public hearing. Immediately she recognized her kidnapper standing there, currently a high-ranking police officer surveying the scene. His name has still never been revealed. Her denunciation was reported immediately to the press:

> For me, seeing him plunged me into a bottomless hole. He was the one who arrested me, rather, kidnapped me in 1977. He was the one who was shifted from Rabat to Casablanca in order to, according to the expression, take special care of me there where I was in Derb Moulay Cherif. How am I to take the fact that I find him again, always, on the day Morocco announces that finally it has reconciled with its past? (Boukhari, 2004)

Encountering one's torturer is a common experience for former detainees and affords rare glimpses into the world of "violence workers" (Higgins, Haritsos-Fatouros, and Zimbardo 2002). Were exact numbers known and the missing accounted for, how would one measure the range of people affected? Political prisoners, for example, were officially recognized but only after they emerged from months or years of enforced disappearance in secret detention centers. For those who will never reappear, how does one measure absence? Whatever these numbers are, they confront contested interpretations of Morocco's history: when do *les années de plomb* (the years of lead) and *al-sanawat al-sawda'* (the black years) begin or end? Why and how does the female voice vanish throughout these decades?

The report by South African TRC indicates the ways in which female voices disappear by their transformation into metaphors for victimization instead of statistical and legal acknowledgements of actual female bodies destroyed by violence. The report concludes that because approximately 61 percent of the violations cited in more than 20,000 victim statements were committed against men:

Men were the most common victims of violations. Six times as many men died as women and twice as many survivors of violations were men. Hence although most people who told the Commission about violations were women, most of the testimony was about men. (TRC vol. 1, 171)

Women testified about abuses to sons, husbands, and brothers. Men did not testify about abuses to women. After that first round of hearings, Mapule Ramashala, one of the seven women South African commissioners, noted that women expressed "the pain of others, not of themselves. If women do not talk, then the story we produce will not be complete. Culturally we think we understand. For example, people may not have told their spouses. We should have special in camera [non-televised closed] hearings, but then do men learn from these?" (quoted in Ross 2003, 23).

The TRC categorized most women's experiences under the category "severe ill-treatment" (TRC vol. 4, 286), defined as sexual assault, abuse, or harassment; rape; mutilation; incommunicado detention; detention without charges; withholding food, water, or medicine during detention, etc. (TRC vol. 1, 81–82 and vol. 5, 256). To counteract what seemed to be women's silences, recommendations by various South African women's organizations included in the section, "Gender and the TRC" report were: women-only hearings (three were held), women giving testimony collectively as a group without television coverage, and commissioners receiving training in gender-related issues (TRC vol. 4, 10; Goldblatt and Meitjes 1998). Women's experiences and, therefore, their stories of harassment, disappearance, or arrest were treated as incidental to main events. Women themselves were reluctant to see their roles as resisters either in society or in the antiapartheid and liberation movements. "Patriarchy," notes Albie Sachs, a judge of the South African Constitutional Court, "is the one truly nonracial institution in South Africa" (Sachs 1990, 1–11).

Women's participation in the public sphere provokes powerful social alliances centering on gender, in which Moroccan and South African protagonists usually at odds with each other seem to collude. Male comrades unwilling to include wives, sisters, and mothers in clandestine oppositional networks were matched by the persecution of governments ferociously eliminating all opposition, both male and female, yet reserving specific apparatuses of control over women who transgress against taboos, for example, Moroccan women imprisoned for their political activism.

THE RIGHT TO SILENCE?

Police torture of silent suspects to induce a confession is common, as is the phenomenon of a suspect's refusal to answer questions. Police and courts routinely interpret silence as evidence against suspects. In contrast and from a legal perspective, many countries maintain the suspect's right to silence. France's *Code of Criminal Procedure* (article L116) makes it compulsory that when an investigating judge (*juge d'instruction*) hears a suspect, the judge must warn the suspect of the right to remain silent, to make a statement, or to answer questions. In South Africa, women detainees who had been tortured under the apartheid regime and became high-ranking government officials, such as Bridget Mabandla, Deputy Minister of Arts and Culture, refused to testify before the TRC. Thenjiwe Mtintso, then chair of South Africa's Commission on Gender Equality, and the ANC's highest-ranking woman member, confessed that she was unable to talk about the sexual abuse she had experienced (quoted in Goldblatt and Meintjes 1998).

Latifa Jbabdi, the only woman commissioner appointed to Morocco's Truth and Justice Commission, wrote about her experiences of secret detention and prison. In 1994, as part of *Ittihad Ichtiraki* newspaper articles on women in prison, appended in 2001 to Fatna El Bouih's memoir, she described accidental privileges accorded women in Derb Moulay Cherif, such as the right to go to the toilet without a guard, which then became the one occasion she could freely remove her blindfold. Jbabdi includes a brief account of the women political prisoner's success at stopping a guard's sexual assault:

> One day our comrade, Khadija Boukhari, was sexually harassed by a guard: our anger burst out and we disregarded everything that was forbidden, which provoked an inquiry that gave consideration to our comrade. (Jbabdi 1994, 5; repr. El Bouih 2001, 108)

While Jbabdi's description is laconic and abrupt, as if reporting facts to Amnesty International, her pride in collective feminine resistance emerges. Fatna El Bouih dates the first women's revolt in secret detention to the same moment when a guard attempted to rape one of the women prisoners after following her to the toilet. El Bouih writes: "It was a memorable night: the walls of that prison heard in its history the first voices of protest, and most amazing, women's voices" (2001, 23). All were blindfolded, manacled, and forced to lie still in complete silence, yet somehow the woman under attack was able to raise an alarm. My October 3, 1999, oral history interview with El Bouih adds vivid details:

> It was our first revolt in Derb Moulay Cherif center, the first voices raised besides the screams of men and women undergoing torture, it was the first cry of denunciation of a particular injustice, sexual harassment. We screamed loudly around three o'clock in the morning during Ramadan, we screamed loudly and we thought they would kill us. We screamed that he was assaulting us, that we were women, it shouldn't be allowed, it was an injustice. Everyone

talked, Latifa [Jbabdi] began, and then it was me. She was terrified but we said
we had to do it. We held a demonstration, we insulted them, we were women
and we were there but we wouldn't be made to accept it. The next day they
conducted an inquiry. They hit us and humiliated us to shut us up. But the next
day, their superiors came, the commanders, even with our eyes blindfolded
there were ways to see. We saw by their shoes, boots, fabrics that they wore
that they were high-ranking officials who questioned us while we were blindfolded and they said they would punish them.

In the diabolical world of secret detention at Derb Moulay Cherif where strict
codes of silence reign except for the screams of the tortured and the utter-
ances of forced confessions, El Bouih proudly describes a women's "demonstration." No matter that they expressed themselves solely by screams and
words while blindfolded and immobilized and that they paid physically for
transgressing the imposed silence. The women still recall their triumph of
reaffirmed gender, dignity, and identity. For that moment, prison officials
conducted a perversion of a formal inquiry, with the result that the torturers
and prison officials acquiesced to limiting their atrocities. To practice abduction and mental and physical torture were routine, but in the fall of 1978, for
those women political prisoners acting together, there was a temporary respite from threats of rape.

HISTORIES OF RAPE

International human rights reports routinely lament the lack of documentation about gender-based human rights abuses exemplified by the South
African and Moroccan cases and women members of their respective truth
commissions who choose silence. The difficulties in transforming women's
experiences of rape into proofs of the governmental role in its perpetuation
are highlighted by an unusual case of a Moroccan woman political prisoner
raped by a prison guard in 1974, unusual due to its history of documentation.
Author Marguerite Rollinde in her excellent chronicle of the Moroccan human rights movement, *Les mouvements marocain des droits de l'Homme*,
emphasizes how rare it was and is for rape victims to denounce publicly
police rapists and to demand remedies.[2] In the early 1970s, women students
active in the national student union formed part of a nascent post-independence feminist movement swiftly suppressed by government repression and
widespread arrests. Rollinde lists the names of some women student leaders:
Saida Menebhi (who would die during the lengthy 1978 political prisoner
hunger strike), Rabea Ftouh (incarcerated five years for political activities),
Fatna El Bouih, and the following anonymous woman detainee whose testimony about rape is quoted at length:

I had already been arrested in 1974 during the fights of the high school students. At the police station, I was raped and there was a national strike in the
high schools to protest against this rape. In 1977, I was arrested again by these
men, searched by men. For them, this was a good time to revenge themselves
against the propaganda that was made about the rape. They waited several
days before interrogating me, but for them, I was public enemy number one.
Each passing policeman slapped me and kicked me. That's her, the snake.
That's her that gave us trouble in 1974, they would say hitting me. You feel
the gaze of strange men always around you. You can do nothing, you cannot
even be minimally at ease because there is the gaze of men on you. If a woman
searches you, you feel humiliated. If it is a man, you feel raped. It's the same
thing at the level of the gaze. (quoted in Rollinde 2002, 219)

Rollinde's 2002 book refers to an earlier text, reprinted by women's solidarity groups outside of Morocco in 1984, in which victims remain anonymous.
In 1980, however, human-rights activists of the France-based Comités de la
lutte contre la repression au Maroc (Committees Against Repression in Morocco) had published the same story of rape in the monthly newsletter with
details:

Rape has been and remains one of the most barbarous methods, more than
other known methods of tortures, used by Moroccan executioners. Fatna El
Bouih, an activist student was pursuing her studies and was also at the same
time a supervisor at the Chawqi High School in Casablanca. On January 24,
1974, a general strike was largely followed throughout the city especially in
the girls' schools. The strike demands were: no to the suppression of the
national union of students; the right to a high school student union; denunciation of the secondary school situation (expulsions, selection, lack of profes-
sors, etc.). Most of the high schools were surrounded by the police force. On
January 25, 1974 Fatna El Bouih was arrested and brought to the police station
in the Maarif neighborhood. She was interrogated about the events of the 24th
at Chawqi High School, which was at the head of the strike. At night she was
guarded in a cell where one of her torturers raped her. Afterwards, he threatened her again with rape and more violence if she dared to speak of it. He
added: "You are neither the first nor the last. Me, I will teach you liberation."
Fatna immediately denounced police savagery and repression practiced in the
police station after her release. High school students in Casablanca protested
and were in solidarity with her in various struggles: boarders at Chawqi High
School went on a hunger strike; other high school students boycotted classes.
Police again intervened in Chawqi High School. Fatna the student was interrogated, and then brought to the police station. The police tried to force a confession that what she said about rape was the fruit of her imagination. In vain. At
Chawqi High School the struggle continued to free the raped student. The
strike lasted a week. Other high schools, teachers were in solidarity, which
forced the police to free her and to pretend to "search for the guilty one" by
opening a legal file. In fact, it was about burying the matter while investigating
the activities of this activist, interrogating family members and other student
boarders. Fatna El Bouih was interrogated two times by the governor of Casa-

blanca (who used the same brusqueness and terror as the police in the station),
by the district attorney, by judges. Finally, they took advantage of the vacation
to announce on the television that the case was closed. (Comités 1980, 10)

The 1980 report concludes that gender-based violence—rape, intimidation,
and police and government cover-up to silence women—was routinely practiced. In her 2001 prison memoir, El Bouih's 1974 rape is alluded to, but not
explicitly reprised, in order to account for the ferocity of treatment in police
custody for the second time in 1977:

> I was met by an important official who appeared very angry and very knowl-
> edgeable about me. "You are the anarchist leader, you led us a merry dance at
> the Chawqi High School. That play comes to an end here: here you are no
> longer the famous anarchist, here the skies are not cloudy because of Fatna the
> oppressed." He was alluding to slogans shouted by fellow students during my
> arbitrary imprisonment when I was a student at the Chawqi High School and to
> the solidarity campaign that enveloped all Morocco. (El Bouih 2001, 14)

The first critic, Abderrahim Tafraout, to review El Bouih's prison memoirs
recognized her as a new Scheherazade, the female vanquisher of royal tyranny according to the article's headline: "Shahrayar was killed by Fatna" (Tafraout 2001). This time, Scheherazade is reconfigured by Moroccan women
writers to represent the survivor who tells the story of her human rights
victimization with fresh details, repeatedly and publicly, in writing and in
speech. The content of her trauma endured longer than a thousand and one
nights. The form of nested interlocking oral testimonies embedded in written
narratives spread over decades strongly parallels the vicissitudes of women
political opponents and their multiple rapes, kidnappings, tortures, humiliations, and travels through the vast and uncharted territory of Morocco's
prison system. Similar to the medieval Arabic text, Fatna El Bouih, the
storyteller, is named, renamed, or anonymous, and she speaks or stays silent
about her torture and rape according to the audience, the reader, and the
framing context of testimony. These survivors' tales, El Bouih believes,
magically convert her listeners into witnesses and in so doing perhaps begins
the work of healing herself, other women sufferers who are encouraged to
break their silences, and the larger social community that her narrative reach-
es.

Latifa Jbabdi, the Moroccan commissioner, directly addressed the dynamic interconnectedness between men's and women's experiences of dissidence
and punishment. In her 1994 newspaper account, (later reprinted in El
Bouih's memoir), she concludes with a story about the police motorcades
and sirens that routinely escorted the women political prisoners from Meknes
Prison to the tribunal for their long-awaited trial. Jbabdi, El Bouih, and other
women political prisoners had undergone seven months of secret detention

and disappearance in Derb Moulay Cherif followed by their prolonged, life-threatening hunger strike in Meknes Prison for the right to trial. Describing her trip to the courthouse, Jbabdi self-consciously oscillates between a narrative of bitterness and humor:

> Once when only I was summoned, as usual I was made to climb into a van surrounded by guards and police armed with machine-guns. In front and behind us were two additional vans similarly armed, not to mention the motorcycle that opened up our route. After I got in, these men revolted, furious at such a grotesque mobilization because of us, especially because of me, a mere woman. They shouted insisting that this was a question of masculinity and honor. I hesitated between laughing at the situation which was genuinely funny, and cursing the machismo that judged me of no importance because of my sex, and did not look to my ideas, my choices and my limits as a human being. (Jbabdi 1994, 6; repr. El Bouih 2001, 135)

Moroccan human rights discourse extends the human rights discourses of witnessing and testifying to public space and beyond male-female inequities to gender-neutral acts of narration by men and women to express suffering publicly. Men too were raped in detention. It is Jbabdi who demands that her tormentors acknowledge her ideas based on a shared humanity and not her gender. But it is El Bouih who narrates the raped body to make audible and intelligible the screams from male and female bodies, penetrated by the torturers' tools and gendered submissive, feminine, and disposable. The primacy of the silenced, disappeared, and tortured body is the salient fact that elicits witnessing and the corroborative social aspects of giving testimony by more than one victim.

Author's note: This is a revised and expanded version of my presentation to Morocco's Justice and Truth Commission, January 14, 2005, Rabat, Morocco. I thank one of the commissioners, Abdelhay Moudden, for his invitation and comments. Unless indicated in the footnotes and bibliography, translations into English are mine.

Editors' note: This chapter originally appeared in *Journal of Middle East Women's Studies* 1:3 (Fall 2005): 73–95. Copyright, 2005, Indiana University Press. All rights reserved. Used by permission of the publisher. For the sake of consistency of style in this volume, we changed all the dates to the U.S. format.

NOTES

1. Fatna El Bouih, *Talk of Darkness*, English translation in progress by Mustapha Kamal and Susan Slyomovics. Translation by written permission of Fatna El Bouih and Editions Le Fennec. (Editors' note: see El Bouih 2008.)

2. In 1993, Casablanca police commissioner Mohamed Tabet was sentenced to death and executed for rape, debauchery, and violence against more than one thousand women. According to Amnesty International reports, this was the first known execution since 1982 (Amnesty International 1994, 214).

REFERENCES

Alqoh, Aicha. 2000. Fatna El Bouih: Ma prison à moi. *Demain* 18, July 7–21: 48–9.

Amnesty International. 1994. Morocco and Western Sahara. In *Annual Report*. 213–15.

Boraine, Alex. 2000. *A Country Unmasked*. Oxford: Oxford Univ. Press.

Bouab, Widad. 1994. al-Sijn alladhi kana maladhan ba'd 'uzlati al-makhafir (The prison that was a refuge after the isolation of secret detention). *Ittihad Ishtiraki*. November 5: 5.

_____. 1999. Interview. December 11.

_____. 2001 Fi Darb Mawlay Sharif (In Derb Moulay Cherif), *al-Ahdath al-Maghribiyah*, August 27: 4.

Boukhari, Karim. 2005. Tatouées par les années de plomb. *Telquel* 166. May 16. Available at www.telquel_online.com/166/zoom_166.shtml.

Brysk, Alison. 1994. The Politics of Measurement: The Contested Count of the Disappeared in Argentina. *Human Rights Quarterly* 16: 676–92.

Charaf, Maria. 1997. *Être au feminine*. Casablanca: Éditions La Voie Démocratique.

Comités de la Lutte Contre la Répression au Maroc. 1980. A propos d'un viol. *Bulletin* 21:2–3.

El Bouih, Fatna. 1994. Ara'u ma la 'uridu (I saw what I don't want to see). *Ittihad Ishtiraki*, November 5: 5–6.

_____. 1999a. Un sommeil court, peuplé de cauchemars. *Le Journal*, June 5–11: 8.

_____. 1999b. Interview. October 3.

_____. 2001a. *Hadith al-'atama*. Casablanca: Le Fennec.

_____. 2001b. This Time I Choose When to Leave: An Interview with Fatna El Bouih by Susan Slyomovics, *MERIP/Middle East Report* 218: 42–3.

_____. 2001c. Pathways to Human Rights in Morocco. Presented at the Genevieve McMillan-Reba Stewart Lecture, Massachusetts Institute of Technology.

_____. 2008. *Talk of Darkness*. Trans. Mustapha Kamal and Susan Slyomovics. Austin, TX: Center for Middle Eastern Studies, Univ. of Texas at Austin.

El Saadawi, Nawal. 1986. *Memoirs from the Women's Prison*. Trans. Marilyn Booth. Berkeley: Univ. of California Press.

Goldblatt, Beth, and Sheila Meintjes. 1998. Dealing with the Aftermath: Sexual Violence and the Truth and Reconciliation Commission. *Agenda* 36: 7–17.

Higgins, Martha K., Mika Haritsos-Fatouros, and Philip G. Zimbardo. 2002. *Violence Workers: Police Torturers and Murderers Reconstruct Brazilian Atrocities*. Berkeley: Univ. of California Press.

Jbabdi, Latifa. 1994. al-Makhfar wa-al-ta'dhib wa-alsijn wa-al-jalladun:shahadat Latifa Jbabdi, (Secret detention, torture, prison, and the executioners: Latifa Jbabdi's testimony). *Ittihad Ichtiraki*. November 5: 6.

Krog, Antjie. 1998. *Country of My Skull*. Johannesburg: Random House.

Laabi, Abdellatif. 1982. *Les chemins des ordalies*. Paris: Denoel.

Menebhi, Khadija. 1999. Istihshad imra'ah (A woman's martyrdom). *Nawafid* 3 (1): 121–27.

Mernissi, Fatema. 2001. *Scheherazade Goes West: Different Cultures, Different Harems*. New York: Simon and Schuster.

Moussadak, Abdelhak. 1999. al-Yusfi Qaddur: huwa almas'ul 'an ta'dhib hatta mawt alshahid Amin Tahani (Youssfi Kaddour: he is responsible for torture until the martyr Amine Tahani died). In *Man qatala al-shahidayni?* (Who killed the two martyrs?), unpaginated commemoration booklet on the anniversary of the deaths of Amine Tahani and Abdellatif Zeroual.

Muhammad VI, King of Morocco. 1999. Premier discourse du trone. *Le Matin du Sahara et du Maghreb*. August 1:1.

Posel, Deborah. 2002. The TRC Report: What Kind of History? What Kind of Truth? In *Commissioning the Past: Understanding South Africa's Truth and Reconciliation Commission*. Eds. Deborah Posel and Graeme Simpson. Johannesburg: Witwatersrand Univ. Press.

Ramphele, Mamphela. 1996. Political Widowhood in South Africa: The Embodiment of Ambiguity. *Daedalus* 125: 99–117.

Rollinde, Marguerite. 2002. *Le mouvement marocain des droits de l'Homme*. Paris: Karthala.

Ross, Fiona C. 2003. *Bearing Witness: Women and the Truth and Reconciliation Commission in South Africa*. London: Pluto Press.

Sachs, Albie. 1990. Judges and Gender: The Constitutional Rights of Women in Post-Apartheid South Africa. *Agenda* 7: 1–11.

Slyomovics, Susan. 2001. A Truth Commission for Morocco. *MERIP/Middle East Report* 218: 18–21.

_____. 2003. No Buying Off the Past: Moroccan Indemnities and the Opposition. *MERIP/ Middle East Report* 229: 34–7.

_____. 2005a. *The Performance of Human Rights in Morocco*. Philadelphia: Univ. of Pennsylvania Press.

_____. 2005b. Morocco's Justice and Reconciliation Commission. *MERIP/Middle East Report*, April 4. (http://www.merip.org/mero/mero040405.html).

Steiner, Henry J., ed. 1997. *Truth Commissions: A Comparative Assessment*. Cambridge, MA: World Peace Foundation.

Summer, Doris. 1988. "Not Just a Personal Story: Women's Testimonios and the Plural Self." In *Life/Lines: Theorizing Women's Autobiography*. Eds. Bella Brodski and Celeste Schenk, 107–30. Ithaca: Cornell Univ. Press.

Tafnout, Abdelrahim. 2000. Shahrayar aladhi qatalathu Fatna (Shahrayar was killed by Fatna). *Al'Amal al-Dimuqrati*, March 8.

Truth and Reconciliation Commission. 1998. *Truth and Reconciliation Commission Report of South Africa*. Johannesburg: Juta.

Chapter Five

The Persistence of Spectacle in PRC Modes of Punishing Criminality and Deviance

Philip F. Williams

Foreign visitors to the People's Republic of China (PRC) occasionally react with astonishment or even revulsion when encountering a PRC criminal sentencing rally or noticing bright red cross marks brushed menacingly through the names of convicts taken away to prison camps or execution grounds in that country. Such public displays of punishment during peacetime have long since practically disappeared in most developed nations such as the member states of the Organization of Economic Cooperation and Development (OECD). Because the PRC has become far more developed economically over the decades since Mao Zedong's death, a question arises as to why that country's prisoners sometimes continue to be made a spectacle of even in the 21st century.

While a chapter-length study would be overreaching to address all of the complex factors at play that contribute to make the PRC Party-state a special case in its public display of prisoners, this chapter focuses upon phases of the internment process that lend themselves relatively well or poorly to the spectacle of punishment in service of the Party-state's interests. For instance, public spectacle during the sentencing phase allows the Party-state to burnish its image as society's protector against apparent miscreants. On the other hand, the avoidance of public spectacle during the transport of prisoners between various jails and labor camps serves security interests—such as by reducing the likelihood of prisoner escapes—and avoids pitfalls such as a negative public reaction to an overabundance of prisoners herded around by an overzealous police apparatus.

There is a fundamental reason why the PRC Party-state continues to set great store by making a spectacle out of punishing what it defines as criminality. While Mao Zedong appears to have feared the revival of market economics and individualistic initiative above all, his less ideological and more pragmatic successors among the Party elite have worried more about political instability than anything else, coining slogans such as "Stability above everything else" (*wending yadao yiqie*). This overriding fear of regime instability stems in part from the fact that the Chinese Communist Party (CCP) has seen its legitimacy as the sole ruling party diminished by CCP-instigated disasters such as the Great Leap Famine (1959–62), the Cultural Revolution (1966–76), and the Lin Biao Affair (a failed apparent coup plot by Mao Zedong's "most loyal successor" in 1971). By publicly showing how effectively the regime can crack down on those who dare challenge or oppose the Party-state or its laws, the Party-state aims to intimidate anyone who might be considering doing something similar.

In reference to developed nations such as OECD member states, Pieter Spierenburg has argued that "the display of physical punishment as a manifestation of [political] authority was still considered indispensable in the early modern period, because the existing states were still relatively unstable in comparison to later times" (202). In contrast to the developed OECD states, the PRC remains relatively unstable politically, though masking this with a state-controlled media blackout of coverage of the many tens of thousands of public protests and anti-government demonstrations that occur annually in that country—mostly in provincial areas far removed from the presence of international media. While outwardly powerful and resilient, the PRC Party-state has become somewhat brittle from a decades-long crisis of authority that became even more severe with the decline and fall of the old Soviet bloc of single-party Leninist regimes by the early 1990s. Under these circumstances, an early-modern or pre-modern throwback to mass sentencing rallies and the Party-state's posturing as society's protector against supposed miscreants and "the enemy within" is understandable from a standpoint of regime preservation.

An aesthetics of spectacle is well suited to promote the Party-state's manipulation of public sentiments against prisoners, for as Andrew Darley has pointed out, such an aesthetics encourages intellectual passivity and an absorption with surface appearances at the expense of deeper meanings of an event such as a mass sentencing rally (4, 192). Spectators at a PRC mass sentencing rally are not expected to critically weigh the various factors that led the judicial authorities to pass down the sentence they chose to impose on the defendant, but simply to applaud and cheer the authorities' punitive ritual authority and raise their voices in mutual condemnation of the defendant. The periodic PRC "strike-hard" crackdowns on drug trafficking and other relatively apolitical criminal behavior is something that relatively few PRC citizens would actively oppose, even though most PRC intellectuals with a background in legal studies or criminal justice are well aware of how the state's rush to judgment and punishment in such crackdowns tends to create many miscarriages of justice that could be avoided if normal procedural safeguards were observed.

A MESSY, INCOMPLETE TRANSITION FROM PRE-MODERN TO MODERN FORMS OF PUNISHMENT

The PRC criminal justice system provides an important counterexample to hypotheses about an abrupt and once-and-for-all change from traditional forms of punishment to their "modern" counterparts. An extreme set of claims about such a discontinuity appears in Michel Foucault's *Surveiller et punir* (1975), which dramatically contrasts the spectacularly gruesome and cruel public execution of the premodern regicidal convict Damiens with the modern-day sequestering of convicts under tight surveillance behind high prison walls. Foucault's *Discipline and Punish* (1995), as the treatise is known in English, would have us believe that the state's practices of punishment made an irreversible and total shift from horrific premodern public spectacle to the routinized and hidden "modern" warehousing of inmates due to an entirely unprecedented kind of totalizing power that suddenly materialized in the 18th century.

However, this is a greatly oversimplified and schematized account of what happened even in France, where neither the pace of prison construction nor the supposedly Panopticonic model for prison construction that Foucault's hypothesis would have predicted has been borne out by the facts (O'Brien 1982, 19). Foucault's hypothesis of abrupt and total discontinuity in a society's practices of punishment may be found even more questionable if applied to countries such as Russia and China, where the incorporation of spectacle and sometimes even corporal punishment within state-sanctioned penal practices lingered on through the nineteenth and twentieth centuries— and in China's example, has persisted into the 21st century, with the continuation of state-administered mass sentencing rallies under the periodic PRC "strike hard" (*yan da*) crackdowns on crime, to give but one example (Williams and Wu 2004, 53–54; Moise 1986, 240–41). As truly rigorous research by David Garland and Abby Schrader on systems of punishment indicates, no lone factor tends to account for the rise or decline of any major mode of punishment—and a mixture of continuity and discontinuity in the development of these modes of punishment is to be expected (Garland 1990, 277–92; Schrader 2002, 190). In other words, the PRC officials who handle criminal justice tend to avoid making a spectacle of prisoners in circumstances that are difficult to orchestrate or keep under control, while embracing spectacle in circumstances that lend themselves to elaborate choreography in the service of the single-party regime's perceived interests.

AVOIDANCE OF PUBLIC SPECTACLE, PARTICULARLY IN THE TRANSPORT OF PRISONERS

Especially during the post-Mao Reform era, the officially forbidden but often tacitly condoned practice of torturing prisoners has been almost invariably handled in secrecy, particularly when guards or cadres have been doing the torturing. Yet less extreme practices by the authorities have also been treated with the utmost secrecy, and the PRC remains the only major world power that has forbidden the Red Cross to make routine inspections of its prisons, in spite of occasional promises to change this policy.

As was usually the case in the former Soviet Russian gulag, tight secrecy has typically been enforced in the transfer of PRC convicts to a prison or labor camp (Shalamov 1980, 151–70).[1] Information about the final destination of PRC inmates has frequently been withheld from them until their arrival at a given penitentiary or labor camp.[2] For example, Cong Weixi's questions about where the guards were transporting him repeatedly met with the obfuscating reply that he would find out once he had arrived there (Cong 1998, 90).[3] During the initial stages of imprisonment in a camp or jail, the prisoner's family members have tended to be even more in the dark as to their incarcerated relative's whereabouts, as the practice of incommunicado detention has been common in the PRC.

PRC prisoners have often been especially reluctant to be dispatched to prison in distant borderland regions. Living conditions in such regions have often been severe; some prisoners might also be prevented from returning to their home city after completing their sentence, as the PRC government shares to some extent the Qing Dynasty's interest in reducing overcrowding in its large eastern cities by permanently resettling some urbanites in sparsely populated borderlands far to the west or the north. Moreover, the likelihood of seasonal family visits has generally diminished in proportion to the remoteness and isolation of a given prison camp.[4]

To reduce the likelihood that prisoners in transit to a distant jail or camp might escape into the crowd on a railway station platform, trains that carry prisoners would usually load or unload their inmates either at an empty station platform, or else alongside the railway tracks approximately a hundred meters away from the main station platform. By unloading prisoners far from crowded areas of the railway station, prison officials would thereby avoid attracting unwanted attention from ordinary passersby—which also accounts for the common practice of transporting prisoners under the cover of evening darkness (Wu 1994, 98).[5] The manner in which a casual onlooker would often direct his curious gaze at such prisoners during a relatively rare daytime prison transfer is an indication that the sight of prisoners in transit has not been a common occurrence in the PRC.[6] The PRC government's carefully ritualized mass spectacle involving the public humiliation of sentenced prisoners is one thing, but its tight-lipped approach to the unmanaged exposure of ordinary prisoners to the public eye is quite another matter.

THE CCP'S REVIVAL OF THE SHAMING SPECTACLE OF *SHIZHONG*

One type of abusive shaming practice utilized in some PRC camps and prisons is functionally equivalent to a certain mode of pre-modern torture, but has adopted specific forms and terminology that are more appropriate for modern times. There was a category of pre-modern punishments that were intended both to chastise the offender and exert a deterrent effect upon the local populace by placing the convict on "shameful public display" (*shizhong*) in some sort of awkward posture or uncomfortable restraining device. Prisoners subject to such punishment would often be put on display in a crowded section of town with a yoke-like cangue around the neck or else standing inside of a "stand-up cage" (*zhanlong*). In relatively severe cases where capital punishment was applied, the executed convict might have his severed head displayed atop a pole at a busy intersection or in the marketplace, there to serve as a warning to others. A latter-day version in PRC prison culture was to force the prisoner to "pose for a photo" (*zhaoxiang*) by being tied to a post or a tree in town somewhere that was exposed to the elements; the "poser for a photo" would have to go without food or water for an extended period of time. Zhang Xianliang witnessed this form of torture in his northwestern PRC prison camp various times in 1958, and has described it in his diary-like memoir (1995, 115).

The inmate protagonist of Cong Weixi's novel *The Deer Turned Its Head* (*Lu huitou*) also suffers this torture and is tied up naked to a post under the blistering summer sun, defenseless against swarms of mosquitoes (1988, 143–153). The resulting mockery and other unwelcome comments from passersby would be especially difficult to endure if the prisoner had been stripped mostly or entirely naked, a practice that occurred largely for the purpose of exposing the inmate's skin to biting mosquitoes (Cong 1988, 150).[7]

Another modern PRC variety of shaming punishment has been known as "controlling the blood" (*kong xue*), whereby the prisoner would be tied to a long and sturdy carrying pole, and then turned almost upside down at approx-imately a 75-degree angle to the ground (Zhang 1995, 115). Similar to a widespread practice in the Cultural Revolution, some prisoners in the Jiang era have continued to be forced to hold themselves for a long period of time in the awkward and painful "jet plane posture" (*zuo feiji* or *penqi shi*); in this posture, the prisoner would be required to bend forward deeply at the waist while raising his arms high above his back and head (Gao 1991, 51). An even more common holdover during the 21st century is the continuation of the public shaming of convicts in mass sentencing rallies, during which the Party-state mobilizes hundreds or even thousands of local townsfolk to cheer the severity of the sentences handed down by the authorities and to glare or even jeer at the assembled convicts.

PRISONERS TURNING THE TABLES ON THE AUTHORITIES WITH SPECTACLES OF THEIR OWN

Some particularly embittered PRC citizens have occasionally stricken back at the Party-state's heavy-handedness by making a spectacle out of their own deaths. Some released prisoners who were prevented by the authorities from leaving the locale of the labor camp and blocked from returning to live in their home cities have committed suicide as a gesture of protest against the government by taking their lives in a place with symbolic overtones such as the nation's capital; this final act of defiance resembles the pre-modern sui-cide of a sorely mistreated daughter-in-law who wished to kill herself at her in-laws' residence as a way of shaming her abusive mother-in-law (Williams and Wu 2004, 143).[8] To be sure, in anticipation of an unending string of various frustrations and disappointments awaiting them in their future, other PRC inmates have instead taken their own lives in a non-dramatic, self-effacing manner.[9]

Although the prosperous southeastern provinces far from Beijing's heavy hand have seen many Deng Jiang Hu–era criminal cases tried in ways that have limited the state's great advantage over the individual defendant, the connection between criminal justice and spectacle has remained prominent. An example is the January 1990 trial in Xiamen, Fujian, of the novelist Tang Min for libel (Tang 1994, 41–44). A number of small-town officials in the general vicinity of this prominent Southeastern seaport jumped to the conclu-sion that one of Tang Min's satiric novels included slanderous comments about their own conduct. These officials thereby angrily demanded that the local government bring Tang Min to trial and impose a stiff fine and a multi-year prison sentence. However, Tang Min's attorney delivered a well-argued defense that led the panel of judges to set the monetary compensation due the plaintiffs at merely two thousand *yuan*, a token amount that was but a small fraction of what the plaintiffs had been counting on receiving from the defendant (Tang 1994, 43).[10] Even though Tang Min was still sentenced to a year's imprisonment, she made a point of behaving like the winner of the case, repeatedly waving and flashing a triumphant smile at the assemblage of news photographers and ordinary onlookers who thronged the area around the courtroom. While inside the courtroom, she defiantly insisted upon her complete innocence and criticized the libel judgment against her as an illegal punishment. When one of the judges subsequently stared at her with a reproachful expression on his face, she glared back at him with such ferocity that he quickly averted his eyes. The plaintiffs' expectation that the trial would amount to a public shaming of Tang Min thus backfired, as she turned the tables on them by winning favorable publicity and scoring a sort of moral victory over both the disappointed plaintiffs and the discomfited judges.

One of the major reasons that resorting to public spectacle in matters of criminal justice has fallen into disfavor in most modern nations is that the authorities are justifiably worried about the unpredictability of public reactions to such spectacle. For instance, in the early spring of 1989, the CCP authorities in Tibet under then provincial Party Secretary Hu Jintao decided to intimidate restive dissident Tibetan Buddhist monks by carrying out a public execution of two Tibetan "counterrevolutionary" prisoners. However, instead of breaking the spirit of the Tibetan protestors, as might have been the result among many Han Chinese if this measure had been taken in China proper, the public executions instead had the effect of infuriating the local Tibetan populace, thereby catalyzing one of Tibet's largest protest marches ever seen. This in turn led to Hu Jintao's imposition of martial law over Tibet and an especially bloody crackdown by the predictably intolerant PRC authorities. The crackdown in Tibet that peaked in March 1989 created some negative public relations fallout for the PRC internationally, along with prefiguring the imposition of martial law and the harsh military crackdown on nonviolent demonstrators in China proper during the summer of 1989.

CONCLUSION

As what Foucault might have called a "schema of individual submission" (*schéma de la soumission individuelle*), the PRC's continued practice of parading bowed-down or tressed-up prisoners in front of a scornful crowd at a mass sentencing rally allows the regime to burnish its image as the protector of the citizens' security while branding the convict with a level of shame and dishonor that can sometimes be psychologically debilitating (1975, 246–247; 1995, 243). Whenever the latest cycle of the Party-state's "Strike

Hard" campaign against crime has begun, this post-Mao successor to the Mao-era *pidou hui* or struggle meeting has followed in train, especially in provincial areas where there is less reason to be concerned about critical reportage from foreign correspondents. [11]

Even as the PRC criminal justice system has seen some significant improvements in areas such as greatly downsizing the forced exile of released inmates, the continued use and abuse of prisoners in the public spectacle of mass sentencing rallies is a sign that significant continuities with both the Maoist and pre-modern criminal justice systems still exist in the 21st century. In focusing onlookers' attention at a superficial level of immediacy and discouraging critical reflection on the mass sentencing rally and other forms of Party-state grandstanding and self-serving discourse, the aesthetics of spectacle continues to provide the Party-state with an important tool for preserving its dominant role within PRC society—often at the expense of the citizens it arrests and incarcerates.

NOTES

1. The inmate narrator in the Soviet author Varlam Shalamov's story "The Lawyers' Plot" is not allowed to know his destination while in transit within the gulag: "Where was I being taken? North or south? East or west? There was no sense asking, and besides, the guards weren't supposed to say" (160).

2. PRC prison authorities did not provide either Harry Wu or Wang Xiaoling and her group of female transit prisoners with any information about their final prison destination, as recounted in Wang Xiaoling (1988, 96) and Wu (1994, 99).

3. For more details about Cong Weixi's anxiety stemming from the prison guards' and cadres' excessive secrecy about the transit prisoners' destination, see Cong (1989, 169).

4. Cong Weixi mentions the hardships his elderly mother would face merely to visit him at the frigid and remote Xingkaihu Prison Camp in Manchuria, and mentions this fear and his anxiety about not knowing his destination (Cong 1989, 141, 167).

5. Harry Wu's arrival at the Qinghe labor camp's train station of Chadian is described in Wu 1994, 98. Taking pains to conceal the loading and unloading of transit prisoners from the ordinary citizenry in a given locale was also a typical practice of Soviet Russian gulag officials, as indicated by Aleksandr Solzhenitsyn (1974, 567).

6. Harry Wu had not come across any ordinary civilians for a year when he noticed a group of them gazing curiously at him and his fellow inmates while the latter were transiting a civilian area (1994, 98). Cong Weixi has also remarked upon the apprehensive and curious stares from public bus riders during an unusual instance when he was being transported to a different prison camp on an ordinary city bus (1989, 143).

7. Tying up a naked or practically naked prisoner in an area infested with mosquitoes is a type of punishment that was not uncommonly inflicted upon army deserters by the Guomindang (Chinese Nationalist) military during the Second World War. In the PRC beginning from 1949, this practice tended to be inflicted on prisoners instead of military deserters.

8. Cong Weixi specifically identifies the factor of protest in the manner of the chemist inmate Zheng Guangdi's suicide (Cong 1998, 256).

9. This is the manner in which Harry Wu's fellow Tuanhe camp inmate Ao Naisong committed suicide (Wu 1994, 188–189, 268).

10. The 2,000-*yuan* penalty that the judges decreed in Tang Min's trial would not have even covered the plaintiffs' legal outlays and related expenses of bringing the case to trial, as it was

equivalent to well under US$400. They were shocked and disappointed at having been awarded so much less than the tens of thousands of *yuan* that they had insisted they deserved to receive from the defendant.

11. The first "Strike-hard" (*yan da*) campaign was launched in 1983. These campaigns have continued to occur in the 21st century. A photograph of a group of drug dealers rounded up for execution during one of the first Strike-hard campaigns may be viewed in Moise 1986, 240. Mass sentencing rallies held by the Party-state to parade convicts and sometimes even unconvicted suspects in front of assembled crowds have continued in the 21st century, such as one held in Chenzhou, Hunan province, in late March 2009.

REFERENCES

Cong Weixi. 1988. *Lu huitou* (The Deer Turned Its Head). Beijing: Zhongguo qingnian chubanshe.
———. 1989. *Zou xiang hundun* (Heading into Chaos). Vol. 1. Beijing: Zuojia chubanshe.
———. 1998. *Zou xiang hundun sanbuqu* (The Heading into Chaos Trilogy). Beijing: Zhongguo shehui kexue chubanshe.
Darley, Andrew. 2000. *Surface Play and Spectacle in New Media Genres*. London and New York: Routledge.
Foucault, Michel. 1975. *Surveiller et punir: naissance de la prison*. Paris: Éditions Gallimard.
———. 1995. *Discipline and Punish: The Birth of the Prison*. 2nd edition. Trans. Alan Sheridan. New York: Vintage Books.
Gao Xin. 1991. *Beiwei yu huihuang: yige "Liu si" shounanzhe de yu zhong zhaji* (Disgrace and Glory: Prison Jottings of a Victim of "June Fourth"). Taipei: Lianjing.
Garland, David. 1990. *Punishment and Modern Society: A Study in Social Theory*. Chicago: Univ. of Chicago Press.
Moise, Edwin E. 1986. *Modern China: A History*. London: Longman Group.
O'Brien, Patricia. 1982. *The Promise of Punishment: Prisons in Nineteenth-century France*. Princeton: Princeton Univ. Press.
Schrader, Abby M. 2002. *Languages of the Lash: Corporal Punishment and Identity in Imperial Russia*. DeKalb, IL: Northern Illinois Univ. Press.
Shalamov, Varlam. 1980. "The Lawyers' Plot." In *Kolyma Tales*, trans. John Glad, 151–170. New York: W.W. Norton.
Solzhenitsyn, Aleksandr I. 1974. *The Gulag Archipelago, 1918–1956: An Experiment in Literary Investigation*. Vol. 1. Trans. Thomas P. Whitney. New York: Harper and Row.
Spierenburg, Pieter. 1984. *The Spectacle of Suffering—Executions and the Evolution of Repression: from a Preindustrial Metropolis to the European Experience*. Cambridge: Cambridge Univ. Press.
Tang Min. 1994. *Zouxiang heping—Yu zhong shouji* (Heading toward Peace—Prison Jottings). Urumqi: Xinjiang Daxue chubanshe.
Wang Xiaoling. 1988. *Many Waters: Experiences of a Chinese Woman Prisoner of Conscience*. Hong Kong: Caritas Publishing.
Williams, Philip F., and Yenna Wu. 2004. *The Great Wall of Confinement: The Chinese Prison Camp Through Contemporary Fiction and Reportage*. Berkeley: Univ. of California Press.
Wu, Harry and Carolyn Wakeman. 1994. *Bitter Winds: A Memoir of My Years in China's Gulag*. New York: Wiley.
Zhang Xianliang. 1995. *Wode Putishu* (My Bodhi Tree). Beijing: Zuojia chubanshe.

Chapter Six

The Cocoons of Language

Torture, Voice, Event

R. Shareah Taleghani

OF "EXTRAORDINARY RENDITIONS"

The "Complaint and Demand for Jury Trial" in the case of Syrian-born, Canadian citizen *Maher Arar vs. U.S. Attorney General John Ashcroft (et al.)* contains a nearly ten-page subsection entitled "Facts Specific to the Plaintiff."[1] The *facts* of Arar's case are detailed in a day-by-day, sometimes hour-by-hour, linear narrative offered in the third person. The account begins with Arar's detention for "suspected terrorist activity" on September 26, 2002, at JFK by U.S. immigration officials. It describes his initial interrogation without legal representation by FBI and INS agents, and then it goes on to offer the details of the U.S. government decision to "render" him to Syria. We then read of Arar's "removal" first to Jordan where he was interrogated and beaten, and then to Syria. Accordingly, he spent almost a year in Syrian prisons, mostly in Palestine Division, an interrogation headquarters of the Syrian military intelligence, where he was tortured, physically and psychologically, forced to sign a false confession, and eventually released on October 5, 2003, after the Syrian Supreme State Security Court found no evidence of a connection between Arar and al-Qaeda.

The narrative of *Arar vs. John Ashcroft* details the detainee's initial experience at Palestine Division in the numbered passages typical to the standardized format of a legal document:

> 51. For the first 12 days of his detention in Syria, Mr. Arar was interrogated for 18 hours per day. He was also subjected to physical and psychological torture. Syrian security officers regularly beat him on the palms, the hips, and

117

lower back, using a two-inch thick electric cable. They also regularly struck Mr. Arar in the stomach, face, and back of the neck with their fists. The pain was excruciating. Mr. Arar pleaded with them to stop, to no avail.

52. Syrian security officers continued also subjected [sic] Mr. Arar to severe psychological torture. They placed him in a room where he could hear the screams of other detainees being tortured. They also repeatedly threatened to place him in the spine-breaking "chair," hang him upside down in a "tyre" and beat him, and give him electric shocks.

53. To minimize the torture, Mr. Arar falsely confessed, among other things, to having trained with terrorists in Afghanistan. In fact, Mr. Arar has never been to Afghanistan and has never been involved in terrorist activity. (16)

Three brief sections retrospectively account for Arar's first twelve days at Palestine Division. Accordingly, what is considered relevant for the purpose of documentation is the specific duration of interrogation (eighteen hours), the abbreviated details of his physical and psychological torture (the parts of the body where he is beaten is presented in list form, how he is forced to listen to the sounds of other prisoners being tortured), and the material instruments used (the 2-inch width of the cable, the threats of the "spine-breaking 'chair,'" the tire, electric shock). Almost as an addendum, the complaint reminds its readers directly that "the pain was excruciating" and that Arar pleaded with his torturers to stop.

Maher Arar's indifferently termed "removal" or "rendition" to Syria and his subsequent torture and imprisonment in one of the more infamous sites of Syria's "carceral archipelago" is but one example of a now well-documented, systematic, long-standing, and internationally condemned U.S. policy of "outsourcing" the torture of detainees both prior to and during the current "war on terrorism" (Foucault 1995, 297).[2] "Maher's Story," as it is titled and tabulated on his official website, belongs to the annals and corpus of the punitive practices *and* prison literatures of *both* the United States and Syria. However, I evoke it here neither merely as another reminder of routinized U.S. government complicity in, exploitation of, and deployment of torture in Syria or elsewhere abroad nor solely as an additional indication of the connective threads between transnational, globalized prison literatures and documentary human rights discourse.[3] Rather, I want to pause for a moment to consider the ways in which "Maher's Story," especially the "excruciating" details, the *facts specific to* his experience of torture, are concisely *rendered* in this particular legal document as well as another *rendition* of the events surrounding his case (discussed below). I do so in order to raise an initial point of comparison and contrast for the central focus of this chapter—the issue of torture of political detainees at the hands of agents of the Syrian state and the question of its depiction in contemporary Syrian prison literature.[4]

By examining a selection of works by Nabil Sulayman, Faraj Bayraqdar, and Hasiba 'Abdalrahman, I consider the various ways in which different authors represent, reify, displace, marginalize, and efface torture as an embodied and inscribed event—a recurrent event that under the normative parameters of the discourse of international law and human rights must be described in detail, catalogued, classified, and rendered categorically, rationally, and visibly *readable* through documentary and physical evidence as well as "I-witness" testimony. The portrayals of torture in these literary works offer alternative modes of depiction, a series of aesthetic interventions, through which Syrian authors mimic, traverse, and problematize the narrative boundaries of reportage common to descriptions of torture in human rights discourse. As will be shown below, a series of more recent literary works seek to blur the line between the truth effects offered by aesthetic representations of state-inflicted corporeal assault and the necessary truth claims made against the same political regime by those who have endured the most abject of human rights abuses.

"MAHER'S STORY": TORTURE AND THE NARRATIVE IMPERATIVE

"Maher's Story" articulates a series of truth claims not only about Arar's experience as a detainee both in the United States and in Syria, but also about the specificities of the forms of torture he was forced to endure. It is a story that also speaks to more abstract formulations of the relationships between the literal inscription of political power wrought by torture on the detained body and the question of the voice of an incarcerated subject. In *The Body in Pain*, one of the most widely disseminated theoretical analyses of torture, Elaine Scarry has outlined how torture simultaneously targets the voice and the body of the tortured in order to convert both into a form of political power. For her, torture and interrogation function to create a "fiction of power" that relies on the infliction of pain by the state. Accordingly, pain, including that caused by torture, is inherently resistant to language and actually destroys the human capacity for speech that would normally be a "source of self-extension" for the tortured subject (Scarry 1985, 54). In an exaggerated form, torture reenacts and objectifies externally pain's ability to destroy speech (20, 54). Together, although they are believed to be motivated by the need for information, torture and interrogation actually deconstruct the victim's voice and appropriate it as the political regime's own voice (20). In torture, according to Scarry, the pain inflicted is continually amplified to the degree that it becomes objectified and becomes visible to those outside the detainee's body. Pain's "totality" becomes "separated from the sufferer and referred to power, broken off from the body and attached instead to the regime" (56). In turn, this makes the regime and its power over the detainee's body "incontestably real."

The political regime that employs torture will deny the existence or use of torture, and hence its status as the cause of pain or injury inflicted on the body. Even in the midst of this denial, however, it is to the regime's benefit to have the fact of the use of torture made known in the wider public in order to generate fear of its use. Thus, victims who speak of torture can be enveloped in a kind of eternal catch-22. When they make their experiences of torture known so that they will not be forgotten, they also reinforce the "fiction of power" of the regime. That is one of the reasons why narrating torture remains fraught with ambiguity.

Although not without its critiques, Scarry's reading of the structure and function of torture offers an indication why victims of torture, whether through their own voices or through alternative channels, consistently confirm and reiterate the imperative to narrate the experience of torture.[5] The idea that "Maher's story" must be told and then heard or read, recognized, and responded to once again reiterates the link between "human rights discourses, norms, and instruments" and "an international commitment to narratability" when it comes to the question of rights claims (Schaffer and Smith 2004, 3). Above all, in order for Arar to seek justice, his story must be simultaneously narratable and readable.

The passage from the legal complaint cited above is but one, albeit abbreviated, version in which Arar's own voice is made absent and the narrative of his torture and interrogation is re-presented and re-framed by the requirements of legal documentation. Just as legal interpretative acts "signal and occasion the imposition of violence upon others," so too do the documentary demands of human rights claims visit a kind of narrative violence on the stories of those who have suffered from violations (Cover 1986, 1601). As a casualty of the U.S. policy of "extraordinary renditions" as well as torture at the hands of the Syrian state, Arar provides his story as testimony that instigates a rights claim. His act of witnessing must then be "coded to rights' instruments," and in this case, the experience of the first twelve days of torture is presented in less than 180 words (Schaffer and Smith 2004, 3). This and the other modes of telling through which the account of Arar's torture and detention have unfolded demonstrate once again that "human rights in general, and human rights law in particular, can be productively formulated in terms of narrative genres and narrative voices" that not only necessarily differ from one context to another but also inevitably reflect gaps in their representation (Slaughter 1997, 407).

The divergent forms and voices of "Maher's story" include a personal statement offered to international media on November 4, 2003, shortly after Arar's release.[6] In the following passage taken from that statement, Arar himself, in the direct intimacy of the first person, testifies to and describes the forms of torture he endured from the second day he spent at the interrogation division:

> Interrogations are carried out in different rooms. One tactic they use is to question prisoners for two hours, and then put them in a waiting room, so they can hear the others screaming, and then bring them back to continue the interrogation.
> The cable is a black electrical cable, about two inches thick. They hit me with it everywhere on my body. They mostly aimed for my palms, but sometimes missed and hit my wrists. . . . Interrogators constantly threatened me with the metal chair, tire and electric shocks.
> The tire is used to restrain prisoners while they torture them with beating on the sole of their feet. I guess I was lucky, because they put me in the tire, but only as a threat. I was not beaten while in the tire. They used the cable on the second and third day, and after that mostly beat me with their hands, hitting me in the stomach and on the back of my neck, and slapping me on the face.[7]

In general terms, this second version of Arar's description of his torture repeats many of the same facts as the first version offered in the complaint. Yet, in this case, Arar does not directly mention his pain, but he reminds us of the physical effects of torture and the fear it elicits from the detained subject. In doing so, he emphasizes both his physical and psychological "vulnerability" as a detainee and calls on his audience to "recognize" how his human rights have been violated through selective details (Turner 2006). Thus, for example, he notes that his wrists were "sore and red for three weeks," that "my skin turned blue for two or three weeks but there was no bleeding," and that "I was ready to confess to anything if it would stop." With the emphatic rhetorical effect of repetition, his description also focuses on the soundscape of the space of interrogation—especially the fact that he could hear "other prisoners being tortured, and screaming and screaming." Noticeable as well is Arar's oscillation between general, explicative observations on the space and instruments of torture at Palestine Division and his description, chronologically, of his own, individual experience. He feels the need both to comment on the tactics and spaces used by interrogators in general; in doing so, he speaks not only for his individual case but also for a detained human collectivity.

The forms, instruments, tools, or vehicles of torture that Arar describes are more than familiar to Syrian political detainees and have consistently appeared as the subjects of description in many works of Syrian prison literature since the 1970s and even earlier. In 1983, at the height of what *Middle East Watch* termed the "Great Repression" of both Islamist and secular opposition to the regime of Hafez al-Asad, Amnesty International reported that as many as thirty-eight different forms of torture were systematically being used against political detainees.[8] Although Syria's accession to the UN Convention Against Torture occurred on August 19, 2004, as of 2005, despite several prisoner amnesties following the death of al-Asad, torture in myriad forms is still "widely reported."[9]

Both Arar's statement and the passage cited from the legal complaint hint at only a small part of an extensive lexicon of torture that exists as part of the punitive practices of the Syrian state: the tire (*dulab*) and the chair (*al-kursi al-almani*) as well as electric shock and beatings with cables. Other accounts speak of the *falaqa* (beating on the soles of the feet) or the *bisat al-rih* (translated as the "flying carpet" when a prisoner is strapped to a flat sheet of wood and subjected to beatings and electric shock) (*Middle East Watch* 1991, 149–51). However, just as torture "lacks a stable definition," the explanation of these terms and the ways in which they are detailed constantly vary from the testimony of one prisoner to another and from one work of prison literature to another (Posner 2004, 291).[10] Despite, or perhaps precisely *because of*, experienced and descriptive discrepancies, the imperative to narrate that exists in the telling or recounting of being tortured stands as an attempt to subvert one of the primary functions of torture itself. If torture is "paradigmatic in its implementation as a tool to destroy the speaking subject," then "Maher's story," along with much of the work of human rights organizations is emblematic of the necessity of the restoration of the voice of the tortured after the work of torture is finished (Slaughter 1997, 407).

In many ways, particularly when it comes to the representation of torture, works of prison literature are easily interpreted as narratives of witnessing that offer the same impulse to restore and render visible the voice of the tortured seen in the different versions of Arar's story. Yet, the modes and stylistics that authors employ when attempting to inscribe torture vary greatly and therefore offer far different effects than what can be gleaned from the two passages taken from Arar's case. From social realism to poetic memoir, these authors demonstrate both the imperative to narrate *and* the need to question and efface the event of torture through the stories they tell.

TORTURE AND THE "IDEOLOGY OF PRISON"

While the issue of torture is at the center of the controversy over Maher Arar's story, in many works of contemporary Syrian prison literature, torture, physical abuse, and corporeal punishment are not the primary focus of the depictions of the experience of the political prisoner. Some authors, such as the short story writer Ibrahim Samuil, marginalize or avoid entirely direct depictions of acts of torture and the immediate suffering that results from them.[11] In Samuil's works torture is almost entirely absent but exists as a threat to his protagonists that both disappears from the main body of his short narratives and remains hovering at the edge of the text in the mind of the reader.[12] By sidelining descriptions of torture, Samuil's tales focus on how his characters perceive a loss of humanity that is caused by the system and routine of detention as a whole.

This is not to suggest, of course, that torture is not represented in Syrian prison literature. One paradigmatic representation of torture in modern Syrian prison literature appears in writer and critic Nabil Sulayman's novel *The Prison (al-Sijn,* 1972). A social realist text, *The Prison* tells the story of the heroic Wahab, a young man who is arrested, tortured, and imprisoned along with a large number of his colleagues who belong to an unnamed, underground, leftist political organization in the 1950s.[13] Sulayman's novel follows a common plot pattern of many prison narratives. It begins with Wahab's arrest after months of being a fugitive. It then moves on to depict his torture and interrogation, his solitary confinement, and finally his entry into the collective, routinized life of a communal cell.

In the 1970s, Sulayman's advocacy of social realism and "commitment literature" bordered on the "totalitarian" (Firat 2007).[14] *The Prison* presents a portrait of the endurance and resistance of both the individual, "committed" political prisoner and a group of political detainees that fall within the parameters of what Yasin al-Hajj Salih has called the "ideology of prison."[15] Shaped by this ideology, much of earlier Syrian and Arabic prison literature generally is plagued by the perceived need on the part of authors to represent resistance to a political regime's oppression solely as a collective, coherent, and unwaveringly heroic project. In the case of Sulayman's novel, Wahab successfully endures his own torture, does not give away any information (despite the fact that other characters have informed on him), and then easily adapts to prison life.

In *The Prison,* Sulayman deploys a heavily detailed, realist style of depiction that both frequently evokes the narrative style of traditional human rights reportage of torture and leaves little doubt as to the validity or authenticity of the description offered. Through Wahab's story, he serializes the forms of torture that his hero must face. Seemingly, no form of torture is left unrepresented in the novel. Yet, the protagonist never gives in to the pain inflicted upon his body. Wahab is beaten, whipped, flogged in the "tire," forced to endure electric shock treatment, deprived of sleep, left in solitary confinement, exposed to sound and light torture, and finally raped by his torturers. In addition, the interrogators threaten members of his family and friends. In one scene after another in the first part of the novel, Wahab suffers but resists, and in the end, he triumphs against the systematic torture used by the regime.

An example of Sulayman's representation of Wahab's torture and his unwavering resistance to being turned into an informer can be seen when Wahab is taken to the "inner salon" and faces torture by the "tire":

> They tossed him down on the ground, and one of them stroked his head with the edge of his shoe, unkindly. From the corner, another rolled a tire out that was stopped by the body of Wahab who had begun to feel a separation from what was around him, little by little. He wanted to watch them. They put his legs in the tire, then they rolled him up well, and pushed in his head. . . . He discovered that his flexibility was great. He began to be rolled now with the tire. The game made him laugh, just as it caused his heart to bleed. The laughter that didn't surpass his lips provoked the rage of the men. They all took up the canes, and began to try to beat out one another to get to him. In the beginning, his feet were preferred, but then his entire body began to attract them. (Sulayman 1999, 19–20)

Momentarily after this session of torture in the tire, the sergeant prepares to leave, telling the rest of the men that they must get him to confess or "finish" him. The rest of the torture that takes place in this session is not described as Wahab lowers his eyelids, and then the next section picks up with an interruption in the process of his torture as Wahab reflects on his situation and the need for him not to give in to the torture and confess (21).

Sulayman's portrait of resistance is replayed with each session and form of torture. In this scene, as another officer enters the room, Wahab thinks to himself:

> He was enduring in order to keep safe all he knew of the secret hiding places and the meetings of the organization: if you scream, they'll insult you. If you cry, this is not a laudable beginning. Just gnash your teeth. Don't believe the claims of the doctors, for those teeth of the bourgeoisie are damaged by pressure. Be neutral, and with that the game will end to your advantage . . . the pain in his back and hips increased as he sprawled out, (pain) from everything that had been caused by the canes and fists of theirs. (21–22)

Wahab's will to keep silent, to elude confession, and to avoid informing on his comrades remains seamlessly intact throughout the novel. *The Prison* offers no echoes of Maher Arar's false confession under torture; instead, for the "leftist" hero Wahab, the torturers' attempt at appropriating the voice of their victim for the power of the state appears to have failed. Yet, at the same time, the rendition of torture provided here evades the kind of questioning of the problem of describing torture that emerges in other textual examples.

THE BETRAYALS OF SILENCE: TRUTH CLAIMS AND THE SELF-INTERROGATIVE

An interrogation of the problem of description, not just of torture, but also of the entire experience of detention, is at the heart of Faraj Bayraqdar's poetic prison memoir, *The Betrayals of Language and Silence (Khiyanat al-Lugha wa al-Samt)*.[16] In the different fragments of writing that constitute this text, Faraj Bayraqdar provides numerous descriptions of the torture and cruel and unusual punishment that he witnessed and suffered under during his more than thirteen years of detention. A hybrid narrative that appears at different times as memoir, journal, poetry collection, eyewitness testimonial, and direct political indictment, the focus in many of these passages is not on Bayraqdar's own torture or suffering, but the physical and psychological agony experienced by his fellow prisoners.[17]

Bayraqdar's meditations on his own personal suffering under physical torture are brief and come at the beginning of the memoir when he describes his interrogation at Palestine Division. Like Maher Arar and Sulayman's character Wahab, Bayraqdar includes in his description a list of the tools, techniques, and instruments of torture, yet he does so with a difference. As he attempts to recount the methods of his torture, including being "ghosted" on a ladder (strapped to the ladder, hung upside down, and whipped), he directly questions both the believability of what actually happened and as his reader directly to "try to find an explanation for this terrifying, engineered madness" (Bayraqdar 2006, 28). In this section entitled "On the Brink of Insight," he writes:

> What will you say to people when they ask you about that?
> You will be silent. Because you are sure that no one will believe a single word you say.
> In the best of circumstances they will consider your words simply delusions or waking nightmares; it is not proper for you to remain under their force.
> Can you be faithful to your duty of the necessity of exposing the entirety of the experience, from the first rattle to the last hell?

Bayraqdar's depiction vacillates between his attempt to describe the instruments of torture and their effects, his direct pleas to both himself and a distant audience for an explanation of what is happening to his body, and his own personal *recognition* of the possibility that what he is describing will not be taken as truth, and thus be seen as something beyond the realm of believability by those who might be reading or listening. Here, as well as elsewhere in his memoir, the poet reflects on the dilemma of remaining "faithful" to the need to "expose" the reality of his experiences while coping with the predicament of his perception of their potential un-describability. It is thus that he evokes his sense of betrayal—not just his betrayal at the hands of agents of the Syrian state, but the betrayals of the language at his disposal and the betrayals of a subjugating but at times unavoidable silence.

Bayraqdar unveils his memoirs as a deliberately unedited and ambivalent re-cognition of his imprisoned past. The published fragments of *The Betrayals of Language and Silence* stand as his attempt at a "recovery of something once known," a series of scenes of vulnerability that must be recognized by others (Cave 2002, 33). Yet, it is a recovery that is "disquieting" for both Bayraqdar and his readers as he himself interrogates his own representation of the torture of his own body (2). In a plea to the extreme limits of the imagination of his audience, he attempts to describe the other modes of torture, "the mangling" and the "German chair" that he and his fellow detainees were forced to endure. At the same time, he grapples with the realization that his words, even with their conscious poetic resonance or the aid of a picture or a diagram, will never fully capture either the atrocious absurdity of his torturers' tools and methods or his psychological experience of the moment of being tortured. He writes:

> A tyrannical chair . . . deaf. . . . This chair, that they call the "German chair" is a curse. A rabid curse that takes pride in the paralysis of your hands and the crushing of your spinal cord, and that grants you, finally, if they want, the blessing of castration.
> You have now paused on the brink of insight, and ascertained, with sufficient depth, that *this reality is not real at all.*
> But . . . how do you convince people of that when you yourself are aware of the difficulty of absorbing this ambiguity, and these stark contradictions in your naïve linguistic game?! (Bayraqdar 2006, 29; emphasis mine)

As in the section cited earlier, here, Bayraqdar's use of the second person raises an ambiguous connection between himself and his audience; is the "you" of the passage Bayraqdar addressing himself or is it his bid to force his reader to recognize his vulnerable position as a tortured subject, to oblige the reader to put herself in his place? The narrative both attempts a description of other instruments of torture, especially the "chair," while at the same time undermining, momentarily, the veracity of the depiction by telling us that the reality he describes is not real at all.

In the same fragment, as if the narrative offered has somehow failed to explain the experience fully, the former political prisoner leaves an extended endnote: a numbered list of definitions of types of torture used in Syrian prisons which is headed by the title "Simplified explanations approximating some of the means of torture." This list of a specific lexicon of torture appears, at first glance, to be like those found in the reports of human rights organizations, but Bayraqdar offers it in his memoir as a marginalized addendum.[18] Despite the fact that these forms of torture have already been mentioned in the narrative, he provides re-definitions of "the ghost on the ladder," "the mangling," "the tire," "the electricity," and "the German chair" in a direct, stark, and simplified language. For example, the entry entitled "the mangling" states: "this process is implemented by stretching the prisoner out on his back, then a chair is placed in the area of the pelvis, then the legs are made to enter, after folding them and fastening them between the legs of the chair, so the legs become doubled at the knee and opened at the top" (30).

The interrogative narrative reflection in which he himself acknowledges the barriers to "convince" his audience of the truth of his claims is juxtaposed with the explanatory footnotes of forms of torture. It is this element of contrast that gives an indication of the discrepancies and gaps inherent in the imperative to narrate that lies at the heart of human rights claims. Bayraqdar resorts to both poetic prose and a footnoted catalogue, and therefore alludes to the fact that his aesthetic interventions against the human rights politics of the Syrian state not only carry gaps but also cannot be confined to one genre or form of narrative.

THE COCOONS OF LANGUAGE

While Nabil Sulayman's novel *The Prison* serves as an example of a traditional social realist text that presents the protagonist as heroically resisting torture in all its detail, and Faraj Bayraqdar's memoir juxtaposes the definitional catalogue of forms of torture with an interrogation of the believability of torture's description, former political prisoner and current human rights activist Hasiba 'Abdalrahman offers a markedly different portrayal of torture. In 1999, eight years after her release from a prolonged period of imprisonment, Hasiba 'Abdalrahman published her first novel, *al-Sharnaqa*, (The Cocoon). Based on diaries and other writings from her prison experience but nonetheless avowedly *fictional* in the author's own terms, *al-Sharnaqa* can be considered a landmark work not only because it is the first novel about the experience of detention in Syria written by a former female political prisoner, but also because of its fragmented, asymmetrical structure and its non-linear, polyphonic narrative.[19] The unstable stylistics of *al-Sharnaqa* mark a significant departure from the seemingly "transparent" social realism of an earlier generation of novels about political detention, such as Sulayman's *The Prison*, that formed the early corpus of contemporary Syrian prison literature.

When it first circulated in Syria, the novel caused a scandal; 'Abdalrahman was accused of airing the dirty laundry of the Syrian opposition. One of the primary objections to the text was that it depicted an abject lack of solidarity among political prisoners, but the author was also criticized for her implicit and explicit representations of the rape of female detainees, female sexuality, and the misogyny of Syria's political elite. *Al-Sharnaqa*, in many ways, represents the beginnings of a process of deconstruction of the "ideology of prison." 'Abdalrahman's gendered rendering of the prison experience is far from more traditional conceptions of a *riwaya nidhaliya* (a novel of struggle or resistance), and she herself has observed that it is impossible to portray "heroes in the age of defeats."[20]

Yet, it is not solely the scandal of discord depicted in the novel and its reception that makes the text significant. *Al-Sharnaqa* offers a distinct mode of the representation of the *advent* of the torture inflicted by agents of the state on the bodies of political detainees while simultaneously connecting this act of bodily punishment and pain to other major *events* in twentieth-century Syrian history. Most strikingly, the novel stands as one of a few published Syrian literary works that depict, even if only briefly and allusively, the siege of the city of Hama by the Syrian military in February 1982—an event that included a declaration of war against the Syrian state by Islamist oppositional forces and the subsequent massacre at the hand of government troops of what is estimated to be between 5,000 to 10,000 or more people. Hama 1982 has been selectively erased in the rhetoric of more official versions of contemporary Syrian history and, in many ways, remains one of the key "silences" of contemporary Syrian literature (Kahf 2001, 229).[21]

In contrast to the examples above, *al-Sharnaqa* offers a juxtaposed representation of torture and historical event through the voice of the main character, Kawthar, as a detained yet persistently speaking subject. 'Abdalrahman attempts to disrupt the "language-destroying" capacity of torture through her textual rendition of the interrogation experience, and she layers the crime of torture against the individual body of a female detainee upon the atrocities of other events—in particular the crime of a massacre committed against the collective body of the Syrian nation. In scripting both torture and massacre against the "longue durée," the tedious yet contentious routine of imprisonment as well as a broader vision of modern Syrian political history, the author presents language and voice within the narrative imaginary of her characters as a cocoon. Ambiguously spun throughout and around the text and linking characters and events in an erratically constructed "inaugural" continuum, this cocoon of language is posed as sanctuary from the physical and psychological suffering imposed on the political prisoner (Derrida 11). At the same time, the novel defers the possibility that the chrysalis of political consciousness of the characters that led them to imprisonment will result in a positive or productive individual and collective metamorphosis.

Divided into two parts with multiple chapters, *Al-Sharnaqa* begins with the arrest, solitary confinement, interrogation, and torture of Kawthar, a member of an unnamed "leftist organization" and the central but not the only narrator of the novel. This is followed by a second chapter that offers a series of her delusional "visions" during and in the aftermath of the "sessions" of torture she endures. The initial prison of interrogation, the two other main women's prisons, and other sites of detention in the novel are never named nor are their precise locations ever given. Because Kawthar has been detained before, there is a constant vacillation between the time of her current detention and her memories of both her previous arrests and other moments in her personal past.

As the novel unfolds and Kawthar is transferred from the interrogation division to the first women's prison and then a second one, the narrative not only offers descriptions of the space of detention from Kawthar's point of view, but also slips into the stories of other female prisoners who are variously divided into the categories of "leftist"/"Marxist," "fundamentalist," or "criminal." A cohesive sense of linear time is lost as the text presents a depiction of Kawthar's movements between communal cells, the quotidian banalities of prison life, her constant memories of life "outside," and the physical and verbal arguments between inmates over space, material objects, and political and religious beliefs. Kawthar's own narrative coincides and entangles with the individual, personal histories of different characters, but she is eventually taken back to interrogation in order to face another "decisive battle" with her interrogators ('Abdalrahman 1999, 107). Following this, she is brought to a different women's prison, and under the effects of the torture she endured, she suffers from nightmares, including one in which she disjointedly envisions images of her own rape by a soldier in a city in which a massacre has taken place—a city that can be inferred from the text to be Hama.

In the second part, the text vacillates between Kawthar's voice and the voices of other characters depicted not only through dialogue but also through the metafictional references to their diaries and other papers that are included as part of the over-arching structure of the narrative. The novel dwells on both the states of interpersonal conflict between the different women that is described in the text as a continual "state of war" and the fraught relationships within the political organizations that they are involved in. Because of their lack of solidarity and the continual tension, Kawthar eventually isolates herself from the collective life of the prison and literally describes herself as having entered a "cocoon" (263). Kawthar's cocoon in the second half of the novel is one of imagination, memory, and fantasy that serves as a refuge not from torture and bodily pain but from the ongoing arguments between prisoners. In the end, while dozens of other prisoners have been released, it is unclear if Kawthar has been freed or if she is merely once-again hallucinating in a solitary cell as she narrates the conclusion of the novel in a dream-like state.

Throughout much of *al-Sharnaqa*, the presence of torture is indicated briefly in a distanced and abstract fashion. These indications emerge through the direct use of the term "*ta'adhib*" (torture) and its derivatives—a female prisoner is awakened by a nightmare of "torture," another detainee is said to have given information about the hiding places of the organization after being "tortured," the women hear that a comrade has died "under torture." The description of torture figures most directly in the novel toward the end of the first chapter and in the second chapter when Kawthar endures a series of torture "sessions."[22] In these two chapters, the relationship between torture and 'Abdalrahman's creation of a "cocoon of language" comes prominently into play.

In the scenes of *al-Sharnaqa* representing Kawthar's interrogation, torture's capacity to destroy language, to deconstruct the detainee's voice, and to cause the obliteration of the content of his/her consciousness is seemingly demonstrated by the disintegration of linear narrative, the overwhelming presence of disconnected imagery and dialogue as well as the fading of realist detail in the description of pain. Yet, just as the fracturing of linear narrative does not occur merely under the effect of a character's torture, Kawthar's "world, self, and voice" are not entirely "lost" in the pain of torture nor are the "objects of consciousness . . . swept away and annihilated" (Scarry 1985, 35, 32). Despite their fragmented nature, Kawthar's streaming meditations, memories, and hallucinations partially reverse the function of torture as they work, even if in mutated form, to restore her voice as an indirect "denunciation" and "diminution" of the pain being inflicted on her body (50). Though her voice is seemingly ignored by her torturers, its textual presence within the novel reveals that the process of torture and interrogation has not completely erased her capacity for speech and therefore for her self-extension.

Instead, 'Abdalrahman offers a *surplus*, an *excess*, of articulation in depicting Kawthar's reaction to the torture of her own body. Kawthar's voice, her reflections, and her fantasies, surface to interrupt and efface the presence of the interrogator and the advent and event of torture. Thus, her textually rendered speech acts literally flood the narrative and serve to "occup(y) a space much larger than the body," her body in pain (33). In this sense, unlike the once-silenced subject of Scarry's analysis whose recourse to expression comes *after* the infliction of corporeal pain, 'Abdalrahman's tortured subject always remains in the process of speaking-the-self. Kawthar does not have to wait for the structures of traditional human rights reportage to perform and articulate a disruptive and necessarily distorted but nonetheless generative act of witnessing.

In the first chapter, while she is forced to wait in solitary, Kawthar's recollections move backward and forward in time, her story vacillates between the "enchanted world" of her childhood, her family's poverty, her teenage love of literature, references to coup d'états and war, her growing political awareness as a secondary student, and her first sexual relationship at the age of nineteen. She is abruptly brought back to the present time of the novel by the sound of bowls clanging in the hall (a sign of the quotidian routines of incarceration) and eventually, the voice of the prison guard re-intrudes on her musings. As Kawthar is confronted with the interrogator's questions, the narrative begins to focus on sounds, voices, and her memories of her grandfather. As the physical torture begins, what actually occurs to her body under torture is *not* precisely described; rather, the "atrocious" acts committed by the interrogator are referred to as "the bats of night, twittered in the sky, jumped over my body, tore me to pieces" ('Abdalrahman 1999, 24). While the voices of her torturers occasionally surface in Kawthar's narrative, her voice, in the first person, reflects on her relationship with her grandfather, his ghostly presence in her memory as providing a kind of mediation between her and the cruelty of her interrogators, and the protective amulet he had given her that still remains in her possession at the moment of her torture. Although the voices of those inflicting pain punctuate the text, the actions of the torturers are referenced in a figural rather than literal sense not only through the image of "bats" attacking her body but also through references to entering a vaguely defined "swamp." Although the "bodily event" of torture and its resulting pain are acknowledged and represented in the text, their presence becomes subsumed, undermined, and eventually ex-punged through the character's voice—a voice that cannot be "bypassed" by the reader (Scarry 1985, 7).

As Kawthar is left to recover from the session of torture, she does not contemplate the pain of her injuries; instead, her self-expression focuses on her encounters with her political comrades and her last meeting with her lover ('Abdalrahman 1999, 25–26). Only occasionally does the reality of detention intrude on her thoughts, reflected through the mention of the coughs of men and women in adjacent cells. Yet, in the midst of her reflec-tions on her lover, the narrative shifts back to the present when the interroga-tor tells her to enter another room. Here, however, the chapter does not end with a description of the torture she endures, but with Kawthar entering into another zone of hallucinations and dreams that will serve as the framing structure of the next chapter.

The second chapter opens with Kawthar's "first vision"; she offers a deluge of narrative imagery in the form of delusions, dreams, and nightmares that, despite their sometimes jarring and frightening imagery, initially dis-place the description of actual torture: "A towering mountain, the ghosts of dogs pursuing me, I run alone, I search for a point of balance, gravity flees, I search for it, I tumble . . . the soil of the earth seizes me without guidance . . . awe . . . fear . . . I scream: this is my bed, in its place, the jar of water is just as it was . . . I drink . . . I go back to sleep again (27; ellipses in the original). The next vision begins with a scene of war and then shifts back to images of Kawthar's childhood and the interpretation of her dreams, previous and present, as she begins to enter a state of "waking dreams"(29). Briefly moving beyond the "boundaries" of her current place in prison, her mind returns to the present in anticipation of the return of the interrogator and the forms of torture she will endure.

When another "session" begins, the description of the means of torture is more elaborate and is interspersed, yet again, with the voices of the interrogators. Facing a series of questions, Kawthar's external silence is mediated by her brief interiorized descriptions of what she perceives. She refuses to provide the information requested even when tortured by electric shock. Silent in providing answers to her interrogators' questions though she may be, she is not represented as mute in the text:

> I run . . . hop, jump like a skillful athlete. . . . Sports are useful amongst torturers, and the lashes follow me . . .
> "Skin her (alive). . . . Your goal is resistance?! . . . Take this."
> "Oh God . . . Oh Muhammad, but . . . "
> The damned rag . . . smothers my voice . . . oxygen . . . air . . . the damned rag wasn't there. . . . I was screaming . . . breathing but now, damn.
> "She fainted . . . "
> "The electricity will wake her up . . . "
> Alone I scream . . . voices in every direction. . . . I conceal myself . . . I hide . . . but I don't know where!!! (34; ellipses in original)

In this passage, the reality of Kawthar's torture emerges to the surface of the narrative as the instruments of torture—electricity, scissors, "the chair"—are named. Yet, Kawthar seeks to "hide" or "conceal" herself, and she chooses to do so in a cocoon of expression. Just as she begins to descriptively articulate her experience of torture without recourse to alternative symbolic imagery, her focus shifts and she begins to create her own "fiction" of power. Given a piece of paper she is told to write her personal information and a confession. After initially writing her real name, she starts to compose a fake story about her identity.

The narrative then disintegrates into a series of loose associations of voices and images in which her torturers as literal figures are rendered more and more absent, and Kawthar experiences a disconnected series of flashbacks of past conversations: conversations with her mother and discussions with her comrades about their organization's activities. The few acts of torture referenced in the narrative are referred to figuratively, such as "scorpions . . . the sting of scorpions . . . poured . . . over my ear" (34).

Several more sessions of interrogation and requisite respites from the torture occur as she recollects conversations from her childhood and her more recent past, attempts to recall her lover's face, condemns the sexism of both her torturers and the male members of her own organization, and ruminates on human nature and the breadth of human history of which her detention, her torture, and *other* events are a part. Framed as feverish delusion, it is unclear if this continual reel of unconnected fragments are a creation of her imagination or if they are part of her past reality. But throughout this jumbled excess of imagery, these reflections emanating through Kawthar's own voice dominate the narrative and act as a kind of cocoon-like refuge while the actual act and effect of torture fades into the background and only emerges through an occasional reference to pain or the voice of the interrogator.

In *al-Sharnaqa*, the torture of Kawthar is but one event among many in different textual levels in the novel—a reference to the Battle of Karbala, to a coup d'état, to a wave of mass detentions and arbitrary executions, to an attempted assassination, to the Gulf War of 1991 is layered over by the discovery and disclosure of a prisoner's diaries, a failed hunger strike, the birth of a child in prison, a "battle" over space or an old army blanket in a communal cell, the arrival in prison of an Egyptian actress accused of smuggling drugs. 'Abdalrahman positions and occasionally privileges the more everyday happenings, past and present, in the individual lives of imprisoned characters *against*, *through*, and *within* a simultaneous chronicling of political-historical events that might mark a time line of larger Syrian, Islamic, Arab, and global history. Through such juxtapositions, the text disturbs the idea that "only certain events have the power to interpellate witnesses" (Douglass and Vogler 2003, 22). Each event in the novel, be it quotidian or geopolitical, "testifies not so much to what it represents as to what it reveals, not so much to what it is as to what it unleashes" (Nora 1998, 432). Throughout the narrative, each event "is subsumed by its (own) reverberations," and because of this, the "constellations" of events that 'Abdalrahman presents momentarily appear "without theoretical limits and boundaries" and "different levels of meaning overlap" to such a degree that the reader can become lost in a textual labyrinth (432, 433). The reader, like the historian and like the characters represented in the novel, is thus compelled to attempt to "distinguish among events, to differentiate the networks and levels to which they belong, and to reconstitute the lines along which they are connected and engender one another" (Foucault 1980, 114).

While a sense of linearity dissolves with the depiction of the effects of the bodily event of torture in the second chapter, Kawthar's so called "attacks of the imagination," her dreams, and her hallucinations also extend to the cryptic portrayal of a siege of a city. 'Abdalrahman never directly names the cities she describes in her narrative, but the reference here provides an allusion to Hama and the resistance of its people to French rule during the Mandate period in Syria ('Abdalrahman 1999, 41, 42).[23] In one section, Kawthar is shown moving around this same city, which is now surrounded and occupied by unnamed military forces. With the narrative structure echoing the same fragmentation and sense of disjointedness as the scenes depicting torture, as she wanders the streets, she is "pursued" by the sound of stray bullets, witnesses "streets of dead without burial or prayer" alongside "parts of children dangling" and hears the "wails of the women" (42).

The city Hama is not named and no reference is made to the date of 1982; yet, it is clear that Kawthar is envisioning a military occupation and destruction of the city as well as the massacre of a civilian population. Although the lack of specific dates and proper names in the portrayal of the event described as well as Kawthar's delusional state places any confirmation of its "reality" in doubt, the passage is situated in conjunction with and thereby is linked to her torture. The injuries suffered by Kawthar's body are thus displaced unto the injuries afflicted on a collective population by the military forces occupying the city.

Later in the novel, after Kawthar is tortured once again and has returned to a communal cell of the women's prison, she suffers from nightmares. In the midst of such nightmares, echoing the previous portrayal of a massacre and directly intertwining it with images of detention, Kawthar remembers the same images of corpses, death, and bullets as she is pursued by an individual soldier (129). She cries out for her mother as the soldier attempts to rape her although the actual rape is not depicted in the narrative. As the passage continues, it is revealed that Kawthar is dreaming as the other prisoners discuss what might have happened to her or what she had seen. As she fades in and out of her nightmarish state, the narrative abruptly shifts, and Kawthar senses her own "inner fear"—not of being killed or of being raped but that her lover will soon be detained (131).

Throughout *al-Sharnaqa*, brief references are made to the occupation, destruction, and mass death of the "closed city," the epithet that 'Abdalrahman uses to indicate Hama. In the examples cited here, Kawthar's individual torture, along with the possible detention and torture of others, is mapped onto the representations of another event, a crime against a collectivity of bodies—the "corpses" lining the streets of the city. Additionally, in the second passage, the atrocity of mass killings is dislodged onto an act of sexual violence against Kawthar as an individual through the brief inscription of rape. The same surplus of language that is an inherent characteristic of Kawthar's nightmarish states and that provides a cocoon of refuge from torture produces another moment of uneasy witnessing of yet another event. In *al-Sharnaqa*, the siege of the city of Hama, like the torture of Kawthar, is scripted as an event that appears to be beyond the realm of what can be grasped by one's imagination. Yet, torture, siege, massacre, and other events unfold, interconnect, and are inscribed in the precarious continuum of the narrative.

Through the destabilizing stories of her characters in *al-Sharnaqa*, through their own reflections, Hasiba 'Abdalrahman offers the uneven fabrication of a cocoon of language, of speech and voice against the silencing produced by torture and other events. Transgressing, at least in part, official

Syrian state discourse, the author's modes of representing such events serve as a reminder that "every event, among speakers, is tied to an excess of speech . . . an appropriation 'outside the truth' of the speech of the other . . . that makes it signify differently" (Rancière 1994, 30). Kawthar is depicted as spinning portions of her own cocoon as a possible sanctuary and type of vindication in and through the act of speaking and narrating, even if such an act comes in fragmented form. Yet, in the context of the ambiguous end of the novel when it is unclear when or if she has been or will be released from prison, this cocoon, as such, can also only be seen as the unfulfilled potential of transformative liberation. There is, in the end, no obvious metamorphosis for Kawthar, and the novel provides indications that her cocoon of language could perhaps become another mode of detention. It is, after all, according to the author of *al-Sharnaqa*, impossible to portray "heroes in the age of defeats."

NOTES

1. *Maher Arar v. John Ashcroft et al.* United States District Court Eastern District of New York, January 22, 2004, http://www.ccrny.org/v2/legal/september_11th/sept11Article.asp?ObjID=zPvu7s2XVJ&Content=377. All translations from the Arabic are my own unless otherwise indicated. I have used a simplified version of the IJMES system of Arabic to English transliteration by eliminating most diacritical markers. I thank Philip Kennedy, Elias Khoury, Kristen Ross, Faedah Totah, and Leena Dallasheh as well as several members of NYU's Department of Middle East and Islamic Studies Dissertation Writing Group led by Michael Gilsenan and Khaled Fahmy for comments on an early draft of this chapter.

2. For a discussion of U.S. outsourcing of torture, see, for example, Mayer 2005. See also Patten 2005.

3. See Arar's official website, http://www.maherarar.ca/.

4. I use the term "prison literature" (*adab al-sijn* or *adab al-sujun*) inclusively to refer to those texts that have been written and produced in, about, or through the experience of detention.

5. Scarry has been criticized for assuming an "already constituted subject" in her analysis due in part to the archival materials (human rights reports) she uses to draw her conclusions (Crystal Parikh, personal communication). Sáez also calls into question Scarry's notion that torture destroys language and the victim's capacity to speak by examining the problem of false confession and deliberate misinformation provided by victims of torture. As noted above, Arar, in fact, has admitted that he signed a false confession. In addition, as will be discussed below in the examination of Hasiba's Abdalrahman's *al-Sharnaqa*, the recounting of the experience of torture can also reveal an excess or surplus of language at the moment and in the aftermath of torture's affliction.

6. Another more detailed account of the events of Arar's case is offered on the website; this account provides "Maher's Story" in narrative segments separated under dated headings. See http://www.maherarar.ca/mahers%20story.php. *60 Minutes* also conducted a lengthy interview with Arar. See http://www.cbsnews.com/stories/2004/01/21/60II/main594974.shtml. Having filed the complaint on behalf of Arar, the Center for Constitutional Rights has also created a narrated video summarizing Arar's case, including a voice-over by Arar himself. See their website at http://www.ccrny.org/v2/legal/september_11th/sept11Article.asp?ObjID=zPvu7s2XVJ&Content=377. Retrieved September 12, 2007.

7. See http://www.cbc.ca/news/background/arar/arar_statement.html.

8. Amnesty International, "Syria: Torture by the Security Forces," September 1984: 18–21. See also Appendix A in *Middle East Watch* 1991.

9. See, for example, Amnesty International's "Syria" in their *Annual Report* for 2005, http://web.amnesty.org/report2005/syr-summary-eng. See also a public statement issued by Amnesty International on September 23, 2004, regarding Syria's accession to the convention: http://web.amnesty.org/library/index/engMDE240692004?open&of=eng-2d2.

10. A consistent, internationally, and/or universally accepted definition of torture has been a source of debate since the 1948 UN Declaration on Human Rights as well as the UN Convention Against Torture and Other Cruel, Inhuman, or Degrading Punishment adopted by the general assembly in 1984; the question of what torture *is* has also reemerged in the United States over the use of torture in the so-called war on terrorism. For more recent discussions of the debates over the definition of torture, in addition to Posner, see also Levison and Parry.

11. The absence or marginalization of the subject of torture in Samuil's numerous prison stories has been noted by numerous critics, including Mamduh Adwan, Isabella D'Afflito, and Miriam Cooke. When depicted, physical punishment is usually only shown indirectly.

12. Other writers, such as Ghassan al-Jaba'i, choose to render their depictions of torture through an allegorical lens in which the pain caused by torture is narrated in the voice of a humanized, but inanimate object. For example, in his short story "The Barrel," the narrator of the tale is a barrel that was used for smuggling weapons and that has been "detained" as a political prisoner.

13. Although published in 1972, the novel has been read as depicting the imprisonment of secular political opponents under the Shishakli regime (1951–54). However, the only major reference to specific historical events in the text is a discussion that takes place among prisoners about their solidarity with imprisoned Algerian *mujahidin* who are fighting the French.

14. See Firat for a discussion of Sulayman's and Bu Ali Yasin's *Literature and Ideology in Syria 1967–1973*.

15. Personal interview. August 2005.

16. Faraj Bayraqdar was born in 1951 in Tir, near Homs in central Syria. He began publishing poetry while still in high school. At the University of Damascus, he and a group of friends started a literary journal, but certain texts published in it led to his arrest and imprisonment for three months. His first poetry collection, *You Are Not Alone*, came out in 1979. He stopped writing in the early 1980s due to activities in the Communist Action Party. In 1987, Bayraqdar was arrested again. His imprisonment lasted more than thirteen years, in three different prisons (Palestine Division, Tadmor, and Saydnaya). Without his knowledge, a group of friends in Beirut published *Dove in Free Flight*, a collection of his poetry written and smuggled out of prison. After an international campaign was mounted on his behalf, Bayraqdar was released from prison during the brief political respite known as "Damascus Spring" in 2000–2001. His memoir is composed of a series of fragments he wrote while imprisoned. Written primarily on cigarette paper, these fragments were smuggled out of prison. After his release, he compiled them into a memoir but left them, for the most part, unedited.

17. Published in the cultural supplement of the Lebanese newspaper *an-Nahar* and disseminated widely on the Internet long before he could find a publisher who would agree to print and distribute his book, the most famous passage details a gruesome scene at the infamous Tadmur Military Prison, when a guard arbitrarily takes a prisoner out to the courtyard and forces him to swallow a dead mouse whole. The prisoner, Bayraqdar tells us, eventually manages to swallow the mouse, but he survives the ordeal only to go insane in the "kingdom of death and madness" that was Tadmur.

18. See, for example, *Middle East Watch* 1991.

19. Born in 1958 into an 'Alawi family, 'Abdalrahman moved from a small village north of Latakia to Damascus while she was still a child. Having developed an interest in oppositional politics in secondary school, she became active in underground political activities in her late teens. She was detained by Syrian state security for prolonged periods four times, including from 1986–91, due to her membership in the Communist Action Party, a breakaway faction of the Syrian Communist Party that has been banned and whose members have been persecuted by the Syrian government since the mid-1970s.

20. Review of *al-Sharnaqa* published in *al-Mustaqbal* by 'Ali Dayyub (pre-press copy obtained from author). Also noted in author interview with 'Adnan Husayn Ahmad published in *al-Zaman*, and reprinted on http://www.rezgar.com.

21. The siege of and massacres in the city of Hama in February 1982 are generally viewed as the nadir of a series of Syrian government crackdowns on and reprisals against (what *Middle East Watch* has termed "The Great Oppression" of) oppositional forces (both secular and religious, militant and pacifist) between 1976–82. The city was long considered a major stronghold of Islamist opposition to the Ba'th party beginning in 1963, and it had been the site of major government repressive measures in both 1964 and 1981 that included the massacre of protestors. On February 2, 1982, government forces entered the city in order to disarm militias of the Muslim Brotherhood and other groups based there. A call for general insurrection was issued by the Muslim Brotherhood, and for ten days, a series of clashes between government troops and the armed opposition ensued until upward of 30,000 Syrian troops occupied the city. In response to the armed resistance, the government's forces destroyed large sections of the city indiscriminately with little regard for civilian life. The Syrian Muslim Brotherhood has estimated that the number of people killed by government forces was as high as 25,000. Most English-language historical accounts give the range of those killed as between 5,000 to 10,000 but suggest that the numbers could be higher. It also should be noted that two Syrian writers, Haydar Haydar and Manhal al-Sarraj, have also published novels depicting the siege in 1982, although these works are currently banned in Syria. See *Middle East Watch* for a detailed account of the siege and the events leading up to it (especially 17–21). See also Lisa Wedeen's discussion of the Syrian regime's rhetoric and "official narrative" of the events at Hama in February 1982 (46–49).

22. There is also a very brief description of the character Lama's torture by a guard who knew her from childhood in the chapter entitled "The Decisive Battle."

23. It should be noted that what adds to the ambiguities of the text is that throughout the novel very few proper names of places and very few dates are given; for example, Aleppo is referred to as the "Northern City" and Damascus as "The Capital." 'Abdalrahman's references to particular historical events must be interpreted through her descriptions, as is the case with the siege of Hama in 1982.

REFERENCES

'Abdalrahman, Hasiba. 1999. *Al-Sharnaqa*. (The Cocoon). NA.
____. 2002. Interview with 'Adnan Husayn Ahmad. *Al-Zaman*, March 4.
Amnesty International. 2004. Syria: Amnesty International Welcomes Syria's Accession to the UN Convention Against Torture, September 23, http://web.amnesty.org/library/index/engMDE240692004?open&of=eng-2d2.
____. 2005. "Syria." *Annual Report 2005*, http://web.amnesty.org/report2005/syr-summary-eng.
Bayraqdar, Faraj. 2006. *Khiyanat al-Lugha wa al-Samt* (The Betrayals of Language and Silence). Bayrut: Al-Jadid.
Cave, Terence. 2002. *Recognitions: A Study in Poetics*. Oxford: Clarendon Press.
Cooke, Miriam. 2001. Ghassan al-Jaba'i: Prison Literature in Syria after 1980. *World Literature Today* 75: 237–245.
Cover, Robert M. 1986. "Violence and the Word." *The Yale Law Journal* 95: 1601–1629.
d'Afflitto, Isabella Camera. 1998. "Prison Narratives: Autobiography and Fiction." In *Writing the Self: Autobiographical Writing in Modern Arabic Literature*, eds. Robin Ostle, Ed de Moor, and Stefan Wild, 148–156. London: Saqi.
Derrida, Jacques. 1980. *Writing and Difference*. Trans. Alan Bass. Chicago: Univ. of Chicago Press.
Dorfman, Ariel. 2004. "The Tyranny of Terror: Is Torture Inevitable in Our Century and Beyond?" In *Torture: A Collection*. Ed. Sanford Levison, 3–18. Oxford: Oxford Univ. Press.

Douglass, Ana, and Thomas A. Vogler. 2003. Introduction to *Witness and Memory: The Discourse of Trauma*, ed. Ana Douglass and Thomas A. Vogler, 1–54. New York: Routledge.

Firat, Alexa. 2007. "Cultural Battles on the Literary Playing Field." Middle East History and Theory Conference, May 11–12, in Chicago, Illinois.

Foucault, Michel. 1980. *Power/Knowledge: Selected Interviews and Other Writings 1972–1977*. New York: Pantheon Books.

____. 1991. "Questions of Method." In *The Foucault Effect: Studies in Governmentality*, ed. Graham Burchell, Colin Gordon, and Peter Miller, 73–86. Chicago: The Univ. of Chicago Press.

____. 1995. *Discipline and Punish: The Birth of the Prison*. Trans. Alan Sheridan. New York: Vintage Books.

Kahf, Mohja. 2001. "The Silences of Contemporary Syrian Literature." *World Literature Today* 55: 224–236.

Levison, Sanford. 2004. Introduction to *Torture: A Collection*, 23–43. Oxford: Oxford Univ. Press.

Maher Arar vs. John Ashcroft et al. Complaint and Demand for Jury Trial: United States District Court Eastern District of New York. January 24 2004, http://ccrjustice.org/ourcases/current-cases/arar-v.-ashcroft (Accessed November 24, 2008).

Mayer, Jane. 2005. "Outsourcing Torture: The Secret History of America's 'Extraordinary Rendition' Program." *The New Yorker*. February 14, http://www.newyorker.com/archive/2005/02/14/050214fa_fact6 (Accessed November 24, 2008).

Middle East Watch. 1991. *Syria Unmasked: The Suppression of Human Rights Under the Asad Regime*. New Haven: Yale Univ. Press.

Nora, Pierre. 1998. "The Return of the Event." In *Histories: French Constructions of the Past*, ed. Jacques Revel and Lynn Hunt, 421–436. New York: New Press.

Parry, John T. 2004. "Escalation and Necessity: Defining Torture at Home and Abroad." In *Torture: A Collection*, ed. Sanford Levison, 145–164. Oxford: Oxford Univ. Press.

Patten, Wendy. 2005. Human Rights Watch Report to the Canadian Commission of Inquiry into the Actions of Canadian Officials in Relation to Maher Arar. Human Rights Watch. June 7, http://hrw.org/backgrounder/eca/canada/arar (accessed November 24, 2008).

Posner, Richard A. 2004. "Torture, Terrorism, and Interrogation." In *Torture: A Collection*, ed. Sanford Levison, 291–298. Oxford: Oxford Univ. Press.

Ranciere, Jacques. 1994. *The Names of History*. Trans. Hassan Melehy. Minneapolis: Univ. of Minnesota Press.

Sáez, Ñacuñán. 1992. "Torture: A Discourse on Practice." In *Tattoo, Torture, Mutilation, and Adornment: The Denaturalization of the Body in Culture and Text*, ed. Frances E. Mascia-Lees and Patricia Sharpe, 126–144. Albany: State Univ. of New York Press.

Scarry, Elaine. 1985. *The Body in Pain: The Making and the Unmaking of the World*. New York: Oxford Univ. Press.

Schaffer, Kay, and Sidonie Smith. 2004. *Human Rights and Narrated Lives: The Ethics of Recognition*. New York: Palgrave Macmillan.

Slaughter, Joseph. 1997. "A Question of Narration: The Voice in International Human Rights Law." *Human Rights Quarterly* 19: 406–430.

Sulayman, Nabil. 1999. *Al-Sijn*. Al-Ladhaqiya: Dar al-Hiwar.

Turner, Bryan S. 2006. *Vulnerability and Human Rights*. Univ. Park: Pennsylvania State Univ. Press.

Wedeen, Lisa. 1999. *Ambiguities of Domination: Politics, Rhetoric, and Symbols in Contemporary Syria*. Chicago: Univ. of Chicago Press.

Chapter Seven

A Primer for the Politics and Literature of Resistance

Apparitional Subjectivity in The Collective Autobiography of the New York 21

Ramsey Scott

The virtual disappearance of *Look for Me in the Whirlwind: The Collective Autobiography of the New York 21* hardly registers in the list of bitter ironies that emerge from the government's persecution of the Black Panther Party.[1] Today, *Whirlwind* seems to have been nearly laid to rest in the graveyard American history reserves for documents of its pogroms and purges against political dissidents, its acts of racial violence and genocidal terror. *Whirlwind* is designed by its authors as a political instrument to resist these attempts to erase history; it constitutes a literary, poetic response to the government's efforts to control the narrators' stories. Through its engagement with and subversion of autobiography's frame, *Whirlwind* embodies subjectivity as a collective undertaking, challenging readers to engage with its confounding structure through alternative interpretive practices. The state's use of language to condemn the New York 21 while imposing its versions of individual rights, civics, and so-called just action requires the authors of *Whirlwind* to find unconventional means with which to express their own experiences. Faced with the distorted, distort*ing*, moralizing narrative forms the state uses against them—forms that whitewash the government's use of illegal surveillance and counterintelligence activities while arresting citizens seeking to enact real and lasting social change—the New York 21 defendants search for alternatives. *Whirlwind* thus serves as an experimental text, the culmination of an attempt to construct a dissident literature from inside the state's oppressive juridical and prison regimes.

SHADOWED BY THE STATE / THE STATE'S SHADOW

The original dust jacket of the New York 21's collective autobiography explains the book's content as follows: "Sixteen of the original New York Panther 21 defendants, indicted in April of 1969 for allegedly 'plotting to bomb public places,' collectively tell us their story."[2] The curious difference between the number of autobiographies announced in the book's title and the number of contributors listed on the dust jacket may leave readers wondering at collective autobiography as a textual equation capable of reducing 21 life stories to the product of sixteen narrators. Haywood Burns' introduction to *Whirlwind* fails to mention the calculations necessary to make this odd equation functional. "In these pages the defendants in the New York Panther trial reclaim their personalities and we get to see them as individual people," Burns writes. "They trace in poignant detail their lives," he continues, "and we come to feel we know the defendants as people" (vii).

The apprehension echoing in his promises to allow readers to "see [the defendants] as individual people" and "know the defendants as people" underscores the fundamental crisis of subject formation central to the text's construction. What kind of subject formation can include the excluded narrators, the members of the New York 21 not included in *Whirlwind*, whose apparitions nonetheless haunt its pages? The *New York Times* review of *Whirlwind* states that the book contains "not so much the moving individual story as . . . a cacophony of voices chorusing their protest so loudly that one is deafened," an effect contributing, in the reviewer's mind, to the book's so-called clamorous disharmony (Carew 1971). If *Whirlwind* evokes a sense of "disharmony" for some readers, the government's efforts to build a case against the New York Panthers should elicit a more distinct sense of disquiet. The campaign against them began on the prerogatives of the New York Police Department; some of the earliest members of the New York Panthers were undercover officers, and although this NYPD operation coincided and eventually overlapped with nationwide FBI COINTELPROs (counterintelligence programs) that J. Edgar Hoover initiated against Black revolutionaries, the New York Panthers owe their particular misfortune to the NYPD's long history and expertise in "neutralizing" those it deemed political dissidents.

At a time when the department was mired in scandal, beset by allegations involving corruption, gambling, and drug smuggling, the case of the Black Panther 21 helped to redirect media attention away from the NYPD's own crimes.[3] In *Perversions of Justice*, Peter L. Zimroth's study of the trial, the actions of the NYPD's Bureau of Special Services (or BOSS) receive careful treatment. The undercover division once known as the "Radical Bureau" for its efforts in taking down political activists, Zimroth reports that the BOSS had particular experience in undermining black organizations. Its previous exploits included a thorough infiltration of the Nation of Islam, along with numerous other groups considered dangerous to the legacy of white supremacy in the Big Apple. Eugene Roberts, a BOSS operative and Panther infiltrator who would testify against the New York 21, claimed not only to have witnessed Malcolm X's assassination, but to have attempted to resuscitate Malcolm X himself (Zimroth 1974, 170).

Thus does Murray Kempton describe the depth of police meddling in the New York Panthers in his book on the trial, *The Briar Patch*: "The police own all that is official in the history of the New York Branch of the Black Panther Party," Kempton writes. "Its character was painted by district attorneys; what records it has were compiled by policemen; even the strongest bond its protagonists would share was finally owing to their prosecutors [and] the Department of Corrections" (Kempton 1973, 42–43). In their thorough analysis of the government's campaigns against political dissidents, Ward Churchill and Jim Vander Wall note that "at least five police infiltrators—Eugene Roberts, Ralph White, Carlos Ashwood, Roland Hayes, and Wilbert Thomas—had moved into the New York BPP from almost the moment it was established" (*COINTELPRO* 1988, 361). As police plots against the Panthers intensified, the division between Panther-initiated plans and those initiated by infiltrators became increasingly muddled. Peter Zimroth employs a carefully phrased observation that hints at the unsettling entanglement of police provocation and so-called intervention: "The obvious danger in police methods like these is that the police are . . . promoting the very activities they say they are trying to prevent" (62). Zimroth reports that one of the earliest examples of such "police methods" against the New York Panthers involved BOSS operative Wilbert Thomas, who "supplied a map of [a] hotel and a car" that could be used to rob the hotel. The Panthers were then arrested for planning a hotel robbery (62).

If the ethical standards of such police agents and operatives seemed suspect, the political stance taken by the Panthers sounded in comparison like standard ethics. As part of its ten-point plan, the Party stated, "We believe that this racist government has robbed us and now we are demanding the overdue debt of forty acres and two mules. . . . We will accept payment in currency which will be distributed to our many communities" (Jones 1998, 473). The Panthers' engagement with the logic of restorative justice captured in the above statements unraveled as the impact of police infiltration and provocation forced members underground and consumed the Party's energy in endless legal battles, especially the case of the New York 21 itself. Although such battles provided brief opportunities for political performances and theatrical protests that exposed the gross imbalances and prejudices built into the justice establishment (the infamous binding and gagging of Bobby Seale during the trial of the Chicago 8, for example), they also mired Party members in layers of legalistic doublespeak.

In the case of the New York 21, the Panthers and their lawyers were forced to downplay notions that they actively worked toward an "over-all plan to harass and destroy the power structure," even as envisioning such a plan was integral to the image the Black Panther Party held for its supporters as much as its detractors (Zimroth 1974, 238). Confronted with a court system based on a code of morals and a system of self-representation inimical to their collective and individual identities, the Panthers faced fundamental challenges to their carefully wrought claims of authenticity. "The defendants could not have it both ways," Zimroth writes. "They could not . . . present themselves as serious, committed, idealist revolutionaries at the same time that their lawyers were emphasizing their disorganization, confusion, lack of competence, and seeming lack of purpose. . . . Nonetheless, the defendants seemed willing to risk this political point in order to win an acquittal" (172). Aside from such seemingly existential questions of authenticity and identification raised inside the courtroom, the mere fact that so many Panthers faced arrest proved devastating to their political aims. The high bail regularly set for Panther defendants (most of whom would be acquitted in cases that often exposed the law enforcement establishment's attempts to manipulate justice) eviscerated Panther leadership and redirected its organizing efforts toward fundraising and away from the community programs that had been the party's most effective organizing tools (Zimroth, 172).

Indeed, just months after the founding of its New York branches, and even before the arrests that would mark the beginning of the case against the New York 21, numerous New York Panthers languished behind bars. Those not arrested were forced to spend most of *their* time attempting to raise bail money for jailed comrades. The Harlem branch became the center of activity, in part because of the recruitment efforts of the BOSS undercover agents that staffed its office. William King, who would become a central target in the New York 21 case because of his training as a U.S. Marine and his authorship of a manual on urban guerilla warfare, was one such recruit. "King had arrived in September [of 1968]," Murray Kempton writes, "a stranger to all of his new comrades except Eugene Roberts, the police detective." Kempton claims that King was "at first so distrusted that only Roberts' recommendation finally won him admittance" (68). As federal officials learned of the degree to which the New York Panthers had been infiltrated by the NYPD in the months leading up to the indictment of the New York 21, the case came to be viewed as the final chapter of Panther history not only in New York, but in the United States at-large. Peter Zimroth concludes that the case of the Panther 21 was part of a plan to "emphasize the criminality of the Panthers *as an organization*" (his italics, 46). A federal agent interviewed by Zimroth about the case of the New York 21 suggests that media coverage of earlier cases against various Black Panther leaders too frequently focused on the individuals themselves. When Panther leaders successfully fought off the charges against them, their popularity grew (46). The media had overlooked the government's preferred theme in such cases, that which law enforcement agents hoped the case of the New York 21 would advance: the inherent criminality of the Black Panther Party.

Thus, when New York District Attorney Frank Hogan announced the 156 charges against the 21 defendants, he presented accusations that the government hoped would be ratified as facts in future histories chronicling the Black Panthers and the era of civilian discontent they helped to define. He had already hand-picked Supreme Court Justice John M. Murtagh to handle the case, believing Justice Murtagh the judge most capable of upholding a façade of impartiality while remaining faithful to the police department and its witnesses. It was a department, after all, that had once served as Murtagh's own place of employ. The fact that he had faced indictment for his failure as commissioner of investigation to scrutinize completely a gambling scandal that occurred under his watch was a point in his favor. As Murray Kempton explains, the police had once spared him the humiliation of an arrest; thereafter he treated police testimony as though he possessed an "undamaged faith in the word of anyone in uniform" (28). Thus, even after extensive police surveillance, infiltration, and provocation of the activists who supposedly posed such a threat to the state, prosecutors sought out the judge whose demeanor they believed would lend itself most generously to the collective biography they wished to write for the accused.

COLLECTIVE IDENTITY AS REPRESSION, COLLECTIVE IDENTITY AS RESISTANCE

If this focus on the creation of a collective criminality underscores the dominant strategy in the prosecution's case, it also outlines the tactic *Whirlwind* pursues as a text, a mode of resistance and subterfuge founded upon de-individuated radical action. As Michael Hames-Garcia notes of *Whirlwind* in his book, *Fugitive Thought: Prison Movements, Race, and the Meaning of Justice* (2004), the New York 21's collective autobiography embodies what Hames-Garcia describes as "a collectivist conception of the self," one "committed to complex solidarity" (194–95). As envisioned in *Whirlwind*, the construction of this "collectivist self" involves a careful erosion of the seemingly natural boundaries between those who speak and those who remain silent. It asks us to question on whose authority one speaks, and who the purported authorities speak for. Zimroth thus observes, "Even before the proof was in all the [New York 21] defendants were lumped together, the fact that they were alleged Black Panther terrorists obliterating the differences between them" (33). Although the prosecution would on numerous occasions

single out particular defendants as leaders or key organizers of specific con-
spiracies, the "complex solidarity" displayed in *Whirlwind* coincides with the
prosecution's own legal strategy of collective criminality.

In one particularly startling example of the government's tendency to
view the defendants through the lens of collectivity, Murray Kempton notes
that the prosecuting attorneys could not keep the defendants straight. In the
court transcript Kempton cites, Mr. Phillips, attorney for the prosecution,
attempts to identify Dharuba Moore after Moore interrupts the court proceedings:

> **THE DEFENDANT MOORE:** This is a farce. You're a racist judge—a
> racist pig judge.
> **JUSTICE MURTAGH:** What is the name of the defendant who spoke out
> there?
> **MR. PHILLIPS:** Your Honor, Lumumba Shakur and the gentleman standing
> next to him.
> **JUSTICE MURTAGH:** This gentleman who is number two, what is his
> name?
> **MR. PHILLIPS:** Tabor, I believe, Michael Tabor.

And Moore, defendant number two, confused at this sign that Mr. Phillips,
otherwise master of their intimacies, could not tell any one of them from any
other, could only shout back, "You can include me," at which there was
applause and Justice Murtagh cleared the courtroom (39–40).

The confusion of identities that typifies the prosecution's efforts to crimi-
nalize "the Panthers *as an organization*" thus provides the defendants with
the means of establishing their own textual defenses. What remains striking
about trial of the New York 21 is not only that the prosecution's strategy of
collective or associative guilt fails, but that the authors of *Whirlwind* utilize a
similarly collective, associative strategy in order to produce a document of
resistance.

Consider again the curious mathematics involved in the discrepancy between the subtitle of the book, *The Collective Autobiography of the New York
21*, and the book's sixteen contributors: *Whirlwind* establishes its oppositional stance through the dispersal of individual identities. Sixteen individual
contributors accept responsibility for the life stories of their five missing
compatriots, sprinkling their own recollections throughout eleven numbered
sections so that only the most dedicated readers can connect one person's
memory with a previous memory attributed to the very same person. Although some sections seem to have been thematically assembled, in general,
the eleven sections begin and end without clear purpose or reason. "Part 1"
consists of brief autobiographical sketches in which speakers talk at vastly
differing lengths while rarely deviating from the autobiographical theme,
although one defendant (Joan Bird) doesn't talk at all, and isn't introduced

until "Part 2." Other defendants speak twice in "Part 1." The use of aliases further complicates readers' efforts to account for the ownership of the book's narrative fragments. Contributors with chosen names are first introduced with their chosen names listed alongside their given names—or what some of the narrators would call their slave names—and subsequently referred to by their chosen names, but this pattern does not hold for *all* contributors.

As individuated identities become lost or confused in the midst of the cross-hatched narratives that give them life, the collective contributions of the sixteen seem to multiply exponentially, as if the book represents not one, two, or sixteen narrators, but a virtual army of revolutionaries, not a single one of whom can be fully disentangled from the collective, revolutionary, textual body he or she seems to occupy. This interpenetrating, multiplying, de-individuating author-collective represents a textual illusion quite distinct from the case history itself. Sorting through the relationships between the defendants is a difficult task, significantly complicated by the effort required to extract supposedly authentic Panther activities from those faked, provoked, or otherwise manipulated by government agents. In his testimony in the New York 21 trial, police undercover agent Ralph White describes divisions within the Party subsequently repeated in histories of the Panthers.[4] According to White, "There were those . . . on the political side of the party . . . and then you had the people who were more or less like the military part of the party" (Kempton, 238). These differences gradually metastasized into the fatal split between those loyal to Huey P. Newton and the West Coast Panthers, ostensibly the "political side of the party," and those such as the East Coast Panthers and the New York 21, supposedly aligned with the exiled Eldridge Cleaver, who represented what White called "the militant part of the party."

Although often accepted as an accurate description of the Panthers' disintegration, White's simplistic analysis of the Party's divided factions masks the role of provocateurs such as himself in engineering this division. White attempted to prove himself to other members of the Party by joining those who championed militarism: "If someone said, 'What we got to do is start icing more pigs,' I'm going to say, 'Right on, yeah'" (Kempton, 225). His efforts did not convince the Panthers who knew him that he should remain free from suspicion. Afeni Shakur correctly suspected that he was a policeman, a suspicion she shared with others, including her husband and head of the Harlem branch, Lumumba Shakur. After learning of her accusations, White fired his gun into tabletops at the Ellsmere Tenants Council, where he and Lumumba had been working for tenants' rights. Nonetheless, Lumumba Shakur seems to have suspected White as well. Shakur tested White's interest in violence by offering him access to dynamite and suggesting he make use of it (Kempton, 222–225). White performed more convincingly for his fellow law enforcement officers; unaware that White worked for the same department as he did, fellow BOSS undercover officer Eugene Roberts classified White as "a bad mother" in his reports to superiors. White, similarly unaware that Roberts was a policeman, said of Roberts, "If you blow in his ear, he'd kill someone" (Zimroth, 67). In retrospect, the notion that a division between militancy and politics divided the Party thus becomes difficult to untangle from the role of the government's provocateurs, who regularly advocated violence.

As many commentators have noted, accusations of militancy obscured more complex debates within the Party.[5] Escalating legal costs forced debates between the Panthers over how to allocate resources. The New York 21 was largely comprised of rank-and-file members. In this way, they typified the politically savvy but economically underprivileged citizens President Nixon had come to fear most as threats to his hold on power and to the elective power of the Republican Party itself. Such "militant representatives of the urbanized poor," as Christian Parenti describes Nixon's enemies in his book *Lockdown America* (1999), were the true targets of Nixon's "war on crime," a thinly camouflaged campaign against politically engaged minorities (12).[6] In contrast to the rank-and-file status of many New York 21 defendants, numerous cases against Panthers throughout the country—Huey Newton's appeal, the legal defense of David Hilliard (accused of threatening President Nixon's life), and Bobby Seale's trial for the murder of a fellow Black Panther in New Haven—involved the Party's most powerful representatives.[7] Although members of the New York 21 did not possess the notoriety of Newton, Hilliard, or Seale, New York City proved a profitable place for Party fundraising. Kempton notes that members of the New York 21 believed a disproportionate amount of financial support was being allocated to pay the legal expenses of more well-known Panthers facing trials of their own; some began to advocate robberies and other methods of expropriation as a means of raising money (180–181). The militaristic split envisioned by White took on a life of its own as the trial dragged on and the Party faced impossible financial demands. Meanwhile, FBI agents, now acting as covert mail couriers for Panther correspondence traveling between various offices, intercepted letters and provided their own counterfeit missives, further spreading confusion, dissent, and suspicion among members.

Whirlwind largely conceals the fact that, as tensions between Party offices escalated, the New York 21 defendants increasingly found themselves at odds with one another. In her book-length biographical interview with Afeni Shakur (*Afeni Shakur: Evolution of a Revolutionary*, 2004), Jasmine Guy reports that Afeni was disgruntled from the trial's inception. Lumumba Shakur and other higher ranking Panthers decided that she and Joan Bird would be represented by the only female lawyer made available to the defendants (97). Rather than accepting the lawyer the men had rejected for themselves,

Afeni Shakur defended herself, rebuffing Lumumba Shakur's insistence that she accept the legal representation chosen for her. As bail money accumulated, the group decided that the women—Afeni Shakur and Joan Bird—would be released first. Next, Cetewayo and Dharuba made bail; they had been chosen for their speaking abilities, and were expected to campaign for bail money to free the rest of the defendants.

From the beginning, Cetewayo and Dharuba struggled to raise the necessary funds. Cetewayo fled to Algeria, where he joined Eldridge Cleaver in exile. Dharuba had planned to accompany him, and after failing to appear in trial it was widely reported that he *had* gone to Algeria, as stated on the book jacket of *Whirlwind*. However, according to Murray Kempton, when the time came to enact this plan, distrust had reached an unprecedented level of intensity; Cetewayo and his traveling partner, Connie Matthews, decided that Dharuba was not reliable enough to travel with them (183). Perhaps both Cetewayo and Dharuba believed their inability to raise adequate bail for the remaining defendants had already sufficiently damaged their relationship with the group to make disappearance necessary; other evidence suggests that FBI agents helped erode their trust in one another and in their fellow Party members.[8] Whatever the reasons, both abandoned the promises they had made to their fellow defendants. As a result, Afeni Shakur and Joan Bird were forced to return to jail. While Cetewayo joined Cleaver in Algeria, Dharuba went into hiding. The undercover operations that likely influenced their actions would eventually entangle many of their co-defendants. In their 2002 edition of *The COINTELPRO Papers*, Churchill and Vander Wall note that, "as of this writing, all but a handful [of the New York 21] are either dead or serving lengthy sentences in maximum security institutions" (361). Perhaps because of this common fate, the disagreements, betrayals, and suspicions that damaged the relationships between members of the New York 21—and that *Whirlwind* helps to conceal through its innovative structure— have largely dissipated through time. The feelings of intimacy members share for one another are evidenced in Shaba Om's recently videotaped greeting to political prisoner and fellow *Whirlwind* author Sundiata Acoli: "No matter what the circumstances may be, no matter what the physical barriers may be . . . there was a bond of companionship, a bond of unadulterated trust for one another, to the extent of putting . . . our hands in each other's lives and our lives in each other's hands. So you know, you just don't find that. You know. You just don't find that."[9]

THE BIRTH OF APPARITIONAL SUBJECTIVITY IN THE
COLLECTIVE SHARING OF INDIVIDUAL EXPERIENCE

Shaba Om's reference to a connection that exists outside of language and that permeates physical barriers, that allows for the transferal of one's hands and life into the hands and life of another, provides a useful perspective from which to view the dissolving boundaries between textual identities crafted by the contributors. His reflections cast *Whirlwind*'s collage-like, collaborative, and sometimes confusing text, in which an anecdote from one person's life provides a window through which one reads the life story of another, as one element in a larger process of resistance that relies upon constantly transforming identities, provisional selves that can be disassembled and exchanged among one's closest compatriots. Sundiata Acoli's memory of the writing process involved in constructing *Whirlwind*, captured in an address entitled "On Marcus Garvey's Birthday Celebration," grounds the transposition of hands and lives facilitated by the fragmented body of the narrative in the collective acts leading to the book's composition: "We passed around the mike [Acoli says], spoke into a tape recorder and the publishers, Vintage Press or somebody [Random House] transcribed the tape into a book" (1998, 3). The dialogical process Acoli describes—the tape recorder exchanged between the narrators' hands before reaching the editor's desk—remains legible in the text itself. The authors build off the preceding narrator's words, sometimes taking up where the previous speaker left off or commenting obliquely on a single element of the previous monologue.

The sharing of compositional labor that contributes to the text's final form results in many fascinating passages; and yet, the flatness of some sections, the relaying of details that seem almost formulaic, provokes readers to wonder who stands to benefit from this process, and whose curiosities or commands authorize its progression. Portions of *Whirlwind* suffer from what might be called *clinical* neglect. The editors seem to have taken a holiday. Rudimentary errors go uncorrected. When Sundiata Acoli speaks of his college years, "colege" appears in full irony with a single "l." Most puzzling is the misidentification of Kuwasi Balagoon, known to the state as Donald Weems. When he first speaks, his given name is listed as Walter Johnson, another defendant in the case who also contributes to the book, but who only appears under his chosen name of Baba Odinga (33, 27). This error sows confusion and enables further misidentifications, an outcome diametrically opposed to the book's purported purpose, as described in the introduction, "to allow readers to know the defendants as [individual] people." I would like to suggest that such confusions form part of a provisional strategy adopted by the narrators to disable the autobiographical text's guilt-ridden history of confession and personal disclosure leading to self-revelation. What the *Times* reads as "clamorous disharmony" marks an innovative, subversive discourse of narratological seduction and deception, a performance of disembodiment that trades in phantom limbs and donated textual organs in an attempt to liberate its contributors from the very narrated bodies their labors seem to inscribe. Considering the level of police infiltration the trial had already revealed before *Whirlwind*'s composition began, it seems likely that at the very least, the contributors would have viewed with suspicion the editors granted unprecedented access not only to the jail itself, but to meeting rooms capable of accommodating the defendants as a group. The book's editor or editors go unlisted; it remains unclear who oversaw the process of recording and transcription leading to publication. Regardless, many of the guarded yet personal narratives suggest a level of wariness on the part of the contributors, a willingness to talk but in talking to say nothing that stands out too distinctly as a personal revelation, provokes suspicion, or provides too-private an insight.

Nonetheless, cultural critiques woven throughout *Whirlwind*'s narrative remnants provide ample room for further analysis. For example, Cetewayo follows the autobiographical sketches provided by Shaba Om and Robert Collier, each of which begins with reflections on the hospitals in which they were born, with a joke about the hierarchy of New York City hospitals. In so doing he threads his narrative together with their preceding narratives, mentioning that Harlem Hospital, the site of Shaba Om's birth, was known in the neighborhood as "the butcher shop" (7, 3). The repeated invocation of "the butcher shop," or hospital, as a deeply embedded sign within the early lives of *Whirlwind*'s first three narrators conjures failed attempts at the elimination of death's presence in the midst of the living. Sharon Holland notes that the hospital itself, the structure meant to both contain death and define its limits, recalls modernity's ongoing struggle to banish death, at the same time that death's inevitability motivates so-called scientific experimentation on black bodies. In her book *Raising the Dead*, Holland notes that "To achieve the separation between the happy (living) and the miserable (the dying / almost dead), the hospital was created as the perfect institutional replacement for this uncomfortable meeting" (33). Black bodies, she notes, become the primary site for the investigation of the "dying/almost dead." "The death of black subjects . . . serves to ward off a nation's collective dread of the inevitable," Holland writes.

The hospital, and in particular, the understaffed, underfunded Harlem Hospital known as "the butcher shop" thus gives birth to the collective autobiography of the New York 21 amid death's resonance. Afeni Shakur recalls the death of her girlfriend after a mishandled operation; instead of receiving the complete hysterectomy she needs and expects, Shakur's friend retains her reproductive potential, and she ultimately dies as a result of her unexpected pregnancy. Shakur thus concludes, "We don't go to doctors . . . till we're

dead" (85). The theme of the hospital as an institution for the industrializa-
tion of (black) death thus connects the seemingly haphazard narratives that
begin *Whirlwind* to Afeni Shakur's subsequent recollections; in light of Holland's remarks, these narrative threads appear as prophetic insights steeped
in a modern signage that makes from urban legend cold, hard, historical
facts. Harlem Hospital's suggestive nickname, "the butcher shop," also provides a fitting image for various narrative organs in the text that serve as
prostheses for different individuals. As Shaba Om suggests, a sharing or
exchange of organs and limbs between bodies of narrative as well as the
bodies that narrate distinguishes the New York 21's literary, historical, and
political project. The effect of these transposed hands, lives, and words is a
kind of composite body, an apparitional subjectivity [10] partially grafted, elsewhere amputated, the parts of which drift alongside the real-life identities of
the contributors, their words, their own *and* someone else's all at once.
Whirlwind attempts to embody text as a connective tissue capable of
transcending individuals, transplanting stories from one living subject onto
the living textual body of another.

The fact that the text bears few signs of the group's internal unrest points
to ways in which its disorderly narratives strategically refocus the case history on the concept of the collective. Such efforts also obscure the roles different defendants played in the trail itself. The two female defendants, the
aforementioned Joan Bird and Afeni Shakur, were important figures in the
trial, but their contributions recede into the background of the autobiographical fragments *Whirlwind* collects, along with the dispute over which lawyers
would represent them. In Bird's case, a supposed confession to the attempted
assassination of police officers played a key part in the prosecution's representation of the Party's activities. Bird and her lawyers argued that her confession had been extracted through torture. Nonetheless, after the acquittal of
the New York 21, the events related to Bird's controversial "confession"
would result in the only conviction for a crime named in the original indictment, that of Kuwasi Balagoon, convicted on the very same attempted assassination for which the jury had cleared the other defendants.

Although it might be easily overlooked by readers, Afeni Shakur contributes a significant document to *Whirlwind* that hints of the group's internal
difficulties. Squeezed between the "Publisher's Note" (a time line of the
trial's essential dates and events) and a transcript of a letter from the defendants to Justice Murtagh (written during the recess from the pretrial hearings
the judge imposed after repeated interruptions by the defendants), Afeni
Shakur's letter seems an afterthought. To Shakur, however, it was essential.
"I wasn't very cooperative," Shakur tells Jasmine Guy of her contributions to
Whirlwind. "They had to print this letter if I was to participate" (89–90). The
letter is addressed "to Jamala, Lil Afeni, Sekyiwa, and the unborn baby
(babies) within my womb," and in some sections it threatens the tranquility

of the collective structure *Whirlwind* otherwise appears to maintain. Noting that the defendants have been "caught up in this funny situation where everyone seems to be attacking everyone else," Shakur suggests that the defendants, and members of the Panthers in general, must correct the distrust with which they have dealt with one another, before they will be ready to succeed in any revolutionary capacity: "We still must face the problems of purging ourselves of the larceny that we have all inherited. . . . I cannot get rid of my dream of peace and harmony. It is for that dream that most of us have fought—some bravely, some as cowards, some as heroes, and some as plain old crooks" (360–361).

For all practical purposes a footnote to the volume itself, Shakur's poignant address serves as a subtle yet powerful signal of the illusion the rest of the text embodies. Even when she appears to speak for the group, Shakur actually draws distinctions between those still in jail, and those who have skipped bail or evaded capture: "Joan and I, and all the brothers in jail," she writes as she begins her letter; this list includes just thirteen of the original New York 21 for whom the volume claims to speak, thus hinting at the frustration of the imprisoned defendants. In addition, the word "larceny" calls attention to significant contradictions. Larceny refers to the theft of personal property, thus gesturing toward the legacy of chattel slavery. At the same time, to understand larceny as a crime aside from slavery, one must acquiesce to the notion of personal property as a right, a concept many of the defendants—students of Mao and Lenin, Marx and Engels—would likely disavow. The statement nominates the defendants as both the victims and perpetrators of larceny: committed to an alternative set of values, but also tempted by the values their professed political stance would require them to reject. Perhaps it is this compromised position that explains why Shakur also confesses in her letter to have "deviated from . . . revolutionary principles."

Regardless, Afeni's letter derives power from the vagueness of its statements, its apparent oscillation between the personal and the generic. What she wants to say seems to have been carefully edited in order to become what she thinks she *can* say. This wavering between the personal and the generic, the specific and the vague, is most evident in the apostrophe that begins the letter. This apostrophe includes names of children barely familiar to her readers and appeals for forgiveness for "mistakes" that go unnamed and ultimately unexplained. The uncertainty surrounding these "mistakes" becomes all the more curious given the reference to them in a text that makes no effort to illuminate the contributors' abbreviated, dialogical, autobiographical fragments or the text's discordant, fragmented structure, not to mention the relationship between these textual features—the court case itself. In its understated generalities, Afeni Shakur's personal letter thus speaks for the defendants at-large, even as it allows her to record her own displeasure with actions of the group into whose illusory image her words fade: it stamps the text with the shame and anger of the accused who would like to confess certain deeds, not only because they feel these deeds have been justified, but because they also feel that they have failed. Afeni Shakur's letter thus records the despair of the unsaid in a text full of words that speak not for the defendants so much as to the illusion of their camaraderie in the face of jailhouse and courtroom humiliations. The fact that the image of unity presented in the collective autobiography of the New York 21 cannot be found in any other literature or documents from the era—that all other documents point instead to the dissolution of the group—raises essential questions concerning the intangibility of the Black Panther Party itself. The most visible Panthers become memories before the very eyes of their comrades. The collective spirit *Whirlwind* captures is that which never existed; in its reconstituted unity, it traces a dream of the Black Panther Party that never materialized.

Nowhere is this intangible essence more legible than the half-written autobiography contributed by Cetewayo. The sketch of his life story emerges in a written contribution that departs from the dialogical, tape-recorded sessions described by Sundiata Acoli. It does not appear until almost seventy pages into the text, far removed from the rest of the autobiographical sketches, and continues for almost fifteen pages, making it one of the longest continuous entries included in *Whirlwind*. Italicized transitions added by the editors lead the reader across gaps in the unfinished narrative. Cetewayo's former heroin habit is his primary subject; an editor's note explains that the entry has been "Excerpted from Cetewayo's autobiography to be published by Bantam Books" (69). Between the italicized transitions—"*he went with a man named Spike that night for some 'real stuff* . . . '" (76); "*Eventually he got some heroin* . . . " (82)—Cetewayo's story recalls classics of the addiction narrative, such as William Burroughs' early novel, *Junkie* (Ace, 1953): "I was in my coat, going out the door. That was a victory. But it was a perverted victory. . . . I was going out the door to resume my quest for death . . . to search for a fix" (82). Aside from Cetewayo's first comment on Harlem Hospital as "the butcher shop," the story of his addiction constitutes his only contribution to the text.

Interestingly, in both Cetewayo's contributions, subjectivity names the slide toward death. The aboveboard, official institution of the hospital facilitates mortality's arrival as much as the underground, unofficial social network of dealers and addicts that map his neighborhood. The hospital, like the loose-knit community that ushers him into the alleyways and dead-ends where heroin reigns, reproduces qualities of the prison. Cetewayo's hospitals and Harlem street corners become appendages to the prison's sanctioning of social death and enforced, profound, immobilizing alienation. Thus does Dylan Rodríguez describe the contagious spread of the prison regime's impenetrable logic, the way in which "structures of human captivity and bodily punishment, though perhaps most spectacularly actualized at the locality of the jail or prison, necessarily elaborate into other, at times counterintuitive, sites of targeting: the school, the workplace, the targeted neighborhood or community" (58). By authorizing the prison regime's amplifying force to occupy their text as negative inscriptions—breaks, interruptions, deletions, disjunctions—*Whirlwind*'s contributors document the point at which story-telling that embraces resistance must forego the rationality, linearity, and cohesiveness favored by the court, the law, and the state. In doing so, they allow *Whirlwind* to embody the polyvalent voices of resistance the prison regime attempts to isolate and silence, the voices that the prison regime would like to eliminate from discourse altogether.

CONCEALMENT AS EXPOSURE: KUWASI BALAGOON AND THE "DECLARED EXTREMES" OF THE AMERICAN LEFT

Despite its collective structure, *Whirlwind* nonetheless provides the space for fragments of individual voices to emerge. One such voice belongs to Kuwasi Balagoon, whose subsequent writings and activities are usefully prefaced by Murray Kempton's observation regarding the American Left, made as an aside to his account the trail of the New York 21. While pausing to reflect upon the destruction of the Panthers as a legitimate political force, Kempton writes, "American liberalism has never been comfortable unless provided with some pariah to its left for good men to repudiate and thus allow liberalism its claim to a place somewhere in that center between declared extremes" (171–172). For Kempton, the Black Panther Party thus provides American liberals with a revolutionary stance that is sufficiently extreme so as to allow the Left to reclaim some position closer to the conservative center of American politics. In order for the Party become such a pariah, it needs to be closely identified with the activities of individuals such as Kuwasi Balagoon.

As much as Balagoon seems acutely aware of the phenomenon Kempton describes, and as much as he seems to become increasingly dedicated to embodying the "declared extremes" against which others recoil, his writings nonetheless continue to mask fundamental aspects of his identity. Balagoon's entries in *Whirlwind* master the act of exposure that also conceals; his subsequent writings continue this strategy in some ways, and in others, abandon it entirely. In his political and literary explorations of concealment and exposure, Balagoon thus provides further evidence of apparitional subjectivity as *Whirlwind*'s structuring principle. As previously noted, *Whirlwind* erroneously lists Balagoon's given name as Walter Johnson instead of Donald Weems. This apparently innocent error nonetheless serves as a useful emblem for Balagoon's distinctive narrative contributions, in which substitutions and replacements pepper passages that offer personal disclosures. His activities as a self-declared revolutionary also deserve attention: he would persistently draw the government's attention in a variety of high-profile cases, beginning with the New York 21, escaping from prison on two occasions, being charged as an accomplice in the famous robbery of a Brinks armored car (known as the "Brinks Case"), and attempting to organize political prisoners until his death in prison in 1987. His most noticeable moment of "exposure" in *Whirlwind* appears in a reminiscence about school. As a third grader, Balagoon recalls that his schoolwork began to suffer after he became infatuated with his teacher, "too stunned by her beauty to understand anything else" (104–5):

> I remember one day she wore a red dress to school with no bra. I came out of a daydream just long enough to see one of her small but ample, succulent breasts fall from the dress. Good God Almighty—it sprang up and stared out into my eyes. Embarrassed, she was caught off guard. She whipped it right back behind the bright red barrier, then followed my straight line of vision until our eyes met, then nixed it and me off. One could tell that she didn't feel like working that day, but in time it passed. Let it be understood, the value of the whole experience, especially at such a young age. (104–5)

The uncovered, animated nipple that stares back at Balagoon mirrors the prosthetic function of narrative throughout the text. In the absence of a coherent story line, the narrative body is reduced to parts, pieces of the bodies that narrate and the narrative body (a body which is never completely assembled). Such pieces of narrative deflect and (as in the breast that "stare[s]"), reflect the reader's own desire to see clearly what appears to be exposed. In Balagoon's paragraphs, memory re-creates the process by which parts of the (remembered) body are replaced by narrated substitutes. As the narrative plays with parts of a disassembled female form—hips, "ample legs," "succulent breasts"—the teacher's body becomes a single surveying eye. Balagoon thus conjures the seemingly taboo topic of surveillance that shadows *Whirlwind*'s amputated narrative(s). Like the breast that "stare[s] out into [Balagoon's] eyes," *Whirlwind* confronts the government's gaze, freely exposing details of the contributors' lives that covert agents have been seeking in the years leading up to the trial. And yet, like the supposed revelations contained in other entries, the blatant eroticism of the encounter Balagoon describes, emblematized by the literally and figuratively colorful detail of the teacher's red dress, conceals as much as it reveals.

In this act of revealing-concealing, the red dress episode reproduces a pattern that repeats throughout much of the text, in which the declared purpose or intention of a given cultural institution masks its actual function (thus the previously noted role of Harlem Hospital as the neighborhood "butcher shop"). This pattern also holds for many of those sections dedicated to pedagogical experiences. School educates the authors in realities, histories, and socio-cultural facts entirely different from its intended lessons or the purported purpose of those lessons. Many of the authors' anecdotes describe schools as primers for racism's inevitability. "The school in my hometown in rural Texas was like thousands of others, a monument to the way of keeping blacks, Mexicans, or any oppressed minority ignorant, uneducated, unskilled, and, in fact, miseducated," writes Sundiata Acoli (110). Arriving in New York City after spending her earliest years shuttling between family homes in North Carolina and Virginia, Afeni Shakur finds herself for the first time surrounded by white students: "A kid named Myron Cohen said that I looked like something from outer space and I kicked his ass. . . . I was really scared of all those white people around me. I wasn't used to that" (103). "Every day going to and from school we had to pass the white school. . . . Every day some cracker kids would be waiting by their school, calling us and our mothers every derogatory name under the sun," recalls Lumumba Shakur (109). The disappointments, humiliations, and violent episodes recalled in these anecdotes establish a consistency. As a result of the similarity between such recollections, Balagoon's narrative of sexual awakening—if it *is* a narrative of sexual awakening—becomes all the more distinguishable.

Aside from the unlikelihood of his teacher's bra-less red dress exposure occurring in a 1950s American schoolroom, the oddity of this purported recollection lies in the manner through which its retelling unfolds. "Let it be understood," he writes, "the value of the whole experience." What *is* "the value of the whole experience"? Balagoon's language furnishes mysteries through its disorderly divulgences. It ties itself into logical knots with short, declarative sentences that betray themselves before reaching their conclusions. The use of what rhetoricians call anacoluthon (the lack of grammatical sequence, employed in sentences such as, "Embarrassed, she was caught off guard") and anastrophe (the transposition of normal word order, as in, "Let it be understood, the value . . . ") dislodge the recollection's clarity from the sanctuary of sense perception and nudge it toward the incoherence of the unconscious. This movement underscores the way that linguistic play allows the contributors to reformulate the introduction's claims regarding *Whirlwind*'s function as the purveyor of individual identities: the text is, on the contrary, an exploration of the political possibilities contained in identity's mysteries, a testament to the illusiveness of individuality as a concept, and a vehicle for personal expression through collectivity. Balagoon's recollection stages an incidental self-exposure by an authority figure as if to channel the mechanics by which the establishment accidentally reveals the power vested in its covert operatives.

The confounding, disassembling linguistic features that "stare out" from Balagoon's anecdote await the reader's notice, just as his subsequent activities deserve further scrutiny. His *Whirlwind* contributions preface a career equally dedicated to leadership in revolutionary struggle, self-sacrifice, and deception. In April of 1969, when the NYPD began its predawn raids to arrest the Black Panthers who would become known as the New York 21, Kuwasi Balagoon awaited trial in a Newark jail on robbery charges along with Richard Harris, another defendant in the case. Balagoon's status as a prisoner in a bordering state resulted in his absence from pretrial hearings. Over the course of the trial, his lawyers would successfully argue that this absence made him deserving of a separate trial altogether (Zimroth 1974, 13; Maitland 1981). Eventually, the court would grant this request; remarkably, less than five months after the other members of the New York 21 had been acquitted of all charges, Balagoon would plead guilty to assisting an un-named sniper who supposedly fired on police on January 17, 1969. A *Times* article reporting Balagoon's conviction notes that "The allegation that a shootout had taken place . . . was an important event at the trial of the 13 defendants who were acquitted. It consumed several weeks of testimony from the patrolmen who were fired upon" (Vasquez 1971). The shootout was one the few accusations that included physical evidence, as opposed to state-ments regarding possible future acts of resistance supposedly made by the defendants in the presence of police informants; as such, it formed an essen-tial part of the prosecution's more general charges of conspiracy.

Balagoon's narrative presence as a member of the New York 21 thus masks the legal efforts to separate him from the group during the trial itself. His guilty plea and subsequent writings also distance him from the defense strategy of proclaimed innocence; Balagoon is one of a handful of revolu-tionaries from this era who freely admit to have engaged in many of the activities of which the government accuses them. Others, such as Marilyn Buck and David Gilbert, would become colleagues of Balagoon's, sharing his understanding of the American government as the criminal, colonizer, and terrorist. For Balagoon, such an understanding suggests that many forms of resistance, including strategic "appropriations" such as bank robberies, might be justified (Hudson 1983).

In the context of his life's work, Balagoon's memory of his teacher's self-exposure becomes more curious. In the recollection itself, his perception of his teacher's innocence vanishes alongside her pupil's; Balagoon's identity as a member of the acquitted New York 21 similarly vanishes from almost all documents besides the text of *Whirlwind* itself, in which his presence sug-gests his own acquittal. By pleading guilty, Balagoon steps out from the shadow of the group and of *Whirlwind* as a text, even as he enters prison. In subsequent statements and writings, Balagoon pushes the act of exposure ever further. After his arrest in 1981 for his part in the "Brinks Case," Bala-goon refused to participate in the trial proceedings. Instead, he declared himself a prisoner of war and tried to explain his position to the court in his opening and closing statements. His words reverse the standard claims of innocence so often heard in cases of leftist radicals, openly embracing the "declared extremes" Kempton's American liberalism disavows by attempting to explain the logic behind "expropriation raids":

> i believe that the people . . . deserve an explanation of the event, the expropriation and related actions that took place on October 20th, 1981. Not a mere criminal defense in relation to it, that type of legal mumbo jumbo could have matters more confused than ever . . . it is not the people but the United States Government and its oppressive apparatus that we are at war against. . . . Expropriation raids are a method used in every revolution by those who have got to get the resources from the haves to carry on armed struggle. (*a soldier's story*, 59)

Balagoon died of AIDS in prison in 1987; in one of the dedications to him contained in the posthumous collection of his writings, *a soldier's story*, an associate describes him as "closeted," and references his transvestite lover. These facts of his life had remained unknown to many who knew him, even those within the movements he championed (Starr 2003, 18). The exposures that mark Balagoon's writings thus disguise fundamental, yet closeted, parts of his identity.

Here one must once again note the fingerprints of the government's covert operatives on the blockages that prevent more forthcoming personal writings: in the summer of 1970, Huey Newton's call to unite with members of any and all oppressed groups, and specifically the gay community, resulted in yet another FBI COINTELPRO operation. The FBI fabricated letters ostensibly written by Panthers critical of Newton's remarks and thus designed to alarm homophobic Party members, ideally isolating Newton and alienating his supporters (Grady-Willis, 374). The teacher's exposed breast that distinguishes Balagoon's schoolroom memory underscores the virtual absence of discussions concerning sexuality throughout *Whirlwind*, a deficiency that points to the Black Panther Party's reputation for being insensitive to the ways in which its own discourse might be enriched through an engagement with the politics of gender and sexuality. The heterosexual dynamic the exposed breast operates within also gestures to the sexual identity of which Kuwasi Balagoon could not speak while participating in the liberation movements that defined his life story. The revealing in the red dress episode presages his subsequent acts of textual self-sacrifice and self-exposure; yet even these acts mask, conceal, or closet vital aspects of his identity. If Balagoon offers an unexpected glimpse of flesh as his preferred vision, this same fragment of personal narrative provides him with the cover to pass as yet another Panther, one part of the apparitional body politic *Whirlwind* constructs.

CONCLUSION: WHIRLWIND AND APPARITIONAL
SUBJECTIVITY

The ghostly quality of the *Whirlwind* narrative, its apparitional effect, recalls Marcus Garvey's spectral presence in the text as the author of the quotation that provides the book's title and its epigraph. Like the New York 21, Garvey was arrested after a government counterintelligence operation. The Department of Justice's forerunner to the FBI, then known as the Bureau of Investigation and headed by future domestic surveillance and FBI czar J. Edgar Hoover, employed its first black agents in order to infiltrate Garvey's Universal Negro Improvement Association (UNIA).[11] While caged for his supposed crimes, Garvey wrote the letter from which *Whirlwind* draws its epigraph: "Look for me in the whirlwind or the storm, look for me all around you, for, with God's grace, I shall come and bring with me countless millions of black slaves who have died in America and the West Indies and the millions in Africa to aid you in the fight for Liberty, Freedom and Life" (Garvey 1923, 239). Not only does Garvey's arrest and prison sentence prefigure the infiltration and arrest of the New York Panthers by NYPD undercover officers almost fifty years later; when Garvey's own jailhouse letter introduces the text, a literary lineage connects *Whirlwind* to a nearly forgotten archive of resistance and revolutionary imaginings.

Thus recalled by the New York 21, Garvey's ghost unearths his imaginary army from underworlds in which legacies of genocide reside. The apparitional army Garvey envisions as reinforcements for the struggle waged by the living presages the invocation of what I call apparitional subjectivity in *Whirlwind*. As Sharon Holland reminds us in her meditations on the hospital and modernity, the definition of death changes with science and history; in *Whirlwind*, the assurance life brings of death's absence erodes. Apparitional subjectivity provides a provisional answer to Holland's question, if "the dead figure as the folk with no recourse to discourse . . . if they have no discourse of their own, no defense, whose discourse must they *borrow* in order to speak?" *Apparitional subjectivity* describes a textual strategy of countersigning, interleaving, and counterposing: in the lending of the autobiographical act to those who remain silent, personal narratives cross over and confound individual voices, claim collective origins, and construct a dialogical portrait both detailed *and* generic; apparitional subjectivity names a process that carefully de-composes autobiography as a genre, and that simultaneously nominates the very concept of individuality as a foundation myth helping to formulate America's legacy of racial injustice. Apparitional subjectivity articulates its discourse in the uncomfortable no-man's-land between the living and the dead, the speaking and the silent; its purpose is to tunnel under the confines of personal, autobiographical narrative to reconvene as a collective political force fully alive, yet moving in the presence of the dead whose murders at the hands of the state make collective action imperative.

NOTES

1. I am thinking of the many unjust arrests, endless trials, imprisoned innocents, victims of violence, and lives wasted as a result of the government's campaign against the Panthers; in truth, the examples are too numerous to list briefly.

2. The original 21 included Lumumba Shakur, Afeni Shakur, Dhoruba Bin Wahad, Kwando Kinshasa, Cetewayo, Ali Bey Hassan, Abayama Katara, Sundiata Acoli, Curtis Powell, Robert Collier, Baba Odinga, Shaba Om, Joan Bird, Jamal, Lonnie Epps, Lee Berry, Mshina, Sekou Odinga, Larry Mack, Kuwasi Balagoon, and Richard Harris. The sixteen included in *Whirlwind* were Balagoon, Bird, Cetewayo, Collier, Bin Wahad, Harris, Hassan, Jamal, Katara, Kinshasa, Odinga, Om, Powell, Afeni Shakur, Lumumba Shakur, and Acoli; thirteen would go through the entire trial and be acquitted.

3. Robert Daley's book *Target Blue: An Insider's View of the NYPD* (Delacorte, 1973) covers these scandals in some detail, including corruption investigations involving gambling and narcotics, while providing a glimpse into the department's use of the press (Daley, a writer and journalist, was hired by the NYPD to serve as media liaison) to shape public opinion.

4. A useful chronicle of the disagreements between supposedly "militant" and "political" factions can be found in Ollie A. Johnson's article, "Explaining the Demise of the Black Panther Party: The Role of Internal Factors," in *The Black Panther Party Reconsidered*, edited by Charles E. Jones (1998), 391–409.

5. Numerous essays in *The Black Panther Party Reconsidered* (1998) discuss this subject from the perspective of many different groups and interests within the Party itself.

6. For more on Christian Parenti's indictment of Nixon's so-called anti-crime measures as elements of state terror designed to strengthen boundaries of class and race, see *Lockdown America: Police and Prisons in the Age of Crisis* (1999), 6–26.

7. Churchill and Vander Wall's chapter on "COINTELPRO—Black Panther Party" contains a concise chronicle of the major covert operations against the Panthers during this time (*Agents of Repression* 2002, 63–99); for Hilliard's arrest and indictment, see Caldwell, "Panther Charged in Nixon Threat" (1969).

8. An FBI Airtel dated February 2, 1971, suggests that the FBI contributed to Cetewayo and Dharuba's respective decisions to abandon their fellow defendants. The Airtel notes that the "dissension [stemming from the New York 21 trial] coupled with financial difficulties offers an exceptional opportunity to further disrupt, aggravate and possibly neutralize this organization [the Black Panther Party] through counterintelligence" (Churchill and Vander Wall, *COINTELPRO*, 161). Cetewayo and Dharuba failed to appear in court on February 8, 1971, six days after the above Airtel, and several months before the verdict; as a result, Afeni Shakur, now five months pregnant, was forced to return to jail, along with Joan Bird. Dharuba apparently believed that someone had ordered his assassination from within the Party, although accounts differ over whether it was Newton or the New York 21 themselves that he feared (Churchill and Vander Wall, *COINTELPRO*, 157; Guy, 107–08). If he had once been misidentified in court as either Lumumba Shakur or Cetewayo (Michael Tabor), the government's prosecutors made a careful study of Dharuba after the New York 21 trial. He was arrested soon after the trial's verdict was announced, along with his fellow defendant Jamal, for the robbery of a Bronx social club. After his arrest, Dharuba was charged with the shooting of two officers guarding the home of New York D.A. Frank Hogan, an event leading to a series of confrontations between the NYPD and the Black Liberation Army. Subjected to yet another trial, Dharuba would this time be convicted. Subsequently, documents originally sought by his defense team and withheld by the FBI would reveal his conviction to be part of a COINTELPRO operation. Specific evidence that would have led to his acquittal was withheld; one letter in the FBI files suggests that President Nixon himself ordered the operation called "Newkill" that led

to his conviction (Churchill and Vander Wall, 158; Grady-Willis, 380). The state refused to grant Dharuba his freedom for nearly twenty-five years, citing a New York State legal technicality that ostensibly prohibited his release. In 1990 Dharuba was finally released, the courts having finally acknowledged that his conviction was obtained through the government's manipulation and withholding of key evidence (Churchill and Vander Wall, 408).

    9. "Shaba Om Greets Sundiata Acoli," http://youtube.com/watch?v=5T5KwxMUtWU& feature=related, posted July 9, 2007.

    10. Though the phrase "apparitional subjectivity" shares the adjective "apparitional" with Terry Castle's "apparitional lesbian" (*The Apparitional Lesbian: Female Homosexuality and Modern Culture*, Columbia UP, 1995), I intend my use of the term "apparitional subjectivity" here to refer specifically to phenomena that emerge through collective forms of authorship, autobiography, and "life writing" practiced in *Whirlwind* and discussed in the chapter that follows.

    11. Winston A. Grady-Willis discusses this operation in his contribution to *The Black Panther Party Reconsidered*, ed. by Charles E. Jones (Black Classic Press, 1998); more thorough treatments of the same incidents can be found in Theodore Kornweibel's *Federal Surveillance of Afro-Americans, 1917–1925* (Univ. Publications of America, 1986).

REFERENCES

Acoli, Sundiata. 1998. "On Marcus Garvey's Birthday Celebration." http://www.geocities.com/standingdeer1/acoli7.htm .

Balagoon, Kuwasi. 2001. *a soldier's story: writings by a revolutionary New Afrikan anarchist.* Montreal: Kersplebedeb.

Balagoon, Kuwasi, Joan Bird, Cetwayo, et al. 1971. *Look for Me in the Whirlwind: The Collective Autobiography of the New York 21.* New York: Random House.

Caldwell, Earl. 1969. "Panther Charged in Nixon Threat." *New York Times.* December 4.

Carew, Jan. 1971. "Panthermania." *New York Times.* September 5.

Churchill, Ward, and Jim Vander Wall. 2002 (Orig. pub. 1988). *Agents of Repression: The FBI's Secret Wars Against the Black Panther Party and the American Indian Movement.* Cambridge, MA: South End Press.

———. 2002 (Orig. pub. 1990). *The COINTELPRO Papers.* Cambridge, MA: South End Press.

Collier, Barnard L. 1969. "U.S. Bars 2 Cuban Envoys; Sees Tie to Negro Militants." *New York Times.* April 5.

Garvey, Marcus. 1986 (Orig. pub. 1923). *The Philosophy & Opinions of Marcus Garvey.* Dover, MA: Majority Press.

Grady-Willis, Winston A. 1998. "The Black Panther Party: State Repression and Political Prisoners." In *The Black Panther Party Reconsidered*, ed. Charles E. Jones, 363–389. Baltimore: Black Classic Press.

Guy, Jasmine. 2004. *Afeni Shakur: Evolution of a Revolutionary.* New York: Atria Books.

Hames-Garcia, Michael. 2004. *Fugitive Thought: Prison Movements, Race, and the Meaning of Justice.* Minneapolis: Univ. of Minnesota Press.

Holland, Sharon. 2000. *Raising the Dead: Readings of Death and (Black) Subjectivity.* Durham: Duke Univ. Press.

Hudson, Edward. 1983. "Protest Marks Opening of Brink's Murder Trial." *New York Times.* August 9.

Jones, Charles E., ed. 1998. *The Black Panther Party Reconsidered.* Baltimore: Black Classic Press.

Kempton, Murray. 1997 (Orig. pub. 1973). *The Briar Patch: The Trial of the Panther 21.* New York: Da Capo Press.

Kornweibel, Theodore. 1986. *Federal Surveillance of Afro-Americans, 1917–1925.* Frederick, MD: Univ. Publications of America.

Maitland, Leslie. 1981. "Police Find a History of Arrests." *New York Times.* October 24. "U.N. Assures Cubans on 5 Re-entry Visas." 1969. *New York Times.* May 8.

Parenti, Christian. 1999. *Lockdown America: Police and Prisons in the Age of Crisis.* New York: Verso.

"Shaba Om Greets Sundiata Acoli." 2007. Youtube. Originally posted July 9. http://youtube.com/watch?v=5T5KwxMUtWU&feature=related (accessed 2008).

Starr, Meg. 2003 (Orig. pub. 2001). "Some Reflections on an Unpublished Poem." In *a soldier's story: writings by a revolutionary New Afrikan anarchist,* by Kuwasi Balagoon, 17–18. Montreal: Kersplebedeb.

Taylor, Michael. 2007. "'70s in the Bay Area—Era of Radical Violence." *San Francisco Chronicle.* January 24.

Vasquez, Juan M. 1971. "One of the Panther 21 Admits Helping Antipolice Sniper." *New York Times.* October 8.

Zimroth, Peter L. 1974. Perversions of Justice: The Prosecution and Acquittal of the Panther 21. New York: Viking.

Chapter Eight

Remembering Pain in Uruguay

What Memories Mean in Carlos Liscano's Truck of Fools

Eugenio Di Stefano

In the opening passage of *Truck of Fools* (2001), Carlos Liscano recalls his first torture session: "I am twenty-three years old. They have just brought me from the room where they torture. . . . You can hear screams, one person tortured, then another and another, all night" (17). Written sixteen years after the return to democracy in Uruguay and his own personal return to freedom, Liscano finds himself ceaselessly revisiting this horrific site where the body comes up against the unforgiving realities of torture. "You smell sweat, saliva stuck to the beard and hood, your own and others' hair inside the hood from a dunking in the tank, the smell of urine, the bad odor of weeks without brushing your teeth" (67). Embedded in a squalid prison cell for over thirteen years, Liscano presents the reader a world in which only the beaten, ravaged body continues to exist. Left on full display, Liscano's selfhood is stripped down only to reveal his body's bareness: what it says, the smells it produces and the unfamiliar ways it reacts to a torturer's blows are explained with excruciating precision, held out for the reader to experience. But just as Liscano's testimonio wrestles with the pain of incarceration and torture, it also finds unexpected moments of human endurance and dignity; from inside the torture chamber, Liscano will learn to overcome and ultimately heal in the most harrowing of human conditions. Liscano's *Truck of Fools*, in short, successfully sketches a compelling story of human survival.

This story of survival, however, is not strictly limited to his experience in prison; his testimonio also delves into other periods of his life. After his release, for example, Liscano sets out to find the graves of his parents who

died while he was incarcerated. The search will haunt Liscano, but it ends
well when he finally locates their graves. Liscano also writes about the years
before his arrest; in one passage, he recalls two fond memories that would
stay with him for a "lifetime" (23)—his sister's birth and learning to tell time.
The testimonio, in effect, ambitiously spans Liscano's entire life, revealing
memories of childhood, dinners with friends, the death of his parents, and life
in Norway after his release. Nevertheless, there is one moment that is curiously absent. What Liscano's testimonio does not include are the years in
which he was affiliated with and a principal member of the urban guerilla
group, the MLN Tupamaros—the affiliation and membership that would
ultimately lead to his arrest and imprisonment. In the more than a hundred
pages of detailed testimonio, covering Liscano's entire life, the word *Tupamaro* is never mentioned once.

What does it mean for the Tupamaros and Liscano's experience as a
Tupamaro to be absolutely erased? In Liscano's narrative there are emotional
episodes of his childhood, but there is no account of his past guerilla activities. There are stories that speak to Liscano's guilt-ridden relationship with
his torturer, but there is no story that lays bare the bond he maintained with
other Tupamaros. There are moments that reveal the body's capacity to resist
torture, but there is no moment that displays an organization's fight against
the Uruguayan state. There are horrific images in which Liscano's body is
brutally beaten, but there is little insight as to why that body was beaten in
the first place. There are interrogators who torture, but the motivation for this
torture is never clear; indeed, as we will see, the idea that they even have
motives is called into question. Liscano wants his readers to feel his pain, but
he does not want them to sympathize with, understand or even know about
the Tupamaros's ideology. Why do torture, the body, and pain take prece-
dence over a discourse about the political ideology that put Liscano in jail?
Why does Liscano's narrative incessantly displace his Tupamaro affiliation?

Andreas Huyssen has noted that in the postdictatorial period in Latin
America "issues of memory and forgetting have emerged as dominant concerns [that] . . . determine, to varying degrees, the cultural and political
debate . . . , raising fundamental questions about human rights violations,
justice, and collective responsibility" (26). And, in our brief summary of
Liscano, we have already begun to see what is remembered (torture, the
family) and what is forgotten (the Tupamaros). The subject of this chapter
will be the political meaning of this discourse of remembering and forgetting.
Our question will be, what is being forgotten when Liscano remembers the
body, dignity, and healing? What is the postdictatorial discourse of memory,
citizenship, and reconciliation accomplishing when it remembers the body in
pain? In brief, the aim of this chapter is to show that a politics of remembering has come to occupy the center of "progressive" politics in the period of
democracy (post-1985), and in so doing not only replaces the critique of

capitalism that had once defined the left, but, as we will also see, is fully complicit with the further advancement of neoliberalism.

THE MLN-TUPAMAROS

There is a narrative leap of sixteen years from Liscano's sister's birth in 1956 to the night of his imprisonment and torture. It is May 27, 1972, he explains, and today he has planned to celebrate his sister's birthday with his family; but instead in the early morning the military arrive at his house and place a "hood on my head, tie my hands behind my back, and set me out on the sidewalk, facing the wall" (23). He is taken to a torture chamber where he is tortured and then thrown into a prison cell; he will spend the next thirteen years of his life in prison.[1] Although the reader will learn about the pain suffered during these years of incarceration, he is told nothing about the turbulent political climate in those sixteen years of narrative effacement, including the rise of the MLN-Tupamaros. But in not telling us about Liscano's affiliation with the MLN-Tupamaros, the testimonio makes the political history of Uruguay essentially invisible. So the first step in understanding the political meaning of that erasure is to understand what it was about the Tupamaros' political ideology that brought the military to Liscano's door.[2]

Unlike most Latin American nations, Uruguay had a relatively stable democracy for most of the twentieth century. For the greater part of the 1950s it was still considered "a model country," maintaining a sound middle class, a literacy rate of 95 percent and universal health care. The reputation of this South American anomaly was so great that it became known as "the Switzerland of South America." This stability, however, would monumentally collapse as the decade came to an end, as the ill effects of failed ISI policies [import-substitution industrialization] could no longer be contained. As the national economy spun out of control, tensions quickly rose among a strong mobilized working class. According to Lawrence Weschler, "During the first half of the fifties, the only countries *in the world* with poorer growth rates than Uruguay were Malawi and the Dominican Republic. In 1967, Uruguay's GDP fell 5.4 percent, while inflation rampaged at 89.3 percent (the following year it even topped that, at 125.3 percent)" (99). As the economy crashed, civil unrest grew exponentially. It was during this period of economic collapse and political turmoil that the MLN-Tupamaros (*Movimiento de Liberación Nacional,* National Liberation Movement), an organization of Marxist urban guerrilla fighters, appeared on the Uruguayan political scene. With theatrical savvy and cleverness, the group of mostly young, university-educated revolutionaries had managed to mount a tactically sophisticated and highly successful movement that became a source of admiration and inspiration for leftist radicals everywhere.

Yet, the origins of the Tupamaros were certainly less spectacular than their later endeavors. The movement emerged against the backdrop of the sugarcane worker strikes led by the lawyer and future Tupamaro leader, Raúl Sendic Antonaccio. Their first armed attack would take place in 1963 when a small group of Tupamaros broke into the Swiss Club outside of Montevideo and stole "some old and worthless weapons" (Browne). In the ensuing years, however, Tupamaro tactics would grow more daring, as they would deal out a "series of massive shocks"—including bombings, bank robberies, strikes and riots—that would send seismic waves throughout the nation and then continent. But while these attacks were effective, they were rarely violent. In fact, in these first years Tupamaro "guerrilla warfare" was seen more as a form of radical guerrilla theater than a radical political insurgency. Some of the more memorable moments consisted in stealing food trucks and driving through the poorest areas of Montevideo, distributing turkeys and wine to the poor. Another "spectacular accomplishment" was the kidnapping of Ulises Pereira Reverbel, the head of Uruguay's telephone and electric company and closest friend of President Jorge Pacheco Areco. The Tupamaros held him captive in a people's prison, releasing him four days later. The episode quickly became a point of amusement: "a mere four days [. . .] was long enough to set the Uruguayans laughing at him, at their police department, at the president. When Pereira was released, not only unharmed but apparently a few pounds heavier, the poor in Montevideo were quoted as joking, 'Attention, Tupamaros! Kidnap me!' "(Weschler 231). Weschler also describes another memorable episode in which the Tupamaros "ransacked an exclusive high-class nightclub"—an establishment that symbolized all that was now wrong with Uruguay and was detested by many Uruguayans—spray painting the walls with their most unforgettable slogan: *O bailan todos o no baila nadie*—either everybody dances or nobody does (104).[3]

Although the Tupamaros gained wide recognition for these creative "antics," it was their political objective of "socialist revolution" that was most troublesome for Uruguay's volatile government. A MLN-Tupamaro internal communiqué circulating between 1967 and 1971 thus explains, "The MLN objective and strategic tactic are to seize power for a socialist revolution" (Documento 5).[4] Unlike the Uruguayan communist party that was entangled in bureaucratic red tape and politically paralyzed within the traditional party system, the Tupamaros believed that "socialist revolution" could only be realized through "armed action."[5] "For this armed action is the only way. This is determined by the national and global situation, the experience of all communities throughout the world, the success of our and future perspectives; without armed action no other fight makes sense. It is the only guarantee to carry out the revolution to its natural end" (Documento 5). If the socialist revolution could only take place through armed warfare, the Tupamaros were preparing themselves for "a long and hard fight" (Documento 5) that would begin first with the "national situation," that is, with the total destruction of the "bourgeois nation-state" (Documento 1). What had seemed during the mid-sixties to be nothing more than a nuisance for Oscar Diego Gestido's and Jorge Pacheco Areco's presidencies, by the end of the 1960s had become an effective political front, successfully polarizing the Uruguayan left and right.[6]

Furthermore, the threat posed by the Tupamaros, was articulated not merely as a national but as a continental and even a global project. In the wake of the successful socialist revolution in Cuba, the Tupamaro tactics sought to incite *focos*—strategic strikes that would scatter throughout the globe.[7] Thus, if "Tupamaro activities" were deemed "dangerous," it was not only because they threatened the stability of Pacheco's presidency, but also and more important because they gestured toward a "continental strategy" that threatened to spread, first, to neighboring Argentina and Brazil and then to the rest of Latin America (Documento 5). A 1967 MLN-Tupamaro communiqué reveals the underlying philosophy that sought to awaken the "continental" "consciousness" by "bringing socialism to the people" and destroying "the global imperialist system" (Documento 1). The military regime understood the conflict in similar fashion and employed this continental and global rhetoric of a war between communism and capitalism in order to carry out their repressive tactics. Indeed, in the months leading up to the coup and the years that followed it, the discourse of national security concerned itself primarily with the spread of international communism, "The enemy—the International Communist Movement—is perceived as covertly operating everywhere, all the time, in all fields of human endeavor" (Weschler 121). Liscano's arrest and torture must be positioned within this historical context, where political affiliation and political action involved the active obliteration of capitalism and its replacement with socialism; and where repression meant arresting and torturing Tupamaros in order to *actively* foreclose the possibility of a future socialist revolution.

And repression was very effective in Uruguay. In 1972, several months before the official coup and the year Liscano was arrested, Uruguay's government was already working hard to "[e]xterminate Marxism by its root" (5).[8] In the summer of 1973, the moment of Uruguay's self-coup, the authoritarian regime had already detained the core group of urban guerrillas.[9] "During the next half year," writes Lawrence Weschler, "the military incarcerated thousands of individuals and systematically dismantled the Tupamaro structures" (109). By the mid-1970s the Tupamaros had been aggressively hunted and decisively suppressed. But the repression continued for almost ten more years. Statistics reveal that during the thirteen years of military rule four hundred thousand of Uruguay's three million citizens fled into exile. For those who remained, one in every fifty was detained for interrogation—almost every interrogation included torture—and of those interrogated, one in every five hundred received a long prison sentence for political offenses. And at the very height of the repression, Uruguay held the disgraceful honor of maintaining the highest per-capita rate of political incarceration on the planet (Weschler 87). Within a span of only twenty years, Uruguay had radically transformed itself from one of the most democratic governments in South America to one of the most authoritarian, from being known as the "the Switzerland of South America" to "the torture chamber of South America."[10] It would take thirteen years before the physical repression was removed and Uruguayan citizens were allowed to speak again. What would they say?

On March 14, 1985, Liscano is released from prison. On this day, he sits in a government truck filled with other ex-political prisoners and prison guards who are escorting the inmates to their homes after thirteen years of incarceration.[11] He observes his surroundings, a Montevideo both familiar and foreign, and he is overcome by an immense sense of anxiety and disorientation; he looks at the other prisoners and realizes the difficulty they will have entering a new Uruguayan society. What is next for Liscano? He is entering a radically different world, one that is different from the thirteen years of military rule. One of these changes, of course, is Uruguay's transition into democracy. The Tupamaros will also come to play a central role in redemocratization. Yet it is still uncertain whether the society that released the Tupamaros would be more sympathetic to their cause. Would the resurgence of the Tupamaros within the postdictatorial era signal a shift to socialism in this small Southern Cone country?

FREEDOM OR THE TRANSITION TOWARD AN (ABSENT) LEFT

Liscano returns to freedom in spring 1985, but he also knows that this new life will be a lot more difficult than his years in prison. Will he remain in Montevideo and attempt to integrate himself into the new democracy? Or will he, like many ex-political prisoners, depart and find a future somewhere else? Or perhaps, like some others, will he return to his past political commitments, fighting for the socialist cause in Uruguay? After a thirteen-year forced hiatus, the Tupamaros are also weighing their options; within a few months, however, the Tupamaros are hard at work buying up radio stations, disseminating propaganda, and scheduling national conferences. At their Third National Convention, in September of 1985, the Tupamaros reiterate their goals of agrarian reform, nationalization of banking and export sectors, and a moratorium on the foreign debt (Weinstein 112). Four months after the

September convention, Liscano leaves Uruguay and on December 11, 1985, he lands in Stockholm. From Sweden, the ex-guerrilla would go to Norway where he would reside for the next eleven years, and where he would translate, teach, and publish his first novels and plays.

Meanwhile in Uruguay, the history of politics, and specifically a certain type of leftist politics, was not developing the way that the Tupamaros had hoped. In fact by the end of the 1980s, the Uruguayan government had begun to implement President Sanguinetti's free-market model, ensuring that Uruguay's role for the new millennium would be as the new "financial center" in Latin America, a "future Hong Kong or Singapore" (Weschler 160). Martin Weinstein sums up the situation in this way:

> In certain areas, Uruguay has remained steadfastly committed to the free-market model. Uruguay is the only country on the continent that permits the free buying and selling of foreign currencies. In addition, banks constantly advertise their interest rates for dollar deposits, and the government raises hard currency by issuing gold-backed treasury denominated in dollars. For such reasons, Uruguay has once again been dubbed the "the Switzerland of South America." The title used to refer to its constitutional stability and the civil liberties enjoyed by the population. It now confirms Uruguay's role as a haven for foreign capital. (101)

By the time Liscano returned from Norway in 1996, Sanguinetti had been reelected for a second term as president. And although the economy was still struggling, Sanguinetti had convincingly ensured that the deregulation of business and financial markets would improve economic conditions. Yet not all the news was bad for the left. In Montevideo, where half of Uruguay's three million citizens reside, the socialist leader Tabaré Vázquez of Frente Amplio (FA-Broad Front), won the 1990 mayoral elections. A year prior to this landmark victory, the Tupamaros had forged an alliance with FA and became the largest constituency in the FA coalition. [12] But the biggest victory was still to come: in 2004, two years after the banking crisis that would devastate the Uruguayan economy, the left would finally gain full control in Uruguay, as Vázquez would win the presidency and become the first leftist president in the history of Uruguay. Unfortunately, Vázquez, and the recently elected president José "Pepe" Mujica of Frente Amplio, who have run on a progressive platform, have shown themselves to be resolutely committed to furthering the neoliberal project already begun by Sanguinetti. In January 2007, Vázquez signed a Trade and Investment Framework Agreement (TIFA) with United States, hoping to increase exports in Uruguayan beef and software as well as gain a stronger foothold in the international market. Although some Frente Amplistas (Frente Amplio activists) wince at the idea of negotiations with a government that fully supported the 1973 coup, many others believe that there is no other "choice but to look north" (Fox). Whether or not this is the case, what certainly is true is that the reappearance of the "Switzerland of South America," this time not only as a model for liberal citizenship but also as a haven for neoliberal capital, does not appear to conflict in any way with Frente Amplio's economic agenda. In other words, if Liscano's 1972 arrest and torture illustrate just how far Uruguay had moved away from its moniker as the "Switzerland of South America," then the moniker's reemergence during the administration of Frente Amplio reveals that the socialist left now survives not in its communist, but rather in its neoliberal form. In the postdictatorship, then, the socialist left—from an economic standpoint—begins to look increasingly like the right. But in order to better understand the period in which Liscano writes, we must first return to the moment of transition and the politics of the left. Indeed, a new set of issues emerged in the period of transition and reconciliation, producing a new distinction between the left and the right, giving rise to a different conflict that will not center on the role of the free market but the issue of remembering and forgetting past abuses. [13]

Although the transition from dictatorship to democracy was considered peaceful, redemocratization in Uruguay did not arrive without its pitfalls. The most heated debates—in the government and in the universities—centered on the question of remembering and forgetting the past human rights abuses committed by the military regime. These debates emerged soon after the inauguration of Julio María Sanguinetti—Uruguay's first democratically elected president in over fourteen years—who granted two political amnesties: the first, in March of 1985, freed political prisoners but excluded the military; the second, signed in December of 1986, gave blanket and successive amnesties to all military officials. This second amnesty, *Ley de Caducidad* [Law of Expiration], was met with fierce criticism, because it not only granted complete immunity to human rights violators, but also and more importantly allowed them to continue holding public office. [14] While it was uncertain whether the *Ley de Caducidad* was the price paid in order for Uruguay to return to democracy, what is clear is that the military was not going to permit the Uruguayan citizenry to bring them to trial. Just weeks before Sanguinetti's inauguration, Lieutenant General Hugo Medina warned citizens that "if we are obliged, we will have no choice but to carry out another coup d'état" (Weschler 107). These military threats were common parlance throughout the transitional period and unsurprisingly they did not fall on deaf ears; not only did this intimidation make it unsafe for citizens who wished to "look back," but it is believed to be the primary factor in the failed 1989 referendum that would have revoked the *Ley de Caducidad*.

The military was not the only group that wanted amnesty upheld. Many politicians also felt that talking about past human rights violations would only serve to destabilize an already fragile democracy. On numerous occasions President Sanguinetti scolded those "nostalgics" for having "eyes on the back of their necks" (Hampsten "Seminar"). If Uruguay was going to maintain stability, he argued, Uruguayans would have to "look forward," instead of reopening past "wounds" (Weschler 189). Recalling the words of Ernest Renan, Sanguinetti maintained that "'Nations are a plebiscite every day and they are constructed on the basis of great remembering and great forgettings.' If the French were still thinking about the Night of St. Bartholomew, they'd be slaughtering each other to this day" (Weschler 191). "That's why Uruguay is stable," Sanguinetti continues, "The bottom line is that either we're to look to the future or to the past" (189). As can be imagined, Sanguinetti's comments were met with strong opposition by a large sector of the national and international community, who quickly responded, insisting that true democracy could never be formed unless the past was fully taken into account. "As long as we do not face up to the past," writes the Marxist writer Mario Benedetti, "it will be difficult to move ahead" (Hampsten "Road" 7). Eduardo Galeano proffered up an analogy that also expressed the inability of the government to effectively deal with the past, "On the part of the government and some important sectors of the population, there is a belief that democracy is a fragile old lady in a wheelchair. If she moves too much she will collapse, and if you speak too loudly she will have a heart attack. So a democracy is something that shouldn't be touched. These ideas are actually the enemies of democracy because true democracy must move forward, deepen, and develop" (Weschler 169). For Galeano, of course, moving forward could only mean looking back. In the postdictatorship, as we will see later, it is not only presumed that "true democracy" be equated with the discourse of remembering past human rights violations, but more important that the political conflict between the left and the right be understood no longer as a conflict between capitalism and socialism but as a conflict between remembering and forgetting these abuses.[15] For Liscano, as we will also see, this commitment to "true democracy" involves remembering his torture while forgetting the reasons why he was imprisoned in the first place.

TRUCK OF FOOLS

We began this chapter by observing that in Liscano's *testimonio* there is a lacuna of sixteen years between his early childhood and his arrest. Instead of a narrative backdrop that depicts, for example, the economic crisis of the 1950s or the rise of an urban guerilla movement in the 1960s, Liscano describes, among other things, the day his sister was born and the day he learned to tell time. These are the past events that will precede the central event of the text: the twelve years of incarceration and torture.[16] And what Liscano is interested in here is not so much the "idea" of torture as the experience of it. Liscano puts it this way, "Everyone has an idea about torture. . . . But no one can imagine the details. The details have to do with intimate knowledge of the body . . . only those who have gone through it know what it feels like" (2). The idea here, of course, is that what is important about torture is not a general awareness of it or even a particular contextual understanding of the interrogation method in Uruguay; rather he is interested in the most "intimate" "details" about what the body "feels like" when being tortured. For this reason, Liscano will spend the majority of his testimonio attempting to verbalize and share this singular experience; an experience that does not only mean being interrogated and beaten by his oppressor, but also and more important living through a process in which the tortured subject begins to loathe and feel utter "disgust" for his own body.

But the "intimate" "knowledge" of the body in pain, the minute "details" of the dehumanizing consequences of torture on the body, does not translate into absolute despair in Liscano's testimonio. Indeed, the moments of absolute bleakness immediately give rise to profound insights of personal strength, growth, and self-awareness. Liscano explains it this way, "The body is subjected to asphyxia in the tank, to beating, and to its own filth. These are absolutely new sensations for the body . . . I would realize how physical pain is a door to self-knowledge" (68). For Liscano, it is through the body that he will come to experience pain, but it is also through the pain of the body that he will learn and grow; disgust will give way to illumination, and "filth" to inspiration. In a world where the "only objective is survival," what Liscano "realizes" is precisely the importance of his own body, since it is the sole object that keeps him "alive." Further, the body itself comes to be understood as a strategic site of "resistance" when in the torture chamber. Thus, Liscano explains, "The prisoner under torture holds out because of the body's infinite capacity for resistance. If the body does not resist, he dies" (66).

But the body is not the only site of resistance in Liscano's testimonio. In another poignant moment, Liscano writes that, "It is not ideology, not even ideas, nor does it affect all the same or equally. The prisoner holds onto something beyond the rational, the definable. Dignity sustains him" (66). What Liscano suggests here is that the primacy of "dignity"—like the primacy of the body—is essential to endure and survive in the torture chamber. At the same time, what is absolutely not essential for "resistance" is Liscano's political "ideology." From this perspective, "dignity" does the work that "ideas" can never do. And as we have already begun to see, political "ideology" is not only absent in the torture chamber, it is nowhere to be found in the historical account of Liscano's text either. Indeed, rather than "menacing antics" of bank robberies, kidnappings, or bombings there is a complete silence as to why he is in jail and tortured. Precisely because there is no reference to Tupamaro "ideology," there is no notion of the political motives for Liscano's arrest and his torture. In other words, while the primacy of dignity makes Liscano's "resistance" fundamental, it also and more importantly renders the "ideology" that put Liscano in jail irrelevant.[17] This is also why in Liscano's testimonio the difference between a Tupamaro prisoner and any other prisoner is completely indistinguishable, since the motives that may have distinguished them are rendered unintelligible. In other words, insisting on the primacy of the body and dignity in Liscano's testimonio eliminates the "ideological" distinction between the imprisoned Tupamaro and the imprisoned common criminal.

But it is not just the "ideological" differences between the criminal and Tupamaro that cease to matter in Liscano's testimonio. What also emerges is the complete irrelevance of the political differences between the prisoner and his torturer. This, however, doesn't mean that there are no dissimilarities between Liscano and his *responsable* or that he is not committed to marking a sharp distinction between the two.[18] In fact, one of the central features of the testimonio is Liscano's commitment to exploring the torturer's "psychological experience." David William Foster puts it this way, "What makes [*Truck of Fools*] unusually interesting is the discussion of the psychological dimension from the tortured's point of view and an attempt to evaluate the psychological experience of the torturer" (*Truck* 124). Indeed, throughout the text Liscano insists on how "tough" the torturer has to be in order to work "long hours" and experience the daily "miseries" of torturing. Liscano also describes the torturers' "envy" of prisoners, since they know that "deep down" their acts carry no "dignity" or any "human, cultural, moral, or ethical value" (75). Drawing attention to the psychology of the torturer—his lack of "morals," or his "envy"—is not necessarily meant to demonstrate that Liscano sympathizes with his torturer; he may, in fact, hold him in the utmost contempt. Instead, the point is that the feeling of having more "value" than his oppressor presents Liscano with the possibility of seeing himself as less of a victim. Thus, to "evaluate the psychological experience" of the torturer allows the victim to experience a certain type of victory over the oppressor, since the torturer knows that nothing can give his activity any "value," nothing can justify what he does.[19]

Perhaps the most radical claim that Liscano makes is not simply that nothing justifies what the torturer does—in the sense of giving values—but that the torturer himself seems to need and has no justification for beating his victim. We have already seen how torture makes the history and political goals of the tortured irrelevant. Now we see that it does the same for the torturer, erasing the relevance of the very things the torturer might invoke to justify himself. Thus, reflecting on his *responsable*, Liscano imagines that "One day he is bound to think it through, get to where there are no ideological, political, or professional excuses, nothing" (80). The idea is that the torturer's reasons are here revealed to be nothing but "excuses." Liscano, in other words, is not making the more common point that even if the torturer's goals are good, no goal can justify torture, that no ends can justify these means. More striking still, Liscano refuses to criticize the ends themselves; he is not, despite his own communism, criticizing the torturer's anti-communism. His point is neither that the ends cannot justify the means nor that the ends themselves are wrong. Rather, the ends—the politics, the ideology—have nothing to do with the torture. Just as Liscano's communism ceased to matter the moment he began to be tortured, the torturer's anti-communism ceases to matter the moment he begins to torture.

Hence even the fundamental motive for torture—the desire to get information—becomes superfluous. Liscano describes soldiers who torture neither for political reasons nor to obtain information from their victims and consequently asks himself "why does the soldier do what was not ordered, what is not even torture for information, but plain evil, with no point, no objective?" (71). Of course, acts of torture are commonly described as evil. But Liscano's point here is that "evil" is invoked in the absence of any motive or "objective" whatsoever. From this perspective then, Liscano's torturer does not beat him because he is a Tupamaro or even a political prisoner. Furthermore, what Liscano describes when he is tortured may be understood as being closer to the scenario of a sadist who brutalizes for no other reason than pure pleasure. But even this description would not be entirely appropriate. For although the sadist's motivation may not be to obtain information, he does have an "objective": to obtain pleasure. For Liscano, then, the torturer cannot torture because he is a sadist either. Liscano's point is that neither political ideology nor the personal sadism of the torturer is relevant, since the desire to obtain information and pleasure both count as motives and what Liscano's testimonio is interested in is the way in which torture has no motive. On the one hand, eliminating the "objective" as regards to torture will eliminate any possible justification of torture (e.g., to obtain political information). On the other hand, describing torture as "plain evil," that is, eliminating any possible justification, will necessarily entail the eradication of any and all political commitments in relation to the act of torture. For Liscano, there is no "point," there is no reason for his brutalization. [20]

But if there are no motives, then the "new truths" that emerge from torture can never possess any form of political content. And while this will entail the end of a certain type of politics in Liscano's text, it will also present Liscano with the opportunity to search out other truths that can only be "learned in torture." These "truths," Liscano contends, center on "the disgust one feels toward his own body, the officer who tortures while claiming to be just, the soldier who thinks it's funny for the prisoner to hit his head against a wall" (33). For Liscano, what is learned in torture is the truth of what it means to be a "human being." The force behind the discourse of the body in pain (and the discourse of dignity, evil, and the "human being") functions precisely to render the political motivations (ideas, information, truths) of both the torturer and tortured subject completely irrelevant; that is, they are meant to effectively erase any trace of both the communist and the anti-communist in the testimonio. Or to make the point in a slightly different way, once it is getting beaten that matters, then the distinction between anti-communism and communism ceases to matter; this is because the person who is being beaten and the person who is beating him are neither communists nor anti-communists, but rather two humans who are defined by the complete absence of political ideology. The fact that Liscano's text reduces the torturer's anticommunism to an excuse and eliminates the prisoner's socialism altogether does not mean, however, that the left and the right have simply ceased to exist in contemporary Uruguayan politics. Indeed, in the period of the postdictatorship, the left and right are still very much present, yet their primary political difference now revolves around the question of remembering or forgetting the body in pain.

REMEMBERING AND FORGETTING

If the world in which Liscano went to jail was a world characterized by the conflict between Tupamaros and the "bourgeois nation-state," the world in which he writes today is a world divided between those who want to remember the torture and those who want to forget it. Maren Viñar describes the central conflict in the postdictatorial period this way, "when normality returns and reconciliation is sought, [it] produces a social rift between those who don't want to remember and those who can't forget" (6). The left, which was once committed to promulgating communism and overthrowing the government, is now dedicated—in its most progressive form—to prosecuting those who committed gross human rights violations during the dictatorship. The right, which was once committed to "eradicating" communism, is now interested in—at least as it is imagined by the left—forgetting these past human rights abuses. This type of memory politics is precisely at play when Fernando Reati notes that, "If the 70s are the years of terror [then] the 80s and the 90s are the years of a conflict between the will to remember and the will to forget" (11). Of course, what is interesting about Reati's claim is that regardless of whether it is the left remembering or the right forgetting, what is being remembered or forgotten are the "years of terror," that is, the body in pain. But what does it suggest when contemporary leftist politics and scholarship rest upon the recollection of memories of dignity, terror, and torture? What is at stake in talking or not talking about the body in pain?

Or to ask this question another way, why should the body in pain become the primary means through which political opposition is formed in the postdictatorship? The critic Saul Sosnowski notes that during the years of authoritarian rule the military employed "the common metaphor of health and disease to interpret and justify policies against guerrilla movement and, more extensively, against those who challenged or disregarded their parameters for political life" (521). In this way, the armed forces were regarded as the "healers" working against "cancerous cells" that were now threatening to take over the country. For Sosnowski the metaphor of healing translates into a repressive politics of "normalcy." In other words, in order to "restore the health of the Nation" the military had to insists on a "single version of reality," it had to impose its idea of health over the Uruguayan citizenry. Not only was this regime of "normalcy" concerned with imposing their "single version of reality," of the "normal" state, it was also concerned with a "future" that "needed to be submitted to rigid control. And it was on the battleground for this future that cultural production would be engaged" (521). Thus, if the dictatorship had employed a discourse of health during the period of repression, its legacy lives on today during the period of democratization. From this standpoint, what forgetting entails in the postdictatorship is that those in power continue to enforce a regime of normalcy on their citizenry vis-à-vis their refusal to acknowledge the damaged and diseased bodies of the past.

But if forgetting insists on a regime of normalcy, the discourse of remembering is understood as a discourse that opposes this regime by insisting on the primacy of the body. In other words, it is in the postdictatorship that the conflict between the recognition, *on the one hand*, and the denial, *on the other hand*, of the damaged body emerges as the primary political conflict. But even if the left is concerned with exposing these past abuses, while the right insists that they be forgotten, what brings the left and the right together is the desire that the nation must work through these wounds and finally heal. And this is why Liscano's testimonio not only functions as an opposition to a regime of normalcy, since it insist on remembering the body in pain, but in so doing, serves as a primary narrative to heal the nation. In other words, if the goal of Liscano the Tupamaro was to destroy the Uruguayan state in order to form a new socialist citizen and a new socialist state, the goal of Liscano the memoirist is to heal himself—of course, integrating his wounds—so that he can re-integrate himself as a citizen of the capitalist state.

In this way, the objective of Liscano's memoir specifically, and a politics of remembering in general, operates precisely to heal the state.[21] It is for this reason that Elizabeth Hampsten suggests that "What Carlos Liscano has achieved in *Truck of Fools* . . . is a re-integration of himself as a person . . . and as a political citizen." Of course, from the position of a Tupamaro ("seize power for a socialist revolution"), Hampsten's claim regarding Liscano's "re-integration" can hardly be considered as praise, since the Tupamaros were not rebelling in order to claim Uruguayan citizenship; what the Tupamaros wanted was to overthrow the system, not belong to it.[22] Instead, what

Hampsten is suggesting here—albeit inadvertently—is that talking about torture (and the body in pain) without recourse to ideology, an ideology whose force is the elimination of economic inequality, is precisely the process by which Liscano in particular, and the left in general, are reintegrated into the Uruguayan nation-state. In other words, the moment that one talks about torture bereft of ideology, torture becomes without contradiction the quintessential discourse of the postdictatorial liberal nation—the talking cure of the nation, a national discourse that citizens, scholars, and politicians alike incessantly need to recall and work through in order to heal the nation of its historical wounds. That is to say, healing has become the neoliberal discourse par excellence.

My point here, of course, is neither to suggest that Liscano is at fault because he wants to heal himself from his past wounds nor to criticize the readers who are sympathetic to his experience. Nor is the argument that Liscano "conveniently" eliminates all references to the activities that would allow the reader to either understand or justify his torture. I am not arguing that this is about what Liscano should have said, but rather that what he does say is not incompatible with the logic of capital. My argument, in other words, is not personal but structural. Indeed, whatever its merits as a personal, ethical, or even juridical document, Liscano's testimonio in no way suggests an alternative to the market, not because citizens, like Liscano, wish to remember, forget, and heal, but rather because remembering, forgetting, and healing are not oppositional to the market. Unlike the project of socialism and the new socialist citizen, the project of remembering serves to never forget past human rights abuses while leaving the political and economic mechanisms of class inequality virtually untouched. This is why Frente Amplio (FA-Broad Front)—the left government that has been in power since 2005—can fully press for the imprisonment of former human rights violators while still fully continuing a neoliberal project that has generated a rise in poverty by 108 percent in the last fifteen years. This again does not mean that Liscano's convictions are those of the right but instead that his politics—the progressive politics of healing—do not serve to eradicate the social and economic injustice produced by neoliberalism.

If, however, the Uruguay of today has reclaimed its status as the Switzerland of South America—that is, as the new "financial center" of Latin America—then what does it mean for the left to recall these past abuses instead of combating the rule of the market in the postdictatorship? At this point the answer should be obvious: not only does the logic of the recent testimonio and the logic of this debate over memory render the disagreements between the left and right irrelevant, but it also turns the left itself into a kind of accomplice of the neoliberal nation. In a period where socialism, as an economic project, has slowly withered into a historical relic, the commitment to remembering the torture and the body in pain plays a powerful role of illustrating the ultimate triumph of neoliberal politics. This is precisely the point of Viñar's assessment of the postdictatorial "social rift between those who don't want to remember and those who can't forget" (6). The "social rift" that marks this recent past cannot be the same "rift" that defined the period leading up to the dictatorship. In that period, the antagonism between the left and the right—that is, between socialism and capitalism—was understood as deeply contradictory; in other words, one could not be for the elimination of poverty and still be for the continued exploitation of the poor; nor could one argue for the destruction of the "bourgeois state," while still aiming to maintain it. But in the current neoliberal moment contradictions are eliminated and disagreements between the left and right are turned into diagnostic differences, which only serve to streamline the flow of capital into the neoliberal state. The "social rift" between remembering and forgetting the body reflects more a difference of liberal remedy; one political group feels that the damaged body needs to be claimed, while the other thinks that it should be left behind, but in both instances—whether remembered or forgotten—what is integral is that politics be understood not in corporeal rather than economic or even ideological terms; but, of course, once politics are transformed into question of the body in pain, then it does not really matter where one stands on the political spectrum. In fact, the point has been that if you care about remembering the body in pain disconnected from beliefs then you are already imagining a world in which your leftist politics are no longer relevant.

From the standpoint of neoliberalism, there is no better example of the absolute irrelevance of a politics of remembering (irrelevance to a critique of neoliberalism) than the current government of Frente Amplio. More than any other government in postdictatorial history, Frente Amplio has openly embraced a politics of remembering in Uruguay. The government has not only continued the search for unaccounted *desaparecidos*, but also has actively pursued human rights violators, including the monumental 2005 arrest of the former president and the figurehead leader of the 1973 coup d'état, José María Bordaberry. [23] But even though Frente Amplio's "progresismo" has made a politics of remembering primary, it has in no way challenged the neoliberal framework set forth by the previous administrations. Indeed, Daniel Chávez explains that since the left took power, "In practice, there are no significant changes in the great lines of political economy, in monetary politics, in the gestation of international commerce" (Chávez 177). [24] The point here is not that Frente Amplio in particular, and the left in general (inside and outside of Uruguay), have failed to see the underlying contradiction between neoliberalism and politics of remembering, but instead that there is absolutely no contradiction between the two. [25] Indeed, the importance of politics of remembering should only be understood in its ability to facilitate the market's production without any opposition whatsoever. In other words, talking about torture (or even your memories of torture) has no impact on changing current neoliberal politics; in fact, it perpetuates its logic.

NOTES

1. The police first implemented torture in Uruguay in 1968. By 1971, the military was also using torture. The "most brutal techniques" utilized by the military were electric shock, dragging prisoners by horse and the "submarine." This last technique, also known as waterboarding, involves submerging the prisoner into a tank of water in order to suffocate and provoke the sensation of drowning (Aldrighi 64). The most widely used form of torture was the "plantón" where a prisoner was forced to stand for long periods of time [up to 4–5 days] without moving; other forms included rape, the witnessing of torture of others (including family members), and firing squad simulacrums.

2. Of course, my argument is not that Liscano "asked for it" or that he "got what he asked for." Rather, the idea here is not only to reveal the historical conflict that is central to Tupamaro ideology, but also to trace how the displacement of this historical conflict is central to understanding Uruguayan politics in general and leftist politics in particular in the postdictatorship.

3. Beginning in 1967, the government of Pacheco Areco began implementing the *Medidas Prontas de Seguridad* [Prompt Security Measures], which not only censored newspapers but also arrested and tortured Tupamaros in order to "stabilize" the country. Likewise, Tupamaro tactics also became more extreme with the escalation of state repression. The most publicized (and possibly the most politically detrimental) act of violence in these years would occur on July 31, 1970, when the Tupamaros assassinated supposed CIA operative and AID agent, Daniel Mitrione. The Tupamaros had found strong evidence suggesting that Mitrione was training Uruguayan agents in "more scientifically effective methods" of interrogation (Weschler 67). Whether Mitrione was in fact a CIA agent is still disputed, but what is certain is that until his kidnapping and murder, the Marxist-Leninist guerrilla group was considered to be "unlike other Latin-American guerrilla groups, [they] normally avoid bloodshed when possible. They try instead to create embarrassment for the government and general disorder" (*The New York Times*, August 1, 1970). What is equally certain is that although the Tupamaros had assassinated officers in past operations (e.g., "The Taking of Pando" in 1969), the assassination of Mitrione was a turning point with respect not only to the military repression against them, but also to the manner in which Uruguayan citizens perceived the group, which was rather favorable until then. For a fictional account of the Mitrione affair, see Constantin Costa-Gavras, 1972 film *State of Siege* and Carlos Martínez Moreno, *El color que el infierno me escondiera* (1981). And for more detailed accounts of both the Mitrione case and Tupamaro tactics, see A. J. Langguth's *Hidden Terrors* (1978) and Maria Esther Gilio's *The Tupamaro Guerrillas* (1972).

4. Unless otherwise noted, translations from Spanish to English are mine.

5. Wilson Ferreira Aldunate famously synthesized the distinction between the revolutionary left and the legal left as the difference between "Los tupamaros y los tapamuros" (Campodónico 179). Los Tapamuros—a play on the name of the revolutionary group—literally means "wall coverers," referring to those tendencies indicative of the Communist Party, including verboseness, long manifestos, and covering city walls with propaganda. This Communist Party tendency, as Miguel Ángel Campodónico correctly declares, was completely contrary to what the Tupamaros thought and how they mobilized.

6. Or as Federico Leicht notes, "In little time, the Tupamaro *foco* would represent the biggest destabilizing threat for the Uruguayan government in the entire twentieth century" (Leicht 45).

7. Ernesto "Che" Guevara coined the term *focos*. Tupamaro communiqués drew heavily from Guevara's political philosophy. For example, they explain, "As Ernesto "Che" Guevara correctly stated, an organization need not wait until all objective and subjective conditions exist

in order to carry forward the revolution: the armed struggle (*focos*) can create them" (Wilson 55).

8. The quote is taken from Hernán Valdés's 1974 testimonio *Tejas Verdes* and documents the repression in Chile soon after the 1973 coup d'état, which murdered the world's first democratically elected Marxist president Salvador Allende. Not unlike Uruguay's coup, Chile's fascist regime's primary objective was also the obliteration of Marxism.

9. In 1972, a state of internal war begins—a prelude to the coup d'état that takes place June 27, 1973. It is possible to draw three distinct periods in Uruguay's military period: From 1973 to 1976 there is a civic-military government, from 1976 to 1980 a military government, and finally from 1980 to 1985 a gradual transition to a new civil government, under the tutelage of the military regime. In March 1985, Julio María Sanguinetti (1985–1990) of the Colorado Party becomes the first democratic president, officially ending the dictatorship. Sanguinetti would also be elected for a second term in 1995.

10. Most citizens were well aware of the repression and torture that existed in the nation. It was no secret, for example, that the military was arriving in the dead of the night to take away political dissidents from their homes. Nor was it a mystery that the screams coming from inside the prison walls, located in the heart of Montevideo, were those of detainees being tortured. Those who passed in the street often heard these screams. This, of course, was not because of military imprudence, but rather a well-thought-out tactic to create a "culture of fear" throughout Uruguayan society (Weschler 128). For a more detailed discussion concerning this "culture of fear" that infiltrated Uruguayan society during the military regime, see Juan Rial's essay "Makers and Guardians of Fear: Controlled Terror in Uruguay" in *Fear at the Edge* (1992).

11. The new democracy granted political amnesty to all political prisoners. The majority of the political prisoners were released on March 10; high-profile Tupamaros, however, were given their freedom four days later on March 14, 1985.

12. Frente Amplio represents a "coalition of the Communist, Socialist, and Christian Democrat parties who joined forces in 1971 with the dream of breaking the strangle-hold of the traditional two major parties in Uruguay and carrying out a democratic revolution which would alter Uruguayan society and redistribute the wealth that had been in the hands of the few since independence" (Fox). Their campaign platform in 1971 was entitled "The First 30 Government Measures," and outlined the fundamental pillars of the party, including agrarian reform, the nationalization of private banks, the nationalization of the principal sources of foreign trade, and the invigoration of state industry.

13. In the era of remembering and reconciliation, as we will see later, there are certainly marked differences between the neoliberal left and the neoliberal right; but these differences will serve only to show how far the left has moved away from the class concerns that were once central to its politics.

14. The Uruguayan government did establish a commission in 1986 but it was only designed to account for the *desaparecidos* or the presumed dead. No names were published, since this would hinder future cooperation by military officials.

15. It is certainly true that the debate between remembering and forgetting is intrinsically tied to questions about how the state can legitimately intervene in society in order to maintain order; for example, a discourse of looking back implies creating some kind of democratic consensus whereby military intervention is dismissed as an acceptable option. The discourse also involves a more profound debate regarding the manner in which Uruguayans can create a stable democracy. The point here, however, is not to argue that a politics of remembering or forgetting seeks to create a more stable democratic project, but rather that the commitment to democratic stability for the left and the right has not involved a real commitment to the elimination of class inequality.

16. Considering the temporal structure of the narrative, the fact that Liscano's imprisonment is immediately preceded by his childhood suggests—if only symbolically—that it is through his childhood and not his political affiliation that we should read his prison experience. As we will have time to see later, this conceptualization of the past—a past empty of political motives—reveals that the logic of remembering is central to Liscano's text.

17. For a radical departure from Liscano's account of torture that points to not only the irrelevance of dignity, but also the primary importance of ideology and history during Uru-

guay's military dictatorship, see Ernesto González Bermejo's *Las manos en el fuego* (1985), "Resistance to the machine [torture]—David [Cámpora] would understand—before anything else is an ideological question: the better one understands the terms of the conflict, the easier it will be to define the enemy and easier it will be to defend oneself from the irrationality of the machine" (22). The point here is not to stress the obvious fact that each tortured subject has his or her own mechanisms for overcoming the brutal reality of torture—for Liscano it is dignity and David Cámpora it is ideology—but rather to suggest that the political meanings of those mechanisms are fundamentally different.

18. Liscano explains, "Each prisoner is assigned a *responsable*, a person who is 'responsible' or in charge of him, usually a captain if the prisoner is 'important.' . . . The *responsable* is the prisoner's owner: perhaps not of his life, because to kill intentionally he is supposed to get permission, but he is the owner of everything else. In my case, I'm the property of a captain who arrested me" (58).

19. There is nothing wrong with wanting to understand the motives why one is doing you harm; yet what is striking about Liscano's narrative is that all the excuses given for the harm done to him have nothing to do with the reasons why he is in jail in the first place.

20. One need only think of another scenario in which the idea of "evil" is invoked in order to understand the full force of Liscano's description of "plain evil." This is the infamous "ticking bomb" scenario in which torture is employed as a "necessary evil" in order to "save the whole nation" (Levinson 32). This "necessary evil," of course, is the sort of worst-case scenario that has gained much attention in the wake of 9/11 and is conjured up weekly on a TV dramas like *24*, a show that presents the protagonist, Jack Bauer, with only one day and two choices: either torture the terrorist or watch as millions of lives are lost to a major disaster. Bauer, of course, always chooses to interrogate his suspect; and subsequently, always saves the "civilized" world from almost certain doom. The show has drawn its fair share of criticism—especially from those on the left—who argue that the drama promoted a pro-Bush agenda that legitimated the use of torture. But even as a form of propaganda—if it is that—the television show doesn't exactly eliminate the primary ethical dilemma that surrounds the drama, which is whether the use of torture is defensible when the question of survival is at stake. It is not surprising, then, that once the question is presented as precisely a dilemma that people from Alan Dershowitz on the right to Slavoj Žižek on the left are prepared to see that avoiding "the greater evil" of a major catastrophe might be the only justification for employing "the lesser evil" of torture.

Liscano, however, goes beyond the moralist position. Liscano, of course, is not referring to this kind of "lesser evil" when he recalls his torturer's blows; nor is Liscano referring to the type of "evil" that Dershowitz's adversaries invoke when talking about situations similar to those found on *24*; that is, Liscano is not describing the moralist position that sees torture as an evil that should never be employed in any circumstance, regardless of whether the suspect, for example, possesses vital information regarding a bioterrorist attack. For Liscano, therefore, it is not just that no motives are justifiable, but that no motives can be considered relevant; that is, if the torturer beats Liscano it is not because he is a terrorist or even a possible terrorist. The oppressor beats him for no reason at all, with no "objective" whatsoever. In Liscano's text, in other words, the terrorist cannot exist. But if the terrorist vanishes, then the ticking bomb situation vanishes, since that scenario hinges on the possibility of obtaining information. In other words, the replacement of the torturer who tortures for a purpose with the torturer who is "plain evil," finds a solution to the highly debated issue of the ticking bomb scenario: the torturer never beats his victims in order to acquire information; the torturer beats his victims because the torturer is evil. But even if the ticking bomb dilemma is resolved—or at least, ends up looking like a misunderstanding that continues to happen—it doesn't resolve the issue of torture, since the "plain evil" of the torturer still survives, even if the information does not. It should also be clear that the point that is being made here is not invested in the inefficacy of torture as a form of information-gathering, but rather that torture for Liscano can only be imagined as something done for no reason at all.

21. The literature that has appeared in recent years primarily functions to promote the idea of healing as a necessary step toward entering the neoliberal nation. For a rare exception, see Federico Liecht, *Cero a la izquierda: una biografía de Jorge Zabalza* (2007), which seems to gesture toward a reappearance of ideological conflict within contemporary historical accounts.

22. But, of course, it is not just the writer Liscano and the critic Hampsten who are committed to celebrating this re-integration. In the postdictatorship, a prominent constituency of ex-Tupamaros-turned-politicians have argued that the Tupamaros formed because they were defending democracy. From the perspective of these ex-Tupamaros, then, re-integration is read and celebrated as the consolidation of democracy in Uruguay. In a recent interview with Emiliano Cotelo, the ex-Tupamaro Jorge Zabalza spoke adamantly about this "fairytale" that some MLN members have invented in the years after the dictatorship:

> EC: What is the "fairytale" that has been created around the period of the MLN after the dictatorship?
> JZ: Today, from the perspective of some very important comrades, very much associated with the MLN, like Fernández Huidobro y [José] Mujica, who are in power, the look back is: we organized because we were the defenders of democracy and were against a possible coup d'état. . . .
> EC: You say that the majority of those who were part of the MLN in the 60s did not take up arms in order to defend democracy.
> JZ: We did not take arms to defend democracy. We took up arms in order to overthrow the political regime in order to install another political system with a totally different democracy, which is not the one that the government has now.

For the complete interview see Emiliano Cotelo, "Zabalza: alguien tiene que mantener la llamita encendida," *Tinku*, October 20, 2007, http://www.tinku.org/content/view/2408/6/.

It is indeed true there did exist a discourse in the MLN that was inspired by the liberal revolution. Clara Aldrighi has explained that national heroes—who were also inspired by the liberal revolution—such as José Gervasio Artigas and José Batlle y Ordoñez, and historical events such as the Paso Morlán Civil War were incorporated into Tupamaro revolutionary discourse. Yet, as she also correctly notes, "In search of consensus and also in order to push active mobilization of the country, the MLN appealed to national history as a legitimating source" (78). In other words, the discourse of liberal revolution was purely strategic. Indeed, a quick glance at MLN documents or communiqués written in the course of the 1960s and 1970s reveals that the MLN was never committed to upholding—to take only one example—the liberal right of private property. Indeed, their entire project sought to destroy the structure that legitimated and maintained this right.

23. The shift begins in 2000 with the presidency of José Batlle who formed a Peace Commission to investigate the whereabouts of unaccounted *desaparecidos*. By 2001, the Commission had discovered the bodies of sixteen missing Uruguayans. Nevertheless, while Batlle's presidency saw human rights as a secondary issue at best, Vázquez has made human rights central to his political agenda. Or as Chávez puts it, "human rights is where the Left government has had its greatest impact" (171).

24. Leicht has described some of the horrific consequences that have emerged in the period marked by the "neoliberalization of the left": "After 15 years of experiences within the free market laboratory, poverty has increased 108 percent, affecting more than 40 percent of the population. Unemployment has reached figures that were once never imagined, salaries have dropped and emigration has reached the same level as during the military dictatorship. Settlements have grown at a rhythm of 10 percent per year, accompanied by problems previously unheard of such as infant malnutrition and social ghettoization" (190).

These problems have not gone unnoticed and several political groups within Frente Amplio have decided to leave the coalition. Daniel Perreira, a leader of the Movimiento 26 de Marzo (26M)—the most recent political group to abandon this coalition—in a 2008 interview states that "Frente Amplio formed as anti-imperialist and anti-oligarchy and it proposed paths for development that were not capitalist. But if today, president Vázquez is congratulated by Bush, and the IMF congratulates [Danilo] Astori [Minister of Economy] and the World Bank congratulates the communist minister Marina Arismedi [. . .] [W]ouldn't it be better to realize that they have domesticated Frente Amplio?". For the complete interview, see Gustavo Torres, "Uruguay: ruptura en el Frente Amplio," *Zoom*, April 17, 2008, http://revista-zoom.com.ar/articulo2113.html.

25. Returning to his interview regarding the motivation for publishing his biography, *Cero a la izquierda: una biografía de Jorge Zabalza*, and the polemic that it has caused in Uruguay, Zabalza states that,

> What is most important to me in this moment is to think ahead, toward the future. To say: we who survived these conditions, who survived the genocide in Latin America . . . what do we think about the future. Do we still need to change the base of society, to achieve a society without exploitation, without the oppressed? Do we still think about this? I do, so I would like to have a debate considering these terms. (Cotelo)

It is interesting to note that Zabalza is not committed to a conventional postdictatorial discourse of remembering (looking back) or forgetting (looking forward) the human rights abuses that has defined the left and the right for the last quarter century. This is not only because Zabalza accounts for past "genocide" in "Latin America," but also because the future has less to do with accounting for this "genocide" than achieving "a society without exploitation." The point here is that the true political impetus is neither toward the future nor the past, but rather toward a politics that makes the question of "a society without exploitation" central. It is a complete commitment to these political questions posed by Zabalza that may be the first step toward a new political project for the left.

REFERENCES

Aldrighi, Clara. 2001. *La izquierda armada: ideología, ética e identidad en el MLN-Tupamaros*. Montevideo: Trilce.

Benedetti, Mario. 1979. *Pedro y el Capitán*. Mexico City: Nueva Imagen.

Bergero, Adriana, and Fernando Reati. 1997. *Memoria colectiva y políticas de olvido: Argentina y Uruguay 1970–1990*. Rosario: Beatriz Viterbo Editora.

Browne, Malcolm W. 1969. "A Small, Elite Rebel Band Harasses Uruguayan Regime." *New York Times*. January 23: 12.

Campodónico, Miguel Ángel. 2000. *Las vidas de Rosencof*. Montevideo: Fin de Siglo.

Chávez, Daniel. 2008. "Uruguay: La izquierda en el gobierno: entre la continuidad y el cambio." *La nueva izquierda en América Latina*. Eds. César A. Rodríguez Garavito, Patrick S. Barrett, and Daniel Chávez. Madrid: Catarata.

Cotelo, Emiliano. 2007. "Zabalza: alguien tiene que mantener la llamita encendida." *Tinku*, October 20. http://www.tinku.org/content/view/2408/6/ (accessed January 20, 2008).

Demasi, Carlos. 1995. "La dictadura militar: un tema pendiente." *Uruguay: cuentas pendientes: dictadura, memorias y desmemorias* . Eds. Alvaro Rico and Hugo Achugar. Montevideo: Trilce.

Documentos 1–5 del Movimiento de la Liberación-Tupamaros. October 26, 2005. http://www.chasque.net/mlnweb/.html (accessed July 30, 2006).

Fox, Michael. 2007. "Uruguay's Frente Amplio." *Zmag*, June 19. http://www.zmag.org/znet/viewArticle/15145 (accessed June 25, 2007).

Frens-String, Joshua. 2009. "New Declarations Against Impunity in Uruguay." *Upside Down World*, March 5. http://upsidedownworld.org/main/content/view/1745/1/ (accessed March 5, 2009).

Gilio, Maria Esther. 1972. *The Tupamaro Guerrillas*. Trans. Anne Edmondson. New York: Saturday Review Press.

González Bermejo, Ernesto. 1985. *Las manos en el fuego* . Montevideo: Banda Oriental.

Hampsten, Elizabeth. 1996. "Carlos Liscano's *The Road to Ithaca*." *North Dakota Quarterly* 63.3: 5–18.

———. 2002. "A Seminar in Uruguay on Testimonios." *Radical Pedagogy* 4.2 (Summer). http://radicalpedagogy.icaap.org/content/issue4_2/html (accessed September 25, 2005).

Huyssen, Andreas. 2000. "Present Pasts: Media, Politics, Amnesia." *Public Culture* 12.1: 21–38.

Langguth, A. J. 1978. *Hidden Terrors*. New York: Pantheon.

Leicht, Federico. 2007. *Cero a la izquierda: una biografía de Jorge Zabalza*. Montevideo: Letraeñe.

Levinson, Stanford. 2004. *Torture*. Oxford: Oxford Univ. Press.

Liscano, Carlos. 2004. *Truck of Fools*. Trans. Elizabeth Hampsten. "Foreword" by David William Foster. Nashville: Vanderbilt Univ. Press. Trans. of *El furgón de los locos*. Montevideo: Planeta, 2001.

Martínez Moreno, Carlos. 1981. *El color que el infierno me escondiera*. Mexico City: Editorial Nueva Imagen.

"Patear el hormiguero." 2009. *Brecha,* May 29: 1227.

Rial, Juan. 1992. "Makers and Guardians of Fear: Controlled Terror in Uruguay." *Fear at the Edge: State Terror and Resistance in Latin America*. Eds. Juan E. Corradi, Manuel A. Garretón Merino, and Patricia Weiss Fagen. Berkeley: Univ. of California Press.

Sosnowski, Saúl. 2002. "Political exclusion / Literary Inclusion: Argentine and Uruguayan Writers." *Latin American Literary History Project*. Oxford: Oxford Univ. Press.

Sosnowski, Saúl, and Louise B. Popkin. 1993. *Repression, Exile, and Democracy: Uruguayan Culture*. Durham: Duke Univ. Press.

State of Siege. 1972. Dir. Constantin Costa-Gavras. Perf. Yves Montand and Renato Salvatori. Cinema 5.

Torres, Gustavo. 2008. "Uruguay: ruptura en el Frente Amplio." *Zoom,* April 17. http://revista-zoom.com.ar/articulo2113.html (accessed May 10, 2008).

Viñar, Maren. 2001. *Memoria social: fragmentaciones y responsabilidades*. Montevideo: Trilce.

Weinstein, Martin. 1988. *Uruguay: Democracy at the Crossroads*. Boulder, CO: Westview.

Weschler, Lawrence. 1991. *A Miracle, A Universe: Settling Accounts with Torturers*. New York: Viking Penguin.

Wilson, Major Carlos. 1974. *The Tupamaros: The Unmentionables*. Boston: Braden.

Žižek, Slavoj. 2002. *Welcome to the Desert of the Real*. New York: Verso.

Chapter Nine

Deviating from the Norm?

Two Easts Testify to a Prison Aesthetics of Happiness

Simona Livescu

In this chapter, I set out to isolate an almost totally neglected motif in the prison literature of two Easts: that of a *modus felicitatis*—a state of happiness or bliss—experienced by prisoners of conscience as victims of systematic human rights abuse. Paradoxical in nature and present much more often than even the very authors of traumatic *oeuvres* are inclined to acknowledge, this epiphanic experience transforms its subjects into aporetic citizens.[1] This abrupt initiation into prison happiness, at times individual and at times collective, infuses political prisoners with unique civic values that reverberate in their communities after release.

Before advancing toward the main critical argument of this chapter, an introduction presenting some background information explaining the selection of these two respective regions seems appropriate. Beginning with the last decade of the twentieth century, the "republic of letters" (to use Pascale Casanova's term) recorded an interesting literary phenomena: the blossoming of prison memoirs' publication in the Arab world and in Eastern Europe. In the Arab world, starting with the nineties, prison literature gained unprecedented local and international prominence, while the same type of narratives became national bestsellers in Eastern Europe after the fall of the Berlin Wall. The wind of global political change before the end of the last century— the changes in the dictatorial regimes or authoritarian monarchic dynasties of the Middle East and the removal of the old communist dictators in the former Soviet bloc—brought about unprecedented institutionalized investigation into these regions' traumatic recent historical past. Human rights commissions were finally founded in Morocco and Algeria to investigate and document the massive human rights violations of previous decades; the Advisory

Committee on Human Rights (ACHR) was created in Morocco in 1990, and the National Consultative Commission on the Promotion and Protection of Human Rights (CNCPPDH) was established in Algeria in 2003. In Eastern Europe, a similar process of documenting and analyzing the recent past led to the formation of various institutions such as the National Institute for the Study of Totalitarianism (Romania), the Czech Office for the Documentation and the Investigation of the Crimes of Communism (Czech Republic), or the Institute of National Remembrance (Poland). These and many others were funded and sponsored by either the civil societies or the emergent democratic governments of Eastern and Central European states. Although these similar processes could be seen independent from each other, a comparative perspective on these two world regions must take into account the repeated affirmation of experts on human rights issues in the Middle East; a number of them insist that the regime of the political prisoners across the Middle East changed for the better after the '89 wind of change in Eastern Europe. To offer one example here, Susan Slyomovics draws this inference in her book, *The Performance of Human Rights in Morocco* (2005), when she writes about the results of human rights activists' lengthy struggle to become officially manifest in the nineties in Morocco, "What brought about change? Mohamed Karam indicates that 1989 was a turning point but only after decades of internal and external pressures. The lengthy struggle by Moroccan human rights organizations and activists was coupled with outside forces, such as the power of the international press. Demands for respect for human rights coincided with the fall of the Soviet Union" (Slyomovics 2005, 21).

The correspondences between these two world areas are manifold; political science scholars and historians have already started looking into the connections between these two regions by studying not only the shared ideologies, but also the strong influence that the former communist secret services such as the Stasi, the KGB, and the *Securitate* exerted in the Arab world. However, even within this body of scholarship the transference of repressive practices between the secret services of the dictatorial regimes of the Middle East and those of Eastern Europe remains insufficiently explored. The secret service files detailing this transference between various countries in the Middle East espousing occasional Marxist-Leninist ideologies similar to those of the former USSR during the Cold War remain highly classified or, even more peculiar, have never been written (the reason being that much of this type of collaboration was carried by secret service agents evading official inter-state agreements' paperwork according to the no-trace policy of intelligence agencies in the former Soviet bloc). Therefore, it comes as no surprise that the inquiry into the official and unofficial oppressive practices exercised on a large scale by states in these regions almost invariably has as starting point the prison memoirs of political prisoners; for decades before the nineties they have been the only source of information about the governmental practices—

often highly secretive—of dealing with opposition and dissent. Thus, the writings in this chapter are considered together because the carceral tactics wielded in both contexts emerged out of shared policies to an alarming extent, as recent research shows. [2]

After the above introductory remarks offering preliminary historical background, this chapter will unfold by focusing on a close analysis of one of the seemingly most insignificant effects reverberating from the larger international or interregional interests; the qualitative analysis of this effect will highlight the manner in which repressive practices exercised on a macro level translate into the micro-scale local social suffering which then, in turn, influence the macro social dynamic once again. Prisoners of conscience, exemplarily punished by governmental political repression, bring into their communities upon their departure from prison a renewed commitment to understanding the relationship between collective responsibility and social suffering. This close analysis is focused on the narrative testimony of a few former political prisoners originally from these two areas and fortunate enough to have survived imprisonment and torture in their countries. Going even further, the richness of the critical material stemming from this comparative approach on the repression in these two Easts is so vast in its historical, political, and psychological implications that the current textual selection represents only a fragment of the results relevant to a study of the effects of local and global social suffering. It is therefore implicit that the following exercise in the close reading analysis of key passages in political prisoners' memoirs will lead to intriguing insights significant to disciplines other than cultural or literary studies. Here, I identify a paradoxical prison aesthetics of happiness and attempt to isolate and define this phenomenological state not only as a trope, but also as a social attitude relevant to community life and political interaction on a larger scale. The consequences are multifaceted; one hopes that the complexity of these consequences must and will lead sociologists, psychologists, and political scientists to dedicate a larger critical attention to this phenomenon's implications in the public sphere. Once a new conceptualization affects the "inexpressibility of pain" (as Elaine Scarry formulates in her study *The Body in Pain*), new terminology in the language of trauma modify and re-appropriate the language of agency changing the discourse of power; the expressibility of pain challenges the political consequences of its previous inexpressibility and changes the agency in public arena (Scarry 1985, 11, 18).

MODUS FELICITATIS: WHO TESTIFIES TO IT AND HOW

The list of physical and mental survival strategies of those imprisoned for political crimes is considerable and varies according to each individual and to prison conditions. Besides those already known, a paradoxical coping mechanism displayed with liminal sincerity by prisoners of conscience baffles and raises questions about its authenticity: an invading feeling of joy or happiness. In the midst of extreme suffering under mental and physical torture, a phenomenon occurs that neither sociologists, anthropologists, psychologists, nor the ideologues of the *panopticon* have been able or even interested to explain convincingly. No significant critical efforts have been made to identify possible *universalia* of this phenomenological trope present in prison accounts, in which the subconscious works counter to what is expected after sessions of violent treatment, identifying feelings of happiness in the least expected of places on a convulsive earth. More than a few isolated memoirs mention such states, and protagonists elaborate more or less insistently on the perception and description of such states of being more than once within the same narrative. This narrative is as likely to emerge if the narratives are autobiographical, elaborating on actual lived experience, as if they are fictional or semi-fictional accounts of their protagonists' prison experience. Even more intriguing is that the trope of joy or happiness is present in these books no matter if their protagonists' memories are scripted on paper during the imprisonment period, immediately after their release, or many years later.

Several prison narratives that recurrently address this *modus felicitatis* are Nawal Saadawi's *Memoirs from the Women's Prison* (Egypt), Tahar Ben Jelloun's *This Blinding Absence of Light* (France-Morocco), N. Steinhardt's *Jurnalul Fericirii* (The Diary of Happiness) (Romania), and Irina Ratushinskaya's *Grey Is the Color of Hope* (Russia). These authors can be seen to struggle to find appropriate and convincing ways of rendering crisis, change, and survival. These efforts indicate the difficulty of representing the shattering of previous life-ordering principles. The authorial efforts to convey states of joy, either individually or collectively experienced, suggest the problematic position of working within the experience and language of trauma (or the lack thereof) on the one hand; on the other, the same authors go to great lengths to argue that those states of joy or happiness come to be exactly the mechanism or the process that takes the political prisoner out of psychological traumatic zones. Consequently, the linguistic representation or the reconstruction of these states for self and others needs to be addressed creatively by these authors, and this is handled with a novel writerly technique in each of these memoirs.

Nawal Saadawi began writing *Memoirs from the Women's Prison* in Egypt in 1981, the very year her imprisonment term was luckily cut short after the assassination of Anwar Sadat (the president of Egypt at the time). Saadawi, an Egyptian psychiatrist, women's rights activist, and author, was only one of many Egyptian intellectuals Sadat had arbitrarily sent to prison for having publicly opposed his economic and social policies. Her prison memoirs vividly detail the political prison conditions that Saadawi experienced. The female narrator and protagonist of the book is Nawal Saadawi herself, who, besides the lucid political and social analysis most prominent in the book, also shares with the readers her attempts to explain occasional states of joy experienced during the imprisonment in Qanatir, a famous Cairo prison, "I don't know the secret of that repose or happiness that came over me all of a sudden. . . . Or perhaps it was the feeling of self-discovery, when there appears before one's eyes a new courage or self-confidence of which one was previously unaware, or when one disperses a fear or a phantom with which one has been living" (Saadawi 1986, 33). Constantly fighting a sense of impotence or powerlessness under duress, her un/caged consciousness finds occasionally "something akin to joy" not only in processes of self-reflection, but also in its very physicality or being, "I don't know the secret of the human faculty for adjustment and victory over the worst of circumstances. . . . Perhaps I had begun with the idea of death or paralysis so that everything which followed would appear less grave. Perhaps this is the human being's capacity to adapt: beginning with the worst so that what is not quite as bad becomes utterly tolerable" (Saadawi 1986, 35).

Both these passages begin with a statement of ignorance about how to properly describe, define, or interpret this sudden self-knowledge. Since Nawal Saadawi's name is marked by a multiplicity of references in her triple role of author/narrator/protagonist of this memoir and a medical doctor and tireless, committed activist in real life, her readers are likely anxious to see how she will get through the difficulty of this enterprise—that of associating prison with joy. The exculpatory "I don't know" betrays the author—when writing about happiness, joy, or repose in the filthy prisons marked by the stark signs of deprivation, disease, and torture—as aware that she commits some sort of transgression in the temple of public consciousness. Nawal makes recourse to the word "secret," when describing this survivalist mental tactic, as if justifying her inadequacy to talk about repose and happiness amid the worst of circumstances in a scientific manner. She has only two choices, equally difficult: not to talk about her own unsettling psychological experiences in prison, although this would mean betraying her conscience as a writer when her cherishing of that conscience is what put her in prison in the first place, or to talk equivocally and possibly unconvincingly about something that could discredit her professional reputation; as a psychiatrist, she ought to be able to capture the causes and effects of psychological states.

Innocence, wonder, and self-denunciation are manifest in the inculpatory and disculpatory tone of this enciphering formula that sets off her statements with the negative emblematic "I don't know"; thereafter, she surrenders the solidity and conviction of her professional abilities. The "secret," though, confers upon her the double position of an insider and outsider at the same time: experiencing a state is one thing, narrating it or passing it on, another. Nawal Saadawi, a one-time prison psychiatrist, acknowledges that she has been taken by surprise in terms of her own psychological experiences in prison and is journeying through the process of deciphering this information herself. Why is Saadawi relinquishing her professional authority as a practicing psychiatrist to categorize this psychological reaction? Saadawi the professional seems overcome by Saadawi the writer; by declaring lack of expertise regarding these subconscious reactions to oppression and pain, she invokes her readers' assistance and participation in the search for understanding. Perhaps a collective perspective upon what it means to be and remain human under duress would help make sense of this paradoxical experience of happiness that some political prisoners traverse when jailed and tortured. The reader is not to go away from this ego-document associating her experience of sudden joy with an existential crisis of consciousness; on the contrary, this shattering-of-ordering-principles crisis provides not only a newer, but also a better set of ordering principles, offering its subjects a self-regard punctuated by a sense of strength through rebirth, newfound understandings, and lasting confidence.

It is not entirely new that consciousness, far from being destroyed while oppressed, can eventually access a higher level of awareness and freedom; Hegel developed just this idea in his *Phenomenology of Spirit* (1807) within the dialectical Master and Slave phenomenological stage. During a confrontational process, the slave consciousness overcomes its condition by benefiting from a closer relation to its environment and by finally deciding to stake its very life in the conflict for recognition. The Master ends up neutralized and the Slave consciousness gains both full awareness of the self and recognition from the Master. Nowhere did Hegel suggest that this dialectical transition would bring about any state of joy to the participants in the conflict; on the contrary, the Master-Slave confrontation and its conclusion are marked by the fear, pain, and struggle necessary for destroying the shackles of oppression to make the world (or consciousness) anew. Subsequent Marxist, feminist and postcolonial theories, in Marx, de Beauvoir, and Fanon's vein, insist that the freeing of the Slave from the Master's oppressive bonds can only come about conflictually, even violently when necessary, via revolutionary means. Saadawi, though, like other political prisoners who describe a profoundly surprising state of happiness after painful struggles with oppression and torture, suggests exactly the opposite: that conflict is erased in the dialectical gaining of awareness. The texts I selected for this chapter and many others confess through their protagonists to a changed understanding of self and environment, a more peaceful inner state, and a more all-encompassing attitude to conflicts, either relational or internal.

Further examples of authors and their modalities to express paradoxical joy will demonstrate the solidity and the fragility of its presence and definition at the same time. It speaks to the solidity of its presence that this experience is detailed not only in the ego-documents of former prisoners who themselves script their jailed experience to paper, but in fictional and semifictional prison narratives as well. A well-known case on the contemporary literary scene is that of a novel written by a consecrated author on a horrendous real-life prison experience at the request of the victim, the former political prisoner. Tahar Ben Jelloun, a Moroccan writer of French, agreed to write the book on the infamous Tazmamart prison in Morocco where disappeared prisoners were kept underground in unimaginable conditions for eighteen years. The book, published in Paris in 2001, was quickly followed by an English translation under the title *This Blinding Absence of Light* in 2002; Ben Jelloun was awarded the IMPAC prize in 2004. Salim is the protagonist of this famously (semi)fictionalized Moroccan memoir titled *Cette aveuglante absence de lumière* in its original French and written by Tahar Ben Jelloun at the express request and with the assistance of the former political prisoner Aziz Binebine. Salim (or Binebine, whose consciousness Salim's role is forged upon), confesses that in the darkness of Tazmamart's underground prison where he spent eighteen years of his mature life, some moments of deep meditation become instances of reaching states close to ecstasy. Realizing that he has fallen gravely ill from contaminated food and lacking access to any medical care, he makes recourse to the self-induced vomiting; after succeeding in ridding his tortured body of malignant bile secretions, he describes his state, "I feel light, famished, and prepare to attain ecstasy, that state in which nothing holds me back with any connection to either beings or objects. I leave everything behind, abandoning myself and my companions. . . . I am in superb solitude. . . . There I am inaccessible. I fly like a joyous bird" (Ben Jelloun 2002, 49). The next paragraph clarifies that this has been a thoroughly cathartic episode; he will come out of this apparent coma to fight the next decade of his prison term,

> The instant I realized that my cell stank to high heaven, I knew I had returned to my body. The state of grace was over. . . . That night, I slept standing. . . . The cold strolled up and down my body, making it shiver. I shuffled over the damp ground. I could not let the cold win. I returned to my exercises, mentally saying my daily prayers. (Ben Jelloun 2002, 50)

The entire novel is a first-person narrative, in which Ben Jelloun constantly appropriates the subjectivity or the "I" of the jailed Salim/Binebine.[3] As in

Nawal's case, Salim's experiencing of ecstatic or joyous feelings or life-limit crisis does not indicate an existential crisis in the classical sense. Like Nawal, Salim will find resistive answers and a sense of survivalist order even during his most despairing episodes. Starting with the first few pages of this fictionalized memoir, Salim declares unequivocally:

> On the night of July, 10, 1971, I became ageless. I have grown neither older nor younger. I have lost my age. . . . I came to a standstill over in nothingness, where time is abolished . . . given up to the sky drained of its stars, its images, the childhood dreams that found refuge there, emptied of everything, even God. I crossed over there to learn forgetfulness, but I never succeeded in being completely within nothingness, not even in thought. (Ben Jelloun 2002, 5)

Both Nawal and Salim are aware of the danger of losing control of their sanity within an absurd carceral system and become determined immediately after their initial observations of the life inside to approach it also according to different rules than those provided by the institution itself; they understand that they need to construct a sense of personal mental hygiene by searching for different ordering principles to defy the inapplicability of previous ones. This mental hygiene, attentively cared for, figures in their texts as the prerequisite for later possibilities of joy.

Turning my critical perspective to prison memoirs written by Eastern European dissident writers, I found states and feelings similar to those described by the Arab authors just discussed. Nicolae Steinhardt wrote and edited his prison memoir, entitled *Jurnalul fericirii* (The Diary of Happiness), several times with no possibility of its publishing during his lifetime under the communist rule (his book was officially published only posthumously in 1991). Steinhardt is representative of the vast majority of Romanian intellectuals imprisoned by the communist regime in Romania after WWII, rounded up over imaginary crimes. The author-protagonist was given in 1958 a thirteen-year forced labor sentence for the "crime of plotting against the social order." In reality, he was sentenced for having refused to sell out his friends and become a witness for the prosecution team, which sought to condemn a large group of anti-communist Romanian intellectuals. (The group, of which Steinhardt was part, was nevertheless sentenced exemplarily in order to suppress unrest and dissent in the country and leave the field ready for the creation of a new generation of intellectuals willing to create communist revolutionary literature and art for the proletarian masses.) The scenes preceding his refusal, the moment of arrest and subsequent prison years were written and then re-written after being confiscated twice by the Romanian secret service, first in 1972 and then also in 1984. Although with no possibility of publishing, Steinhardt did not cease writing several versions from memory while his original manuscript was in the hands of the political police agents. His dangerous efforts to get one version smuggled to the West became finally successful in 1988, when his diary was serialized and read by cultural and political editor Monica Lovinescu from Radio Free Europe's microphone in France. In one of the scenes in his prison diary, he relates the end of one of his dreams in jail:

> Beyond anything, I am happy, happy, happy. I am and understand that I am and I say it. And the light seems more luminous than light itself and is seemingly talking to me telling me who it is. This dream seems to last long, very long. Happiness not only lasts continuously, but also grows constantly; if evil has no bottom, then the good does not have a ceiling either, the circle of light spreads more and more, and happiness, after it veiled me in silk, suddenly changes its tactic, becomes rough, throws itself, falls down on me in giant avalanches which—in an anti-gravitational fashion—heighten me; then, again, proceeds differently: compassionate, it swings me—and finally, it replaces me. I am no more. Indeed I am, but so strong that I don't recognize myself. Since then, I am terribly ashamed. Of stupidity, of meanness, and of dirty things. Of moodiness. Of wickedness. (Steinhardt, 1991, 97, transl. mine)

Present here for the political prisoner, as in the two novels discussed previously, are two planes of existence: one is defined by the inhumanity, the torment, filthiness, and suffering of the physical environment, while the other by a sense of humanity, balance, clarity, and joy. The forcefulness of Steinhardt's ethical convictions is equally matched by his literary talent. As in the passage above, he takes great pains to describe elaborately the moments of bliss he experiences in spite of the constant string of disappearances and deaths surrounding him or the stomach disease with which he himself struggles. He will execute five hard years of his sentence, and be released after the general amnesty of political prisoners in August 1964. Steinhardt's prison diary will be seen in print posthumously, after the 1989 bloody regime change in Romania that he did not have the chance to witness. Although many of his books, articles, translations, and interviews have been published and awarded literary prizes, he is mostly known in the consciousness of his countrymen for *Jurnalul Fericirii* (The Diary of Happiness); his memoir was one of the most widely read prison memoirs in the nineties in Romania and is considered a literary masterpiece.

Irina Ratushinskaya's prison narrative is autobiographical and follows in great detail the experience of her four years as prisoner in the women's political prison of Barashevo in the former USSR. A Russian poet of twenty-eight, she was sentenced in 1980 to seven years of hard labor and five years of internal exile for having committed "the crime of slander against the Soviet state" in poetic form. While imprisoned, she was tortured for having conducted hunger strikes and protests against innumerable human rights violations in the prison and the country. Similar to the case of Tazmamart's prisoners in Morocco, Irina Ratushinskaya was placed in a political prison camp, the location and even existence of which not many people knew. Year after year, numbers of inmates were buried in the camp's own cemetery, so that relatives could not claim a body, document traces of torture, or properly grieve their loss. Irina's poems, written on prison soap, quickly memorized by her and fellow inmates and then erased, persistently celebrated the value of freedom and the beauty of human life. Jacobo Timerman[4] is one of the reviewers of her memoir, titled in the English translation *Grey Is the Color of Hope*; on the back cover of this translation published in the States in 1989, he is quoted as having written the following in the *Los Angeles Times Book Review*: "A true, moving revelation. There is something new, original and unexpected in Ratushinskaya's account of her life as a dissident and as a prisoner: humor, happiness, poetry." Timerman, a former political prisoner in Argentina who published his prison memoirs as well, was impressed with the images of joy and laughter that Ratushinskaya's narrative intertwined with the horrors of pain, constant disease, and torture. As a journalist and author, Timerman captured with a "trained" eye one of the special characteristics of another author's narrative style. Most probably, he would be surprised to find out that this *modus felicitatis*, by whose originality he was struck, is not at all a rare occurrence in prison literature.

To read about this trope in Ratushinskaya's own words, it may be useful to offer the example of such a scene of merriment after a hunger strike the political women's ward has just ended. The women prisoners call the hunger strike the "Madrid" strike in honor of the conference held in Madrid to review the implementation of the 1975 Helsinki Accords; the Madrid conference held between November 1980 and September 1983 dedicated the great majority of its proceedings to the Soviet abuses and violations of this international agreement (the war in Afghanistan; the dismal record of human rights in the USSR, the Soviet republics, or satellite countries; the imposition of martial law in Poland; etc.). In Ratushinskaya's memoir, at the end of their strike, the group of female political inmates enjoy a meager meal consisting of a grated carrot divided into seven equal portions, tea, bits of dried black bread, and three candies the size of peas: "What a superb feast that was! Color crept back into our faces, either from the food or from the high spirits. Our voices became stronger, we laughed after practically every word" (Ratushinskaya 1989, 150). The vivid energy and her descriptions of women prisoners' solidarity is close to those of Saadawi; her words almost echo Saadawi's own when she looked for that secret of human nature manifested sometimes as courage, self-confidence, or the ability to adjust and survive the worst conditions. In another instance in the book, Ratushinskaya insists on the importance of laughter and cheerfulness in prison,

The medics are obliged to record an average of 37.5°C in the morning, and 38°C in the evening. This may not seem drastically high, but when it lasts for months on end, it's terribly debilitating. Your knees become weak, there's a constant buzzing in your head, and the slightest exertion makes you gasp for breath as though your head were trapped in a plastic bag. At the same time, life must go on; you have to carry buckets of water, cut firewood, load and unload the dray with the gloves, launder your sheets in a small basin. And conduct hunger strikes. And laugh and maintain a cheerful demeanor; nobody else in the Zone is any better off. Everyone is ill and that makes it all the more vital not to lose heart. Camp regulations don't promote positive emotions, only negative ones, so Heaven only knows what will become of you in seven years if all you do is fret and fume. For this reason, we don't let a single day go by without jokes and mirth. (Ratushinskaya 1989, 188)

Inner discipline and a good daily dose of art represent the recipe for establishing mental fortitude and their constant practice is the indomitable secret of maintaining psychological and physical survival. Ratushinskaya's thoughts on the role of art and joy in prison echo those of all three other authors, who never ceased to practice the same commitment to art in the form of literature, philosophical ideas, visual secular and divine imagery, personal memories, and deep human friendship and solidarity to share the joy of physical and moral survival.

Lightness of heart, laughter, humor, and joy have undoubtly served many times those incarcerated in their efforts to preserve the constantly tried equilibrium of their psyche. I take these prisoners' confessions to represent more than a slippage of their consciousness seeking refuge from horror, more than a psychological side-effect of trauma, and a more serious survival strategy than previously thought. Faced with the impossibility of going away from trauma, some victims do appeal to dissociation (the process of going away in one's mind) to various degrees, up to the breaking point of mental illness. The prisoners from whose memoirs I quoted in this chapter have never been interned in psychiatric wards or ever diagnosed with mental illness, inside or outside prison. While only a psychology expert can appreciate the degree and the duration of their spatial or temporal dissociation from both the prison walls and the community of prisoners or torturers, these prisoners did actively function even more effectively after these experiences. Their memoirs and their dedicated involvement in the life of their communities for many years after release testify to this.

Due to the occurrence of this specific survival technique in different political and cultural contexts, inferences can be drawn about its effects. To return to the Hegelian dialectical metaphor, within the life-and-death struggle between the Master and the Slave, the latter gradually comes closer to nature and leaves behind the Master, who grows increasingly idle in his monologic, limited approach to their environment. Highly important, Hegel did not see the end of the confrontation between Master and Slave as a violent one. If prisoners of conscience would have a chance to interject in Hegelian scholarship, I would say that they could offer an invaluable perspective to the *denouement* of the Master-Slave struggle for recognition. There would be quite a number of them, who, after traversing the long journey of subjection to the most atrocious of Masters, would insert in the last part of their confrontation with the Master the paradoxical feelings of joy or bliss. What Hegel began philosophically and where he identified feelings and states of fear, pain, conflict, and revolt, many political prisoners who had the chance to live and re-live endlessly the Hegelian struggle behind bars would put the final touch of leaving behind the Master with firm and definitive joy.

APORETIC SURVIVAL

Perhaps this psychological reaction or state of mind has not been given proper attention until now, unless pathologized as a psychological malady (associated with temporary madness), because the state itself is so difficult to convey and ridiculous to accept. Whereas concrete coping mechanisms and practical philosophies are constantly shared by political inmates, intense spiritual or phenomenological states are difficult to communicate and impossible to transfer. Practical survival can be shared, aporetic survival cannot. Epiphanies of self are individually experienced; the poetics and politics of perception or memory of trauma are charged with what we forget when we remember and how to find the proper language to express the re-telling of the unheard-of.[5]

An investigation into why aporetic survival cannot be shared invites a necessary attempt to explicate its structural manifestation. Strikingly, protagonists confessing to joyful states often declare that willingly assuming their death proved the necessary step for living behind the walls. What Nawal Saadawi, author, narrator, and heroine of *Memoirs from the Women's Prison*, tells herself after entering an Egyptian prison, Salim, the hero of *This Blinding Absence of Light* by Tahar Ben Jelloun, essentially echoes very soon after reaching the darkness of the Tazmamart prison in Morocco; he tells himself that he is dead. The day of imprisonment becomes the death-marking moment, "I have no past, and therefore no memory. I was born and died on July 10, 1971" (Ben Jelloun 2002, 19). The only alternative left for Salim is to start living a life by creating a present and to insist on creating different memories. Nawal Saadawi also realizes that life within the panoptic system has to be assumed willfully against reason and logic and must start in that place,

> From the moment I opened my eyes upon my first morning in prison, I understood . . . that I had made a firm decision: I would live in this place as I had

lived in any other. It was a decision which appeared insane to me, for it would cancel out reality, logic, the walls and the steel doors.

Everywhere I had gone, wherever I had traveled, however far away the place, however unfamiliar, I would look around me in delighted wonder and concentration as if I had been born in that place and would die there, as if I had never known any other spot and never would. (Saadawi 1986, 35)

She is determined to cultivate a survivalist aporetic mentality, "I would start to believe that I was not waiting, that I had been born here and would die in the same place" (Saadawi 1986, 98). Steinhardt, in his *Diary of Happiness*, goes even further and identifies the death-assuming gesture as ethical, as "the Solzhenitsyn answer" to interrogation and torture, an answer betraying an already established personal philosophy, entitled to its own name. Salim tells himself decidedly at some point in Tazmamart, "I am no longer of this world" (Ben Jelloun 2002, 50). Nawal's inner monologue on the way to prison betrays a similar lucidity, "I no longer belong to the world outside the van, nor to those people walking in the street, nor to the ones in their cars going home" (Saadawi 1986, 9). Death, looked straight in the face becomes the first structural step toward a radical and radicalizing individual position—most strangely, I would say, since it is usually situated among the last stages of every experiential process.

INTERPRETATION AND IMPLICATIONS

I did not find this happiness to be a sort of ad-hoc skeptic or stoic metaphysics, or a Buddhist detachment from the misery of physicality—the tortured body—and oppression, or an escapist attempt to make recourse to alternative worlds. Rather, it seemed to be the very climax of a prison identity crisis: after assuming one's death by entering prison, a new identity must be painfully and illogically "worked through," acquired, or constructed inside. And while this is a prisoner's constant need, no constant surrounding conditions are really present; they are interrupted time and again by different social dynamics: a different type of torture is occasionally introduced, possible new location and new actors, or the disappearance of older ones; some kind of a stable identity-in-death is constantly sought overtly, consciously or not. Since being identity-dead but still alive means that a different, novel identity must be uncovered, the latent prison-consciousness crisis is expressed most often through questioning, doubt, seeking new ways of seeing, appeals to memory, recourse to enriching epistemological perspectives, etc.[6] Most likely, proponents of existentialism would define this as a crisis of consciousness; psychoanalysts would invoke theories of trauma and its language. Yet, as Kay Schaffer and Sidonie Smith pointed out in *Human Rights and Narrat-*

ed Lives (2004), the applicability of the psychoanalytical model of trauma based on notions of working-through, mourning, radical disruption from the past, or non-linear memory is insufficient: "critics argue that the psychoanalytic model privileges stories suffused with traumatic remembering and suffering, and silences other kinds of stories that may not unfold through the Western trope of trauma (see Ball; Berlant; and Boler). They argue that it universalizes diverse and multiple structures of feeling" (Schaffer 2004, 22). My present attempt to identify the state of aporetic happiness, although doomed to psychoanalytical, rhetorical-literary, or philosophical terminological use, ends up appealing to contemporary sociological theory. When analyzing the protagonists' confessed states around the moment of their prison arrival in contrast to those around their departure from prison, how the formerly happy, joyful prisoner-actors inscribe themselves and function into a social community becomes extremely important. Notions of commitment and symbolic interaction help understand the way of relating to self and collectivity inside and outside "total institutions" (Erving Hoffman's term). Stupefying or aporetic happiness is the effect of bringing about a new identity, forged on renegotiating a different form of commitment to self, to the other, to present community, imagined or not.

To invoke sociologist Howard Becker, one could locate the beginning of this novel commitment in "the crucial action which has created the commitment in the person's acquiescence to the system," like in "his agreeing to work under the bureaucratic rules in force" (Becker 1960, 37). Death is the incipient committed acquiescence in the case of our protagonists above; confronted with an inhumane oppressive apparatus that one must face alone, it takes the form of an individual commitment to the self, in spite of these prisoners having confessed commitment to higher collective social ideals before entering prison. The moment of arrest is generally the first moment of sudden awareness of individual adjustment to a social position; more poignant in this context is Derrida's perspective in *The Gift of Death* (1995) when he says that, even if one can live for another and could also claim to die for another, one must still die one's own death. In his view, someone can live for you, but no one can die your death for you. The crisis of happiness (or the epiphany, if you like) marks the moment of coming to terms with an oscillatory novel identity—of life in death—in a particular form; this newfound sense of self has qualitatively shifted its commitment to self and others. Through happiness, the crisis of consciousness had taken the prisoner from a previous specific personal and collective commitment to a calmer and more comprehensive commitment: the non-traumatic shock for the prisoner of consciousness consists in a surprising commitment to an erasure of the binaries dictated by a total institution.

In *Asylums* (1970), Erving Goffman defines five types of institutions controlling human groups, with prison being among them. "The handling of many human needs by the bureaucratic organization of whole blocks of people—whether or not this is a necessary or effective means of social organization in the circumstances—is the key fact of total institutions" (Goffman 1970, 6). Steinhardt's father deconstructs this theory for his son on his way to prison. He warns him not to look hopefully to the world outside since that is only a larger prison, where one lives an existence not only forcibly and unjustly regulated, but even more disquieted by compliance with the repressive policies of the power structures. Since prisoners of conscience are fully aware that life outside as a total institution brought them inside in the first place, their consciousness searches for a sense of self capable of authentically addressing any and every total institution. The epiphany of happiness acquires it by placing various dichotomies under erasure: regardless of the type of institution, the political inmate who has experienced it will be committed to implode opposite distinctions of previous binary constructs, such as "us vs. them," "I vs. the Other," etc. Goffman says, referring to total institutions, that, "two different social and cultural worlds develop, jogging alongside each other with points of official contact but little mutual penetration." And, "the staff-inmate split is one major implication of the bureaucratic management of large blocks of persons," where "each grouping tends to conceive of the other in terms of narrow hostile stereotypes" (Goffman 1970, 9, 7). This is one major distinction canceled by the state of aporetic happiness, not in a complete blurring, but the acquisition of a new understanding of these worlds and of building a new stance toward oppositionalities such as "right vs. left," or "good vs. evil," etc. This is reflected in Salim's way of thinking and positioning himself vis-à-vis his jailers. He cancels out any interaction based on hierarchy or strict institutional rules: he starts helping the guardians bury the bodies of his comrades, addresses them differently, and relates to them not as torturers, but as equal participants in a given symbolic or real situation. Although he had bitter feelings about his father when he entered prison—his father not only had abandoned him and his mother, but had also publicly disowned him and asked the king to punish his son by killing him exemplarily—after eighteen years in jail, Salim feels at peace with his father's cruel and irresponsible attitude. A telling episode occurs at the very end of his prison term, when Salim is examined and questioned by a psychologist in order to check his sanity and his intentions after release,

> *How do you feel about the army?*
> I don't feel anything.
> *Any resentment, desire for revenge?*
> No.
> *What do you think of your family?*
> Family is family.
> *What do you think of your father?*

He's someone who loves his children, but he isn't a father.
Do you resent him?
No, not at all.
What will you do when you leave here?
No idea. Perhaps take care of my health. (Ben Jelloun 2002, 124)

The father who disowned him and wanted to see him dead is more a part of Salim's life than he was during the first years in prison, when the son judged his father harshly. Salim's vision of opposite relationships is not there and will not be until the end of the book, which details the calm meeting between father and son and the slow reinsertion of the former prisoner into his former environment.

Steinhardt will unequivocally forgive all those responsible for his nation's suffering and for his own, beginning with his torturers, jailers, and informants up to the political figures who had maneuvered the collective and individual process of suffering. A confession in his *Diary* reads,

> I entered prison with vague flashes of awareness not about reality, but with a sort of inner flashes lightning the autogenous darkness which split the darkness without dissipating it, and I am getting out with eyes wide open; I entered pampered, spoiled, I am getting out ridden by pickiness and airs; I went in discontent, I get out knowing happiness. I went in nervous, angry, and sensitive to silly things, I'm getting out equidistant. The sun and life were telling me little; now I know how to taste the thin slice of bread, no matter how tiny; I'm getting out admiring, most of anything, the courage, the dignity, the honor, and the heroism. I'm getting out at peace: with those before whom I erred, with my friends and my enemies, and even with myself. (Steinhardt 2003, 313, transl. mine)

Steinhardt's diary comprises a specific blend of moral, civic, and aesthetic components originating from his remarkable erudition and humor colored by vast historical knowledge, folk wisdom, metaphysics, foreign languages, hermeneutics, theology, constitutional right, and ethics. Steinhardt juxtaposes the suffering of human condition permanently to the happiness that the battered human can experience even in a barred existence, making misery and painfulness subordinate to the spiritual joy one can extract from memory, feelings, belief, and meaningful human interaction in the most unexpected places.

CONJECTURAL ETIOLOGY

One additional observation has to be made here regarding the state of bliss detailed by these four authors in their works; critics could point to the fact that for at least one of them such a state is intimately linked to a religious experience. Nicolae Steinhardt converted from Judaism to Christianity while imprisoned and his prison memoir is a deeply moving account of this spiritual search. (Not only Romanian prison literature provides more examples of the behind-bars aporetic happiness linked to religious convictions; Egyptian literature has also seen a famous case—the prison memoir of Zaynab al-Ghazzali, a devout Muslim well known in the Arab world.) It is important to specify that my selection of these four novels was motivated by the great differences between the ideological and religious approaches that the protagonists displayed. These differences cover an entire spectrum of religious and political convictions: Salim and Irina are non-fervent believers (Muslim and respectively Christian), Nawal is a secular Muslim, while Steinhardt converts to another faith in prison and becomes a clerical figure by taking up the garb of a monk after his release. Within the novels discussed, each of these prisoners' reliance on their faith has different degrees of importance in their daily lives as inmates.

CONCLUSION

One of the few critical pieces addressing paradoxical images of prison is Martha Grace Duncan's article "'Cradled on the Sea': Positive Images of Prison and Theories of Punishment" (1988). Duncan entitles one of her sections "To Die And Become: Prison as a Matrix of Spiritual Rebirth" (Duncan 1988, 1225). Here, she gives numerous examples of authors describing their protagonists' radical feelings of losing everything, falling, dying, being transformed, and even experiencing states of joy and bliss while jailed. Among them are Solzhenitsyn with *The Gulag Archipelago*; Graham Greene with *The Power and the Glory*; John Cheever's *Falconer*; and Shakespeare's *King Lear*, to mention only a few. Martha Grace Duncan tries to offer an answer to her question, "Why do these authors view prison as a vehicle for rebirth? The answer seems to be that, for them, imprisonment offers an opportunity to renounce arrogance and separateness" (Duncan 1988, 1227). For Duncan, the protagonists' feelings of harmonization, content, joy, or rebirth when linked to death, prison, and self-transformation translate as "the state of equality with one's fellow man" (Duncan 1988, 1226). The joy resulted from the process of transformation is "the acceptance of equality with others" (Duncan 1988, 1227). Her conclusion is that the sense of submission brought along by this incredibly difficult rite of passage, the prisoners perceive as achievement and strength. Perhaps Derrida's notion of aporetic ethics or responsibility—the impossibility of respecting the demands of responsibility to self, to a singular other and all others at the same time—is solved by Duncan's prisoners-protagonists as an equality or balance in the commitment to self, other, society, and ideology (Derrida 1995, 69–70).

The later evolution of the four authors which I discussed earlier in the chapter—Nawal Saadawi, Tahar Ben Jelloun, Irina Ratushinskaya, and N. Steinhardt—connects their stories to a greatly changed social attitude. This attitude will imply a renewed commitment to speak truth to power in a novel approach. The expressibility of pain rendered either legally or aesthetically, as Elaine Scarry has pointed out, affects its political consequences. Nawal Saadawi is undoubtly the most prominent example of public and political personality here: not only that she intensified her activist stands for women's rights after her release from prison, she has been also expelled from Egypt and received so many death threats that she had to leave her country for a few years; she continued to speak publicly on the injustices at home by holding public talks and teaching at various research universities in the United States. After her return, she was the first and only woman to put forth her candidacy for the presidential elections of 2005 in Egypt, where Hosni Mubarak, the actual president, is perceived as a dynastic figure impossible to replace through a democratic process after more than twenty years in power. Her stated intention was not to win the election, but motivate the Egyptian people to press for the reform of the Egyptian constitution to allow for multiple candidacies for presidential office. Tahar Ben Jelloun is the author who acts as a shadow or false protagonist in *This Blinding Absence of Light*; when Binebine, his Tazmamart informant, confesses that the spiritual path traced in the book is Ben Jelloun's and not his own, he is not aware yet of the subsequent fight between them; this fight will lead to public opprobrium against Ben Jelloun in Morocco; his countrymen perceived him as making a literary profit out of the nation's oppressive past against whom he had never publicly protested while King Hassan II was alive. Although acknowledging that he has never risked his freedom and the privilege of visiting Morocco whenever he wanted, Ben Jelloun rejected the accusations. He claimed to have used his own youthful experience of imprisonment of eighteen months in Morocco's disciplinary camps for having taken part in the student demonstrations of 1966. The controversy prompted him to detail his personal carceral experience in a subsequent book entitled *The Last Friend* (2004). Ben Jelloun is one of the most prominent Maghrebian writers in France today, where he settled in 1971; his writings on exile, racism, poverty, and human rights have been awarded French and international literary prizes. He is invited to meet students in French public schools and talk about racism and other human rights issues. Besides fiction, he contributes articles regularly for major French and international newspapers such as *Le Monde*, *El Pais*, *Corriere della Sera*, or *Aftonbladet*. Nicolae Steinhardt followed a different path: although he held a doctorate in constitutional law, he was not allowed to practice law after his release in 1964, being still considered by the communist government "an enemy of the people." His friends encouraged him to write essays, translations, and literary criticism. In 1980 he took the oath of poverty and became a monk. After submitting to a set of monastic rules that implied among others humbleness and reticence, he asked for permission from his clerical superiors to allow him to continue writing and publishing. In the post-Stalinist years, he found the ways to contribute to the Romanian literary scene in spite of being constantly under police surveillance and labeled as an "unrepentant hostile element" in their files (Vatulescu 2004, 258). After his death, Steinhardt became an important part of the Romanian cultural landscape with his superb pieces of literary and political commentaries and remains the most revered writer of prison literature in this country. After her release from prison, Irina Ratushinskaya lived a number of years in the United States and London. Alison Townsend closes her review of Ratushinskaya's prison memoir, "Upon their arrival in London, Ratushinskaya and her husband were asked to what they bore allegiance. They answered unequivocally: 'Human rights.' But Ratushinskaya also bears allegiance to the creative process" (Townsend 1989, 19). She and her husband continue to be human rights advocates; after returning to Moscow with her husband and two children in 1998, she also continued to write volumes of poems and prose.

My endeavor has been not so much to dwell extensively on the etiology of this critical state or the minutia of its manifestation, but rather to focus on its very occurrence and the potential ramification of its effects in terms of social interaction—symbolic or otherwise—inside prison or in the later communal and political life. Further comparative implications are of interest here, namely, the manner in which these inmates interject in post-conflict national reconciliation involving the legal system—lustration laws and reparation procedures, the re-writing of history, and the justice of memory, etc., compared to those who did not go through or confess to such states. Some of those who did had become part of truth and reconciliation committees, prominent members of political parties, and writers engaged in counter memorial practices by questioning governmental attempts to institutionalize national trauma legitimizing their own power. This chapter meant to present an argument and open further discussion about the manner in which aporetic happiness extends correctively to the phenomena of social suffering, enabling thus a commitment of encompassing and equidistant bitterless affect translated into bitterless politics by bracketing out opposite social commitments.

NOTES

1. The Oxford English Dictionary Online explains the term *aporia* as "a perplexing difficulty" (http://dictionary.oed.com). I make use of it here in conjunction with Derrida's notion of

aporetic ethics. In *The Gift of Death* (1995), he insists that between the responsibility toward another individual (God, the self, or a singular other) and the responsibility toward the collective there remains a constant tension. Jack Reynolds explains in *The Internet Encyclopedia of Philosophy* Derrida's notion of aporetic ethics, by quoting a passage from his *Gift of Death*: "I cannot respond to the call, the request, the obligation, or even the love of another, without sacrificing the other other, the other others" (Derrida 1995, 68). For Derrida, it seems that the Buddhist desire to have attachment to nobody and equal compassion for everybody is an unattainable ideal. He does, in fact, suggest that a universal community that excludes no one is a contradiction in terms. According to him, this is because: "I am responsible to anyone (that is to say, to any other) only by failing in my responsibility to all the others, to the ethical or political generality. And I can never justify this sacrifice; I must always hold my peace about it. . . . What binds me to this one or that one, remains finally unjustifiable" (GD 70).

2. A number of articles and studies detailing the shared strategies of repression between these two world areas started to be published especially in the last few years. See Michael Levitin's article, "East Germans drew blueprint for Cuban spying," in the *Miami Herald*, November 4, 2007, http://www.michaellevitin.com/2007/11/04/east-germans-drew-blueprint-for-cuban-spying/(last accessed February 24, 2009). Also, in *The Foreign Policy of the GDR in Africa* (1990), Gareth M. Winrow writes extensively about the cooperation of East Germany and the USSR with several Arab states before and after the 1967 Arab-Israeli war. The second volume of *The Mitrokhin Archive II* (2005) contains information on the collaboration between secret services of the USSR and former Soviet bloc countries with various governments in the Arab world; *Stasi and Securitatea* is a recent book written by historian Stejarel Olaru focusing on the Romanian–East German sharing of secret repressive operations; *Stasi* by John O. Koehler (1999) details the extent of Stasi's operations in the Third World, etc.

3. Due to the later disagreement between Ben Jelloun and his informant, former Tazmamart prisoner Aziz Binebine, it is somewhat difficult to determine the degree to which the experiential processes described in the book belong to Ben Jelloun or his informant. What is surely known is that Salim (or Binebine) is one of only three people ever to get out alive from Cell Block B of the infamous desert prison, in which twenty-three inmates were jailed and twenty died slowly during almost two decades of unheard-of cruel treatment. An April 2001 article by David Tresilian in the Egyptian weekly *Al-Ahram*, dated from before their disagreement, quotes Binebine as having said that the novel "is Tahar's, even if it has been much inspired by me and by my story. . . . He has traced a spiritual path [in the novel] that is intimately his own."

4. The Oxford English Dictionary Online explains the term aporia as "a perplexing difficulty" (http://dictionary.oed.com). I make use of it here in conjunction with Derrida's notion of aporetic ethics. In *The Gift of Death* (1995), he insists that between the responsibility toward another individual (God, the self, or a singular other) and the responsibility toward the collective there remains a constant tension. Jack Reynolds explains in *The Internet Encyclopedia of Philosophy* Derrida's notion of aporetic ethics, by quoting a passage from his *Gift of Death*: "I cannot respond to the call, the request, the obligation, or even the love of another, without sacrificing the other other, the other others" (Derrida 1995, 68). For Derrida, it seems that the Buddhist desire to have attachment to nobody and equal compassion for everybody is an unattainable ideal. He does, in fact, suggest that a universal community that excludes no one is a contradiction in terms. According to him, this is because: "I am responsible to anyone (that is to say, to any other) only by failing in my responsibility to all the others, to the ethical or political generality. And I can never justify this sacrifice; I must always hold my peace about it. . . . What binds me to this one or that one, remains finally unjustifiable' (GD 70)."

5. Jacobo Timerman is a Ukrainian-born Argentinean journalist, author, and publisher. After criticizing Argentinean government's human rights policies during the Dirty War in his writings, he will be imprisoned in 1977 and released two years later. His prison memoir, published in 1981, carries the title *Prisoner without a Name, Cell without a Number*.

6. Salim, the protagonist of *This Blinding Absence of Light*, starts telling his fellow Moroccan prisoners French adventure stories, after exhausting the Arab ones he knows.

REFERENCES

Andrew, Cristopher, and Vasili Mitrokhin. 2005. *The Mitrokhin Archive II: The KGB and the World*. New York: Allen Lane.

Becker, Howard S. 1960. "Notes on the Concept of Commitment." *The American Journal of Sociology* 66.1: 32–40. Chicago: Univ. of Chicago Press.

Ben Jelloun, Tahar. 2002. *This Blinding Absence of Light*. Trans. Linda Cloverdale. New York: New Press.

Casanova, Pascale. 2005. *The World Republic of Letters*. Trans. M. B. DeBevoise. Harvard Univ. Press.

Derrida, Jacques. 1995. *The Gift of Death*. Trans. David Wills. Chicago: Univ. of Chicago Press.

Duncan, Martha Grace. 1988. "'Cradled on the Sea': Positive Images of Prison and Theories of Punishment." *California Law Review* 76.6: 1201–47.

Goffman, Erving. 1970. *Asylums*. Chicago: Aldine Publishing Company.

Koehler, John O. 1999. *Stasi: The Untold Story of the East German Secret Police*. Boulder, CO: Westview Press.

Olaru, Stejarel. 2005. *Stasi si Securitatea* (Stasi and the *Securitate*). Bucuresti: Humanitas.

Ratushinskaya, Irina. 1989. *Grey Is the Color of Hope*. Trans. Alyona Kojevnikov. New York: Vintage Books.

Saadawi, Nawal. 1986. *Memoirs from the Women's Prison*. Trans. Marilyn Booth. London: Women's Press Limited.

Scarry, Elaine. 1985. *The Body in Pain*. New York: Oxford Univ. Press.

Schaffer, Kay, and Sidonie Smith. 2004. *Human Rights and Narrated Lives: The Ethics of Recognition*. New York: Palgrave Macmillan.

Slyomovics. Susan. 2005. *The Performance of Human Rights in Morocco*. Philadelphia: Univ. of Pennsylvania Press.

Steinhardt, N. 2003. *Jurnalul Fericirii* (Diary of Happiness). Cluj-Napoca: Ed. Dacia.

Timerman, Jacobo. 1989. Back cover commentary for *Grey Is the Color of Hope* by Irina Ratushinskaya. New York: Vintage Books.

Tresilian, David. 2001. *That Blinding Absence of Light*. Al-Ahram Weekly On-line. 529 (April 12–18).

Townsend, Alison. 1989. "Review: Free Spirit." *The Women's Review of Books* 6.8: 18–19. Philadelphia: Old City Publishing Press.

Vatulescu, Cristina. 2004. "Arresting Biographies: The Secret Police File in the Soviet Union and Romania." *Comparative Literature* 56.3: 243–61. Duke Univ. Press.

Winrow, Gareth M. 1990. *The Foreign Policy of the GDR in Africa*. New York: Cambridge Univ. Press.

Appendix

Cup Poems

Cup Poem 1

What kind of spring is this,
Where there are no flowers and
The air is filled with a miserable smell?

Cup Poem 2

Handcuffs befit brave young men,
Bangles are for spinsters or pretty young ladies.

—Shaikh Abdurraheem Muslim Dost[1]

NOTE

1. These two poems are from Marc Falkoff, ed., *Poems from Guantánamo: The Detainees Speak* (Iowa City: University of Iowa Press, 2007), 35. Falkoff translated into English and compiled this anthology of twenty-one poems written by men held in the U.S. military detention center in Guantánamo Bay, Cuba. Copyright © 2007 by the University of Iowa Press, www.uiowapress.org, all rights reserved.

Index

Abdalrahman, Hasiba, vii, 6–7, 119, 127, 128, 129, 130–131, 133, 134, 135n5, 136n19, 137n23
Adorno, Theodor W., 39–40, 44n16
Advisory Council on Human Rights (Morocco), 88, 90
aesthetics, vii, viii, 3, 4, 6, 8, 12, 14, 35, 36–37, 38–39, 40, 42, 44, 55, 79, 80, 108, 114, 187; of happiness, viii, 8, 187; of spectacle, 6, 108, 114
al-Asad, Hafez, 121, 137
Amnesty International, 99, 104n2, 121, 136n8, 137
Anti-Rightist Campaign, 47, 48, 49, 65, 66, 80, 81, 82n7
aporetic: citizens, 185; ethics, 201, 203n1, 204n4; happiness, 197, 198, 200, 203; survival, 8, 196, 197
apparitional subjectivity, 7, 148, 149, 153, 157, 158, 160n10
Arab world, 185, 186, 200, 204n2
Arar, Maher, 6, 117–118, 119, 120, 121–122, 124, 125, 135n1, 137
Ashcroft, John, 117, 135n1, 137
Auden, W. H., 17, 18, 19, 30, 42, 43, 44
Aung San Suu Kyi, 10, 32, 34, 44n11
authoritarianism, 1, 2, 6, 9, 10, 11, 12, 23, 41, 61, 73, 167, 175, 185
autobiography, 7, 8, 41, 104, 137, 139, 140, 143, 144, 149, 151, 152, 158, 160n10

Barashevo, 193
Bayraqdar, Faraj, vii, 6, 7, 24, 119, 125, 126–127, 136n16, 137
Ben Jelloun, Tahar, vii, 8, 188, 191–192, 196, 197, 200, 202, 204n3, 205
Benzekri, Driss, 90
Bettelheim, Bruno, 59–60, 67, 83n28, 84
Beverley, John, 13, 16
bitterless: affect, 203; politics, 203
Black Panther Party, 139, 141, 142, 151, 153, 157, 159n4, 160n11
Borowski, Tadeusz, 19, 44
Bouab, Widad, 93, 95, 96, 104
Bourdieu, Pierre, 37, 44
Brueghel, Pieter, 17–18, 38, 42, 43n2
Bu Naifu. *See* Wumingshi
Bu Ning. *See* Wumingshi

CCP. *See* Chinese Communist Party
Charaf, Maria, 87, 88–89, 104
"Charter 08" ("Lingba xianzhang"), 10, 15n4
China. *See* People's Republic of China (PRC)
Chinese Communist Party (CCP), 4, 10, 25, 47, 48–49, 50, 51, 52, 61, 62, 64, 65, 66, 68, 71, 73, 81, 82n6, 83n23, 108, 111, 113
Chinese prison camp, 2, 4, 27, 43n3, 44, 47, 51, 52, 56, 60, 82n18, 84, 216. *See also* laogai

Clinton, Hillary Rodham, 22, 44, 82n15, 84

COINTELPRO, 140

collective: autobiography, 7, 139, 140, 143, 144, 149, 151, 160; identity, 143

communism, 23, 167, 173, 174, 175, 185

concentration camp, 12, 19, 59–60, 84

Cong Weixi, vii, 4, 5, 15n1, 20, 29, 44n10, 52, 54, 55, 65–66, 67, 68, 69–70, 71, 78, 79, 80, 82n19, 83n26, 84n39, 110, 111, 114n3, 115

"controlling the blood", 111

Costa-Gavras, Constantin, 179n3, 183

Cuba, 160, 167, 204n2, 207n1, 215

Cultural Revolution, 25, 66, 81n1, 82n9, 83n34, 108, 111

Dalai Lama, 48, 137n22

Darley, Andrew, 108, 115

Deleuze, Gilles, 42, 44

democracy, 1, 9, 10, 32, 50, 163, 164, 165, 168, 170, 180n11, 182n22, 183

Derb Moulay Cherif, 87, 88, 89, 90, 96, 97, 99, 100, 102, 104

Derrida, Jacques, aporetic ethics of, 128, 137, 198, 201, 203n1, 204n4, 205

Dershowitz, Alan, 181n20

Des Pres, Terrence, 20, 44, 59, 60, 83n28, 84

desaparecidos, 178, 180n14, 182n23

diary, 8, 24, 25, 71, 72, 73, 74, 75, 111, 188, 192, 193, 197, 200, 205

dictatorship, 1, 8, 9, 11–12, 23, 88, 164, 168, 169–170, 174, 175–176, 177, 178, 179n2, 180n9, 182n22, 179, 185, 186

dignity, 32, 34, 38, 56, 59, 60, 61, 63, 64, 65, 67, 68, 69, 75, 100, 163, 164, 172, 173, 174, 175, 180n17, 200

dissident writers, 1, 2, 5, 6, 7–8, 9, 10, 12, 15n4, 16, 23, 50, 51, 82n9, 113, 139, 140, 141, 180n10, 192, 193

Dorfman, Ariel, 32, 44, 137

Dost, Shaikh Abdurraheem Muslim, 9, 44n15, 207

Eastern Europe, 1, 3, 8, 12, 185, 186

economic inequality, 176

El Bouih, Fatna, vii, 5, 93–94, 95–96, 99, 100, 101–103, 104n1

evil, 39, 174, 181n19, 193, 198

executions, public, 113

extraordinary rendition, 117, 120, 137

Falkoff, Marc, viii, 2, 9, 16, 25, 26, 44n15, 207n1

Falungong, 10

FBI, 117, 140, 146, 147, 157, 158, 159n8, 160

focos, 167, 179n7

forgetting, 19, 21, 22, 33, 53, 82n6, 164, 166, 169–170, 174, 175–176, 177, 179, 180n15, 192, 196

Foucault, Michel, hypotheses of, 109, 113, 115, 118, 133, 137

Frente Amplio, 169, 177, 178, 180n12, 182n24, 183

Galeano, Eduardo, 170

Garland, David, 109, 115

Garvey, Marcus, 148, 158, 160

Great Leap Famine, 108

Guantánamo Bay, viii, 2, 9, 16, 25, 26, 29, 32, 38, 44n15, 207n1

Guattari, Félix, 42, 44

guerrilla warfare, 15n9, 165, 166, 167, 168, 175, 179n3, 183

Guevara, Ernesto "Che", 179n7

Gugelberger, Georg, 13, 15n8, 16, 44n16

gulag, Soviet, 27, 28, 29, 30, 34, 44n9, 52, 84, 110, 114n1, 115, 201

Harlem Hospital, 149, 152, 154

Harlow, Barbara, 12, 16, 35, 39, 44

Hart, Janet, 35, 36, 37, 38, 44n14

Hassan II (king of Morocco), 5, 87, 88, 202

healing, 7, 22, 33, 80, 102, 163, 164, 175, 176–177, 181n21

Helsinki Accords (1975), 194

Herman, Judith, 4, 56, 70, 84

Hoover, J. Edgar, 140, 158

Hu Jia, 10, 15n3, 16

Hu Jintao, Tibetan crackdown led by, 113

human rights, vii, viii, 1, 2, 3, 5, 6, 7, 10–12, 14, 15n2, 23, 25, 35, 40, 50–51, 53, 55, 64, 80, 88, 90, 91, 92, 94, 100, 101, 102, 103, 104, 118, 119, 120, 121, 122, 123, 126, 127, 130, 135n5, 136n10, 137, 164, 170, 175, 177, 178,

182n23, 183n25, 185, 193, 194, 197, 202, 205, 215, 216; abuses, Soviet, 193, 194; discourse, 5, 11, 103, 118, 119, 120, 216; imperative, 6, 120, 122, 127; narrative, vii–viii, 2, 7, 11, 14, 15n2, 23, 25, 35, 51, 53, 88, 92, 102, 119, 120, 123, 126, 127, 130, 137, 185, 193, 216; and vulnerability, 121, 137

Human Rights Watch, 137

hunger, 4, 27, 31, 33, 48, 55, 56–59, 60, 61, 63, 64, 69, 70, 72, 74, 75, 77, 79, 83n23, 93, 100, 101, 102, 133, 193–194

ideology, 14, 50, 78, 122, 123, 127, 136n14, 164, 165, 172, 173–174, 176, 179n2, 180n17, 201

incarceration, vii, 2, 3, 4, 6, 8, 12, 13, 22, 26, 36, 38, 40, 47, 54

incommunicado detention, 98, 110

Jbabdi, Latifa, 93, 95, 99, 102–103, 104

"jet-plane posture", 111

Jiabiangou, 53, 84n39

Jung, Carl G., 41, 42, 44

Justice and Reconciliation Commission (Morocco), 5, 90, 91, 96, 104

Kant, Immanuel, 37, 44n13

Kinkley, Jeffrey C., 52, 54, 84n40

Kolyma, 25, 27, 28, 31–32, 33, 43n6, 44n10, 115

Laâbi, Abdellatif, 15n2, 93, 104

laogai (remolding through [forced hard] labor), 4, 5, 20, 27, 28, 30, 34, 48, 52–53, 54, 55–56, 57, 58, 60, 61, 63, 64, 67, 70, 71, 75, 79, 80, 81, 82n17, 84n39

laojiao (re-education through labor), 55, 66, 83n22, 84

Ley de Caducidad, 170

Lin Biao Affair, 108

Liu Xiaobo, 10, 15n4, 16

Madrid Conference (November 1980–September 1983), 194

Malcolm X, 140

Mandela, Nelson, 22

Mao era (the era of Mao Zedong), 2, 4, 25, 30, 34, 47, 48, 52, 53, 55, 56, 57, 64, 66, 70, 80, 113

Marxism, 167, 180n8

mass sentencing rallies, 6, 108, 109, 111, 114, 115n11

master-slave dialectic, 190, 195

memoir, vii, 2, 4, 5, 7, 8, 12, 20, 21, 24, 25, 27, 29, 33, 34, 35, 38, 40, 43n3, 44, 47, 48, 51, 52, 53, 54, 55–56, 57, 58, 59, 60, 61, 62, 64, 65–66, 67, 68–71, 72, 73, 77, 79, 80–81, 83n23, 84n40, 89, 93, 99, 102, 104, 111, 115, 122, 125, 126, 127, 136n16, 176, 185–187, 188–189, 191, 192, 193–194, 195, 196, 200, 202, 205

memory, vii, 2, 8, 19, 20, 24, 25, 33, 38, 41, 42, 47, 48, 49, 81, 84, 92, 129, 130, 137, 144, 148, 154, 156, 157, 164, 175, 177, 192, 196, 197, 200, 203, 215

Menebhi, Saida, 93, 100, 104

mental hygiene, 192

Mernissi, Fatema, 92, 93, 104

Miller, Flagg, viii, 29, 32, 44

MLN-Tupamaro, 15n9, 163, 165, 166, 167, 182n22, 183

modus felicitatis, 8, 185, 188, 193

Morocco, vii, 5, 8, 12, 87, 88, 89, 90, 91, 92, 93, 95, 96–97, 99, 101, 102, 103, 104, 185, 188, 191, 193, 196, 202, 205, 215

Muhammad VI (king of Morocco), 88, 90, 104

Mujica, José "Pepe", 169, 182n22

Müller, Herta, 11–12

multivalence, 5, 48, 71, 79, 80

national reconciliation, 203

Nationalist Party (KMT, Kuomintang, a.k.a. Guomindang), 53, 82n14, 114n7

neoliberalism, 8, 164, 177, 178

New York 21 (Black Panther 21), 7, 139, 140–143, 144, 145, 146, 150, 151, 153, 155, 157, 158, 159n1, 160n11

normalcy, 175, 176

no-trace policy, 186

OECD, 107, 108

pain, 8, 11, 17, 19, 20, 22, 32, 33, 34, 35,
36, 38, 39, 40, 44, 47, 53, 54, 55, 59,
62, 63, 69, 77, 83n36, 84, 98, 111,
114n5, 117, 118, 119, 120, 121, 123,
124, 128, 129, 130–131, 132, 136n12,
137, 163, 164, 165, 172, 174, 175, 176,
177, 187, 189, 190, 193, 195, 197, 200,
202, 204n5, 205, 215
panopticonic model, flaws of, 109
People's Republic of China (PRC), 6, 10,
15n4, 23, 44n9, 47, 50, 51, 52, 53–54,
55, 56, 61, 65, 66, 71, 81n2, 82n9, 84,
107–108, 109, 110, 111, 112, 113, 114
The Phenomenology of Spirit (Hegel), 190,
195
photo, posing for, 20–21, 30, 111, 112,
115n11
political prisoners, 1, 3, 4, 5, 7, 20, 22, 23,
28, 30, 35, 38, 44n10, 47, 48, 54, 58,
87, 88, 90, 93, 94, 95, 96, 97, 99, 100,
102, 122, 123, 126, 127, 128, 136n12,
147, 153, 160, 168, 170, 174, 180n11,
185–187, 188, 189–191, 193, 195
post-dictatorship, 8, 169, 170, 174, 175,
176, 177, 179n2, 182n22
prison: diary, 192, 193; literature, vii, 1, 2,
3, 4, 6, 7, 11, 13, 14, 15n2, 16, 23, 25,
29, 30, 35, 37, 39, 40, 41, 42, 44, 54,
118, 121, 122, 122–123, 127, 135n4,
137, 185, 193, 200, 202, 216; memoir,
5, 7, 8, 12, 33, 38, 93, 102, 125, 185,
186, 189, 192, 193, 200, 202
Pu Ning. *See* Wumingshi

Qanatir, 189
Qu Yuan, 68, 83n36

Ratushinskaya, Irina, vii, 8, 188, 193, 194,
195, 202, 205
Red Cross, lack of access to prisons of, 110
remembering. *See* forgetting
Republic of China (ROC). *See* Taiwan
rhizome, 3, 41, 42
Romania, vii, 3, 8, 11, 185, 188, 192, 193,
200, 202, 204n2, 205

Saadawi, Nawal El, vii, 8, 24, 26, 27,
33–34, 35, 38, 43n8, 44, 104, 188–190,
194, 196, 197, 202, 205

Sadat, Anwar, 34, 189
Scarry, Elaine, 6, 95, 119, 120, 130, 135n5,
137, 187, 202, 204n5, 205
Scheherazade (Shahrazad), 92, 93, 95, 96,
102, 104
Schiller, Friedrich von, 37, 44
Schrader, Abby, 109, 115
secret services, 186, 192, 204n2
Securitate, 186, 204n2, 205
Shalamov, Varlam, vii, 25, 27, 28–29, 31,
33, 34, 35, 43n6, 44n10, 110, 114n1,
115
"shameful public display", 111
Sima Qian, 68, 70, 83n37, 84
Slaughter, Joseph, 137
socialism, 23, 167, 168, 170, 174, 177
Sontag, Susan, 20, 21, 22, 30, 44
Soviet Union, fall of, 185
Spierenburg, Pieter, 108, 115
stability, regime, 1, 48, 108, 165, 167, 169,
170, 180n15
"stand-up cage", 111
Stasi, 186, 204n2, 205
Steinhardt, Nicolae (N. Steinhardt), vii, 8,
188, 192–193, 197, 198, 200, 202, 205
strike-hard crackdowns, 108, 109
submission, schema of individual, 113
suicide, prisoner, 60, 66, 67, 68, 70, 77–79,
84n38, 112, 114n8
survival strategy, 33, 195
Syria, vii, 6–7, 24, 117, 118, 119, 120, 121,
122–123, 125, 126, 127–128, 133, 134,
136n8, 137n21, 216

Tahani, Amine, 87, 88, 89, 104
Taiwan, 4, 24, 27, 51, 52, 53, 61, 65, 82n14
Tang Min, 112, 114n10, 115
Tazmamart, 191, 193, 196, 197, 202
testimonio, 8, 13, 15n9, 104, 163, 165,
171–173, 174, 176, 177, 180n8, 183
A Thousand and One Nights, 92, 93, 102
Tiananmen Square Massacre, 10, 48, 49,
82n6
Tibet, 48, 49, 51, 81n5, 113
Tibetan protestors, crackdown on, 48, 113
Timerman, Jacobo, 193, 205
torture, 1, 5, 6, 7, 8, 20, 23, 28, 32, 82n15,
88, 91, 92, 98, 99, 100, 101, 111, 117,
118, 120, 121, 122, 123, 124, 127, 128,

130, 131, 132, 133, 150, 163, 165, 167, 169, 170, 171, 177, 179n1, 187, 189, 193; narrative, viii, 5, 6, 7, 18, 28, 32, 39, 26, 56, 87, 90, 91, 92, 93, 95, 96, 97, 102, 103, 104, 111, 118, 119, 120, 121, 122, 123, 124, 125, 126, 127, 128, 129, 130, 131, 132–134, 135n2, 136n8, 136n10, 137n22, 164, 167, 171, 172–174, 175, 176, 177, 178, 180n10, 181n20, 183, 188, 190, 191, 195, 197, 198, 200, 215
transport of prisoners, secrecy in, 107, 110
trauma, vii, 2, 3, 4, 8, 23, 47, 48, 54, 55–56, 59, 68–70, 71, 72, 74, 75, 76, 79, 80, 81, 84n38, 93, 102, 137, 185, 187, 188, 195, 196, 197, 203; language of, 187, 188
Truth and Reconciliation Commission (TRC), 1, 5, 87, 91, 104
Tutu, Desmond, 51

urban guerilla movement, 142, 163, 171

Uruguay, vii, 2, 8, 15n9, 163, 164, 165–166, 167, 168–170, 171, 174, 175–176, 177, 178, 179n1, 180n8, 182n22–183n25

Vázquez, Tabaré, 169, 182n23

waterboarding, 179n1
wind of change (1989), 185
Wu, Harry, 52, 55, 83n21, 114n2
Wumingshi, vii, 4, 5, 15n1, 16, 24, 25, 27, 29, 43n3, 44, 53–54, 55, 61–63, 63–64, 65, 70, 80, 82n18, 83n31, 84

Yang, Xianhui, 53–54, 55, 61, 84n39

Zedong, Mao (Mao Tse-tung), 73, 107, 108
Zhang, Xianliang, vii, 4, 5, 10, 15n1, 25, 27–29, 43n5, 44n9, 52, 54, 55, 57, 60, 65, 71–79, 80, 82n20, 84n40, 111, 115
Žižek, Slavoj, 181n20, 183

About the Contributors

Eugenio Di Stefano is an assistant professor of Latin American literature at the University of West Georgia. He received his Ph.D. in Hispanic studies from the University of Illinois at Chicago. His research is concerned with literature in its intersection with politics. More specifically, his work examines the representations of torture, violence, and pain in contemporary Latin American and U.S. literature.

Simona Livescu is an advanced doctoral student in the Department of Comparative Literature at UCLA. Her articles and translations pertaining to Continental philosophy, the autobiographical genre, and Francophone writing appeared in *The Comparatist, CLCWeb: Comparative Literature and Culture*, the *International Journal of Francophone Studies*, and *Studia Phaenomenologica*. Her dissertation entitled "Francophonie and Human Rights" deals with the cultural production of East-European, North-African, and Cuban diasporas in France after WWII.

Ramsey Scott teaches at Brooklyn College, CUNY. He is completing a book manuscript on fugitive texts and American poetry in the post-Vietnam era. His essays, poems, and fiction have appeared in the *Southwest Review*, the *Seneca Review, Massachusetts Review, Shampoo, Tarpaulin Sky, Confrontation*, and *Mirage #4/Period(ical)*. "Notes on the Narco-Imaginary," part of an ongoing project investigating the representation of drug use, recently appeared in the poetry journal *House Organ*.

Susan Slyomovics is professor of anthropology and Near Eastern languages and cultures at the University of California, Los Angeles, where she is also director of UCLA's G. E. von Grunebaum Center for Near Eastern Studies. Among her publications are *The Object of Memory: Arab and Jew Narrate the Palestinian Village* (1998), awarded the 1999 Albert Hourani Book Prize and the 1999 Chicago Folklore Book Prize; editor, *The Living*

Medina in the Maghrib: The Walled Arab city in Literature, Architecture and History (2001); co-editor, *Women and Power in the Middle East* (2001); *The Performance of Human Rights in Morocco* (2005); coeditor, *Waging War and Making Peace: The Anthropology of Reparations* (2008); and editor, *Clifford Geertz in Morocco* (2010).

R. Shareah Taleghani recently completed her dissertation on contemporary Syrian prison literature and human rights discourse at New York University and is currently teaching at the City College of New York. Her research focuses on the relationships between modern Arabic literary experimentalism, narrative, and the construction of human rights regimes.

Philip F. Williams has published nine books in East Asian studies, the latest being *Asian Literary Voices* (Amsterdam University Press, 2010). He has been professor of Chinese at Arizona State University, Massey University, and more recently the University of Montana.

Yenna Wu is Distinguished Teaching Professor and director of Asian literatures and cultures at the University of California, Riverside. Her research covers gender, thematic, narrative, and prison studies, as well as pedagogy for literature and Chinese language. She has published many articles, books, book chapters, translations, and reviews in both English and Chinese. Her numerous publications include *The Chinese Virago* (1995), *The Lioness Roars* (1995), *Ameliorative Satire* (1999), *The Great Wall of Confinement: The Chinese Prison Camp Through Contemporary Fiction and Reportage* (co-authored, 2004), *Remolding and Resistance among Writers of the Chinese Prison Camp: Disciplined and Published* (co-edited, 2006), *Me and China* (co-authored, 2008), and *Mandarin Chinese the Easy Way* (co-authored, 2008).